The USBORNE BOOK of ART

The picture on the previous page is a
detail from *The Beach at Trouville*
(1870), by Claude Monet. You can
see the whole picture on page 93.

These pages show an enlarged detail
from *Dynamic Suprematism*, by
Kasimir Malevich. The whole picture
is reproduced on page 113.

The USBORNE BOOK of ART

Rosie Dickins

Consultants:
Mari Griffith
Dr. Erika Langmuir OBE
Tim Marlow

Edited by Jane Chisholm
Designed by Mary Cartwright,
Vici Leyhane and Catherine-Anne MacKinnon
Americanization editor: Carrie Armstrong

Internet-linked

Contents

👁 Internet links

Look for Internet link boxes throughout this book. They contain descriptions of websites where you can see more paintings, play games and find out more about art. For links to these websites, go to the **Usborne Quicklinks Website** at **www.usborne-quicklinks.com** and type the keywords '**book of art**'.

Before using the Internet, please read the Internet safety guidelines displayed on the Usborne Quicklinks Website. The recommended websites are regularly reviewed and updated. Usborne Publishing is not responsible for the content of any website other than its own. For more information, please see page 189.

These pages show a detail from *Tiger in a Tropical Storm – Surprised!* (1891) by Henri Rousseau. You can see the whole picture on page 97.

What is art?

The word 'art' can be used to describe anything from prehistoric cave paintings to a heap of junk in the corner of a gallery. It can even be used to refer to music and literature, but most often it means *visual* art, or things which are made to be looked at – especially paintings.

Some surprising things have found their way into galleries.

The great debate

People have argued about art, what it is and why it's so great, for centuries. Artists and experts often have very different ideas, leading to some violent disputes. The French painter Manet disagreed with a critic so strongly, he challenged him to a duel. There are lots of controversial questions, but no right or wrong answers. Everyone has different tastes and opinions, so it is up to you to decide what you think.

Some people think art should be beautiful or lifelike; others think it is more important to capture a mood or feeling. Just compare the two paintings on this page. One looks almost photographic. The other is much sketchier and painted with only a few colours, but very atmospheric.

Madame Moitessier (1856), by Ingres. Although this looks very realistic, Ingres cheated with the angle of the mirror to make it reflect Madame Moitessier's profile.

Combing the Hair (about 1896), by Edgar Degas. Degas used warm, reddish colors to make this scene feel cozy and intimate.

Detail from *A Sunday on La Grande Jatte* by Georges Seurat. (You can see the whole picture on page 94.) Seurat shocked critics by creating grand paintings of ordinary people.

What's it all about?

Some people believe art should be about ideas. Others prefer to enjoy art for its own sake. The Impressionists (see page 93) had some heated debates over this very question. Some of them felt it was important to paint scenes of modern life; others were more interested in exploring the effect of light on things. Even pictures of ordinary people could cause disputes, as Georges Seurat (see right) discovered.

What's it worth?

People often disagree wildly about the value of art. Vincent van Gogh died in poverty, because no one would buy his paintings – even his friends said they looked like the work of a madman. Now, they are among the most valuable pictures in the world. And critic John Ruskin ended up in court in a dispute over *Nocturne in Black and Gold,* by James Whistler.

Ruskin thought Whistler's painting was far too slapdash. He couldn't believe the artist wanted 200 guineas for *"flinging a pot of paint in the public's face."* Whistler's response was that the painting's value didn't depend on how long it took him to paint, but on his genius and years of study. He sued Ruskin for libel and won – although he was awarded only a farthing (a quarter of a penny) in damages. So it seems the judge really agreed with Ruskin.

Nocturne in Black and Gold – the Falling Rocket (1875), by U.S. artist James Whistler. This painting caused a huge row in the 1870s. It's so blurry, it's hard to see what's going on. In fact it shows a firework display. At the time, people were used to glossy, highly finished pictures, so this one seemed very sketchy by comparison.

But *is* it art?

Today, there is an enormous emphasis on making art new and original – and radical artists are constantly challenging our ideas about what 'art' actually is. So there is more and more controversy about it, and about the high prices collectors sometimes pay for it. Things artists have exhibited include a bicycle wheel on a stool, a painting of a pipe labelled *This is not a pipe*, a row of bricks and even a pile of rubbish from a party (later thrown away by mistake). Does that sound like art to you? Some of them weren't even made by the artist – they were just things he or she had found. You might not expect to find them in a gallery at all. Does seeing them there make them art? They can certainly provoke strong reactions and make you see things in a new way – which traditional paintings often do, too.

Styles and themes

This book traces the history of western art, from ancient wall paintings to modern art. It is arranged roughly in order of date, so you can see how styles and techniques have changed over time. Each section covers a major period of art history, introducing its main themes and ideas, and looking at a few important works in more depth. If you can, try to visit an art gallery or museum as well. Then you can examine works in detail and see how big they really are. The sizes of artworks in this book are given at the back or in the captions.

There is nothing quite as vivid and exciting as seeing a real painting in front of you.

Looking at paintings

You don't have to know much about art to enjoy looking at it, but you may find you get more out of it if you do. These pages suggest things to look for and think about in paintings.

👁 For a link to a website where you can explore the different parts of an artist's toolkit, go to **www.usborne-quicklinks.com**

What's it all about?

One of the first things to decide about a painting is what it's about. Paintings are divided into different groups, or 'genres,' according to what they show. The main genres are story-telling scenes, portraits, landscapes and 'still lifes' or arrangements of objects. These are all explained in more detail over the next few pages. This picture, by Raphael, is a scene from a story about a knight and a dream he had. The women are meant to be from the dream, not real people.

How is it arranged?

Scenes are usually arranged, or 'composed,' to make you look at them in a certain way. Important figures or objects may be bigger, brighter or more centrally placed, to make you notice them first. So here, you automatically look at the knight first. He lies in the middle of the picture, beneath the gaze of the two women.

Vision Of A Knight (about 1504), by Raffaello Sanzio, known as 'Raphael.' The knight is asleep and dreaming about the choice he will have to make between duty, represented by the serious figure on the left, and pleasure, shown by the beautiful woman on the right. Raphael probably based the knight on the Roman hero Scipio, who described a dream like this.

The picture has a triangular structure, divided by the tree. The lines of the women's gazes meet on the knight's head.

What does it mean?

Artists often put in hidden clues, or symbols, to help you guess what a picture means. Sometimes, the clues represent general ideas. For example, the book and sword in the picture above symbolize learning and action, while the sprig of flowers represents beauty and pleasure. Symbols can also help identify who's in the picture. Well-known characters, such as saints, are often shown with a symbol from their lives, so experts can tell who they are meant to be. You can see some examples of saints' symbols on page 31.

Paintings are full of clues, if you know what to look for.

Why was it made?

When you look at a picture, it helps to know the motive behind it. Was it meant to decorate a grand palace, or to hang in a church to help people pray? Or was it just made to be seen in an art gallery, where people could admire its beauty or think about the ideas behind it? Was it meant to have a political, social or moral message, or was it made to express an emotion?

Raphael's painting was made to order, so he would have been told what to paint. It was probably a gift for a young nobleman, and was meant to make him think. But the painting on this page was made for pleasure – it doesn't have an obvious message. The artist, Pierre-Auguste Renoir, painted what he wanted, and people bought his pictures just because they liked how they looked.

How was it painted?

The style of a painting, and even the paint itself, is worth looking at, too. Painting materials and techniques have changed hugely over time. And artists' brushwork can be as distinctive as handwriting. Some paint in a smooth, polished way, while others use expressive dabs and swirls. You can see the difference if you look at the two patches below.

At The Theatre (1876-77), by Pierre-Auguste Renoir. Sometimes called *The First Outing*, this shows a young woman on her first trip to the theatre. She is sitting in a box, gazing out at the rest of the audience, looking slightly overwhelmed by the sight.

Raphael used tiny brushstrokes to create a neat, even surface.

Renoir painted in a quick, loose style. You can still see his brushmarks in the paint.

Do you like it?

Another question to ask yourself is whether you like a painting or not, and why. People have very personal feelings about art, so this is a matter of taste – and tastes change. When paintings like Renoir's first appeared, some critics attacked them for looking too sketchy. But now they are greatly admired. There are no rules. It is up to you to decide what you think about the pictures you see.

People often have very different ideas about what makes a 'good' painting.

Story paintings

Until about 150 years ago, the most important, expensive and prestigious kind of painting was something known as history painting. This meant any large-scale picture that told a story – whether real or fictitious – and included Classical myths and Bible stories, as well as historical scenes. History painting first became popular during the 15th century, and remained so until well into the 19th century.

Leon Battista Alberti (see below) had many talents. As well as writing books, he made paintings and sculptures, designed buildings, and studied Latin and Greek.

The Family Of Darius Before Alexander (1565-70), by Paolo Veronese. This came from a palace in Venice.

The hardest challenge

A great 15th-century writer named Leon Battista Alberti described history painting as the hardest challenge for an artist. To choose suitable subjects, he said, artists had to be well-read. Then they had to know how to tell stories without words, using only gestures and expressions. To create lifelike scenes, they had to understand perspective, lighting and anatomy – and they had to be able to arrange everything into interesting compositions. So history painting needed a lot of thought and imagination, as well as skill with brushes and paint. In Alberti's time, most people thought of artists as just craftsmen. But he used history painting to argue they were really intellectuals and deserved greater respect.

The armor is richly detailed, with jewels and gold trimmings – including two lions' heads.

Veronese's painting shows the ancient Greek leader, Alexander the Great, receiving the family of Darius, king of Persia, whom he has defeated in battle. Veronese makes Alexander stand out by giving him red clothes and showing him with his arms spread wide, as he steps forward to reveal his identity.

Touches of white make Alexander's nails seem to glint in the sun.

Top of the heap

When the French Academy of Painting and Sculpture was founded in 1648, its members decided to rank the different genres of painting in order of importance. Pride of place went to history painting. This order formed the basis of art theory for over a hundred years, helping to make these narrative scenes very popular.

In the news

Large-scale paintings used to be reserved for grand religious or patriotic subjects. But that changed in the 19th century, as artists began creating history paintings based on contemporary news stories. One of the first of these was *The Raft Of The Medusa*, inspired by the wreck of a French ship in 1816.

The Raft Of The Medusa (1818), by French painter Théodore Géricault. This shows the survivors of the wreck, adrift on a raft littered with corpses, as they try to signal to a distant ship. When they were rescued, they told how they had been abandoned by their captain, while he sailed to safety in a lifeboat. Starving, they had to resort to eating each other to survive – though this picture makes them look heroic rather than violent.

When the *Medusa* story broke, it caused a huge scandal – as did this painting. Some people thought the artist meant to criticize the French king, who had been involved in appointing the ship's captain.

Notice how the figures are piled into a pyramid, with the man waving the flag at the top.

Art and revolution

History paintings like *The Raft Of The Medusa* showed how art could have a powerful political impact. The picture caused a huge outcry, with critics arguing about its politics as much as its artistic merits. Not long afterwards, another topical French painting, *Liberty Leading The People*, created such a stir, it had to be hidden. This was a very volatile period in French history, and the government feared it might incite public unrest. It was a scene of French revolutionaries storming the barricades, as had happened only the year before.

Liberty Leading The People: 28 July 1830 (1831), by French painter Eugène Delacroix. Delacroix included himself in the scene. He's the one in the top hat, on the left.

Portraits

People have been making portraits for thousands of years. Most early portraits were made to honor and remember the dead. By the 15th century, though, people were having their portraits painted for all kinds of reasons. Small portraits were often made as keepsakes. But grand, large-scale portraits were usually an exercise in public relations, helping to create an impressive public image for someone important.

Portrait Of A Lady In Red (probably 1460-70), by an unknown artist. This profile view is typical of early Italian portraits. The lady has a fashionably high forehead (she would have plucked or shaved her hair) and fancy clothes, showing that she was from a rich family.

True to life?

Nowadays, we tend to rely on photographs to show what people really look like. But, before photography, people had to rely on portraits. So artists had to pay careful attention to facial features, often exaggerating the most distinctive ones – such as a big nose – in order to emphasize the likeness.

But a portrait does more than create a physical likeness. It is also highly contrived and designed to present someone in a particular way. So the pose, expression and clothes are usually chosen to show the sitter from the best possible angle, and to convey a sense of his or her character and social status. Many portrait painters became successful because they were good at flattering their subjects.

Self Portrait Aged 63 (1669), by Rembrandt van Rijn – one of many self portraits he made during his life. He dressed up for some of the earlier ones. But in old age, he no longer seemed concerned with vanity. Here, he shows himself in ordinary clothes, in a frank, informal pose.

In this enlarged detail, you can see how Rembrandt painted his hat and clothes with broad, loose brushstrokes, but used much smaller touches of paint around his eyes and mouth.

Mirror image

After good-quality glass mirrors became available in the 16th century, many artists started painting themselves. This gave them a chance to examine their own appearance and character. It was also a good way for them to practice and try out new techniques without having to worry about pleasing anyone else. Even more importantly, self portraits were a way for artists to show off their skill to people who might pay to have their own portraits done, like an early form of advertizing.

Picking props

Portrait artists put great care into picking the right props and accessories to reflect the lives and personalities of their sitters – for example, to show what they did for a living. Props can also tell stories. Some old family portraits included an empty cot to refer to a baby who had died, which sadly used to happen quite often. Fashions change, too. So 17th-century portraits tended to have plain, dark backgrounds while, in the 18th century, colorful, open-air settings became popular.

👁 For a link to a website where you can investigate the house and studio of the artist Rembrandt van Rijn, go to **www.usborne-quicklinks.com**

Self Portrait In A Straw Hat (after 1782), by Elisabeth Vigée-Lebrun, a successful portrait artist. Here, she chose to show herself with the tools of her trade. Her glamorous outfit does not look very practical for painting, but was the height of fashion at the time, and the kind of thing her clients might wear.

Modern times

Paintings have always been expensive – whereas photography is now so cheap that almost everyone can have a portrait taken. Inevitably, after the invention of photography nearly 200 years ago, many people became less interested in having their portraits painted. But some artists tried to outdo photographs by painting in a radically different way.

Traditionally, portraits only recorded one view of a person – whether a profile, front or three-quarters view – though painters occasionally added an extra one, as a sculpture or reflection in the background. In modern times, artists have taken this idea even further by combining intersecting views of people seen from different angles. This might seem strange, and less lifelike than conventional painting styles. But, by showing several angles at once, artists were trying to create portraits which represented people more completely.

Portrait Of Picasso (1912), by Juan Gris. The artist Pablo Picasso invented the technique of multiple views used here. So this portrait isn't just a picture of Picasso himself – it also reflects one of his best-known achievements.

Landscapes

In medieval times, people didn't really think landscapes made good paintings by themselves. When they were painted, it was usually only as a backdrop to a story-telling scene. Some were no more than a few rocks in the background – one 14th-century artist's handbook actually advised artists to collect rocks. But, in the 16th and 17th centuries, all that began to change.

This 15th-century landscape is the setting for a Bible story. It's not very lifelike. The mountains get smaller as they get farther away, but St. John stays the same size, to ensure he stays the focus of attention.

Saint John The Baptist Retiring To The Desert (1453), by Giovanni di Paolo

Getting things in perspective

In the 16th century, artists made ground-breaking discoveries about perspective, which enabled them to represent space more accurately (see page 42). This meant they could create much more lifelike landscapes. Gradually, painters began to design pictures where the landscape was more important than the people, or even where there were no people at all. By the 17th century, landscape had become a popular subject in its own right. A huge number were produced, especially in northern Europe, ranging from idyllic imaginary scenes to detailed views of real places, like the country scene below.

An Autumn Landscape With A View Of Het Steen (1636), by Flemish artist Peter Paul Rubens. The 1600s saw a massive increase in landscape painting, particularly in nothern Europe, where this was done. It shows the countryside near Rubens' home in Flanders (now Belgium).

Getting out

The first landscape painters didn't paint on location. They would make sketches outside, but return to the studio to complete their paintings. But, from the mid-19th century, there was a new fashion for painting in the open air. Inspired by the changing effects of light and weather, many artists now wanted to paint landscapes directly from nature.

The Water Lily Pond (1899), by Claude Monet. Notice how sunlight catches the leaves and lily flowers, and glints off the bridge.

Monet painted this scene in his own backyard at Giverny in northern France. It shows a calm, peaceful world, very far from the revolutions and wars going on at the time. Even after World War One broke out and troops were going past his home, Monet stuck to painting lilies.

👁 For a link to a website where you can go on an interactive landscape adventure, and create landscapes that show different places, moods and weather, go to **www.usborne-quicklinks.com**

Personal views

Over the centuries, artists' approaches to landscapes have changed as much as the landscapes themselves. In the last hundred years, especially, there has been a huge variety of styles. These range from the startling cityscapes of the Cubists (see page 108) and the atmospheric urban views of Edward Hopper to 'Land art' (see page 150). This is where artists work within the landscape itself, using dirt, stones and other natural materials. From these, they build monuments inspired by the surrounding scenery – works which then become part of the landscape themselves.

Route 6, Eastham (1941), by Edward Hopper. This landscape looks almost photographic. But it is full of emotion. It's a lonely scene, with no people, just houses seen from the side of a long road, as if by someone just passing through.

Still lifes

Still lifes are paintings of objects that can't move, such as flowers and fruit, musical instruments, or whatever else catches an artist's fancy. Until the late 19th century, the goal of most still lifes was to look as realistic as possible. And artists became so good at it, they could create anything from grapes which look good enough to eat, to jugs and bowls which seem to jut right out of the painting.

Tricking the eye

Still life paintings can be very demanding. Artists have to create an attractive composition, while also trying to make everything – the light, the textures – look as lifelike as possible. The most lifelike pictures are known as *trompe l'oeil*, which is French for 'tricking the eye.' These pictures try to fool you into thinking you are looking at real objects, not flat, painted surfaces. But, despite this, until the 19th century most critics looked down on still lifes. They saw them as just technical exercises which didn't require much creativity to make, or thought to understand.

Old Models (1892), by William Michael Harnett. This *trompe l'oeil* painting tries to make you think it is not a painting at all, but a shelf in front of a cupboard.

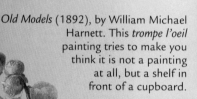

Becoming popular

Still lifes date back to ancient Greece and Rome, when they formed part of the wall decorations in wealthy houses. Later, in medieval and Renaissance times, still lifes mostly only appeared as part of a larger picture. For example, paintings of the Virgin Mary often included a vase of lilies, symbolizing purity. It wasn't until the 17th century that still lifes really became a genre in their own right. They were soon popular with a very wide audience, perhaps because you didn't have to know anything about Classical myths or the Bible to understand them.

Fruit, Flowers And A Fish (1772), by Dutch painter Jan van Os. Sumptuous arrangements of flowers and food are a common theme of still life paintings. Notice the different textures in the enlarged detail on the left.

The Attributes Of The Arts And Their Rewards (1766), by Jean Chardin

Hidden meanings

A still life may be a straightforward picture, or it may contain hidden meanings. Artists often pick objects to represent particular ideas. For example, books mean knowledge, musical instruments symbolize pleasure, and skulls, flickering flames or decaying fruit are meant to make us think about death. Paintings with symbolic meanings are known as allegories. They became so popular, some artists ended up painting little else.

In this still life, the objects were chosen to represent the arts: drawing, painting and sculpture. (See how many art-related items you can spot.) The small replica statue shows the god Mercury, who was supposed to be the patron of the arts.

Express yourself

In the 19th century, still lifes tended to become less lifelike, as artists began experimenting with using them to express their feelings. They often chose objects which had some special significance in their own lives, and used styles and colors which reflected how they felt, rather than how things really looked. According to the French painter Edouard Manet, "A painter can express all that he wants with fruit or flowers."

Today, artists are still experimenting. Now, still lifes don't even have to be painted. Ordinary, everyday objects – previously the subject of still lifes – can appear as works of art in their own right. For example, in the 1960s, the American artist Andy Warhol exhibited life-size copies of boxes of soap powder.

This still life, by Dutch artist Vincent van Gogh, is a kind of symbolic self portrait. It shows a chair and pipe which belonged to the painter – plain, ordinary objects, as rustic and down-to-earth as the man himself.

👁 For links to websites where you can find out about the meaning of different scientific objects shown in paintings, and zoom in on details from a work by William Harnett, go to **www.usborne-quicklinks.com**

Van Gogh's Chair (1888), by Vincent van Gogh. Notice the sprouting bulbs in the box. They are symbols of nature and renewal, and may also be a witty reference to Dutch flower paintings like the one on the previous page.

What is modern art?

Modern art is so different from traditional art that some people think it belongs in a completely separate category. It can be anything from an oil painting to an empty room with the light going on and off. Art historians use the term "modern" to describe art from as far back as the 1850s. That may not sound very modern, but it was about then that artists began to rethink their ideas in a very radical way.

Spot the difference

For hundreds of years, most artists tried to create the illusion of real, 3-D scenes. But in the 19th century that began to change – partly because of the invention of photography in the 1830s. Before then, people had relied on artists to capture appearances. Once photographs could do that, some artists felt they should be doing something else. In the past many artists had been paid by wealthy people to work for them. But that changed too. During the 19th century, artists began to create art first and sell it later. This gave them more freedom to experiment. Just compare the two paintings on this page. Both show arrangements of objects, or still lifes – a traditional subject for painters. But the differences are far more obvious than the similarities.

Vanitas (1600s), by an unknown French artist; oil on canvas. *Vanitas* is Latin for "vanity" – meaning the vanity or emptiness of earthly pleasures when we all die in the end.

Guitar on a Table (1916), by Juan Grís; oil on canvas, 36 x 24in. Notice how Grís uses geometric shapes to break up the picture, and there are odd jumps between one shape and the next, so things don't join up.

Original works

Many people judge art by the technical skill of the artist – so they are more impressed by polished, lifelike paintings, such as the skull, than experimental art, such as the guitar. But for many artists nowadays, originality is more important than technique. The skull might look very convincing, but the simple shapes and vivid colors of the guitar make it a very striking, inventive image.

Is it really art?

Now there is such a huge emphasis on being original, it isn't surprising that artists are constantly pushing the boundaries of what we call "art." If you visit a modern art gallery today, you might find anything from a plain white canvas to a row of pebbles, a huge, hamburger-shaped cushion or a pile of silver sweets.

The word "art" originally meant "crafted by hand," but some of these things weren't actually made by the artist – they were just objects he or she found. Just because they were chosen and arranged by the artist, and put on show in a gallery, does it make them art?

The Physical Impossibility of Death in the Mind of Someone Living (1991), by Damien Hirst; tiger shark, 5% formaldehyde, glass, steel, 84 x 204 x 84in.
This is a real, dead shark, suspended in formaldehyde to stop it from decaying.

The shock of the new

A lot of modern art sets out to be new and shocking, in order to startle you and make you see things in a new way. But, when you look at it closely, It often turns out to be about age-old themes. Damien Hirst became notorious for using dead animals, such as the shark above. But he uses it to explore mortality, just like the 17th-century oil painting on the left. The shark's preserved body, like the painted skull, is meant to make us think about death. But it looks so alive, it is hard to accept it is really dead – illustrating Hirst's title, "The Physical Impossibility of Death in the Mind of Someone Living."

Arguing it out

Modern art can provoke fierce arguments and sometimes even court cases. Everyone has different ideas and opinions, and it is no easy matter to resolve them. Sculptor Constantin Brancusi sued U.S. Customs to prove his sculptures were "art." He won; but artist Richard Serra wasn't so lucky. He made a huge, curving wall of steel entitled *Tilted Arc* for a New York square. The arc angered locals, who said it kept them from using the square. For Serra, that was the point – he wanted to change their awareness of space. But, after a court hearing, judges ordered that it be removed.

In 1998-99, Tracey Emin sparked off a huge controversy by exhibiting her own bed as art. Two visiting artists were even inspired to stage a pillow fight on it in protest.

Looking at modern art

Many people find modern art especially baffling, especially if they expect to recognize what they see, or are looking for traditional skills such as being able to draw accurately from life. But there are lots of other ways to think about it. Here are some questions you could ask when looking at modern art.

For links to websites where you can view a selection of modern art or take an online "art safari," go to **www.usborne-quicklinks.com**

What's it all about?

One of the most puzzling things with modern art is that it is not always obvious what it's really about. But the title may give you a clue – even if it is just *Composition* or *Improvisation*. Vague titles often mean the artist wasn't trying to show a particular scene, but to explore his or her ideas about art or life.

There will also be clues in the work itself – even if they may be hard to spot at first. Look at it carefully and think about what the image shows, and the style and colors the artist used, and how they make you feel.

Some paintings and sculptures don't have clear subjects. They use colors and shapes for artistic effect, rather than as a way of representing scenes. This is known as abstract art. You are meant to appreciate these works as things in their own right, not as images of something else.

The Snail (1953), by Henri Matisse; gouache on cut and pasted paper, 113 x 113in. At first glance, this just seems like a bright, cheerful pattern. But the title suggests there is more to it. Do you think the spiraling arrangement resembles the spiral shape of a snail shell? There is also a tiny snail silhouette jutting out of the lilac shape in the corner.

How was it made?

It is worth thinking about how something was made, too. Modern artists don't just paint and sculpt – they use a huge range of materials or "media." Some make films or photographs, or work with things they happen to find. Others design works, known as "installations," for specific places. And some artists don't actually make things at all, but put on shows or document their thoughts. Their choice of methods will depend a lot on their ideas about art.

Untitled (1985), by Donald Judd; painted aluminum, 12 x 47 x 12in. Judd used metal and other industrial materials because he wanted to explore their particular qualities.

When was it made?

If you know something about when a work of art was made, and what else was happening at the time, it may help to explain why an artist chose to work in a certain way. Big historic events such as wars affect everyone, including artists. And the development of modern art movements such as Expressionism or Cubism, when artists work together and share ideas, can greatly influence an individual artist's style. But it is misleading to see things just in terms of "isms." Art doesn't fit neatly into categories. Each artist and each work is different.

Girl with a Kitten (1947), by Lucian Freud; oil on canvas, 16 x 12in. Freud is known for painting intense, detailed portraits. But it is hard to categorize his style, which is sometimes compared to Realism, sometimes to Expressionism.

Do you like it?

Another important question – whatever kind of art you are looking at – is whether you like it or not, and why. This is a matter of taste – and tastes change. What seemed shocking a hundred years ago may look ordinary today. The Impressionists were considered outrageous in the 1850s. But compared to a lot of very recent art, they actually seem fairly traditional.

Experiencing modern art

You can read more about the history of modern art, from the 19th century right up to the present day, in the second half of this book. It will help you see how radical new ideas developed, and how they related to events at the time.

A lot of modern art is designed to create a strong – and sometimes shocking – impression. You can get an even better sense of this if you visit a modern art gallery or museum, so you can experience the impact of seeing it first-hand.

Maman (1999), by Louise Bourgeois; bronze and steel, 365 x 351 x 403in. This huge spider is just one example of what you can see at modern art museums. It stands outside the Guggenheim Museum in Bilbao, Spain.

ANCIENT AND MEDIEVAL ART

This section traces the origins of art in the ancient world, from the lively wall paintings of ancient Egypt, created almost 5,000 years ago, through the polished elegance of Classical Greek and Roman sculptures, to the richly colored religious art of medieval Europe, up until about 1400.

Detail from *The Wilton Diptych* (about 1395-99), by an unknown medieval artist. You can see the whole picture on pages 32-33.

Art and magic

Many beautiful works of art survive from ancient times – from Egyptian tomb paintings to Minoan palace decorations. But the earliest artists would not have thought of their work as 'art,' the way we do today. Most early art was actually made for ritual or magic purposes.

Walk like an Egyptian

Egypt was ruled by kings, called pharaohs, from about 3000BC to 30BC. Much of the art that survives from that period was made for tombs, including carved stone statues and elaborately detailed paintings. The painting on the right dates from about 1350BC.

Egyptian artists followed strict rules when drawing people. They would always draw a person's head, arms and legs from the side, and usually showed the upper body twisted to face us. This is not a natural pose, but it did show each part of the body very clearly.

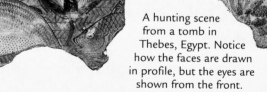

A hunting scene from a tomb in Thebes, Egypt. Notice how the faces are drawn in profile, but the eyes are shown from the front.

Staying alive

The ancient Egyptians believed art had magical powers. They decorated tombs with images of everyday life, because they really believed these would help the person live on in the next world. People thought it was more important to record details clearly than to create natural-looking scenes. For them, art was a way of preserving life. In fact, one Egyptian word for sculptor can be translated as 'he-who-keeps-alive.'

This painting of ancient Egyptians preparing a dead body is from *The Book Of The Dead*, which was full of spells supposed to help the dead in the afterlife.

Island art

From about 2000BC, art flourished on the Greek islands, particularly on Crete, where a people called the Minoans lived. The Minoans were great seafarers and traded with the Egyptians, and their art shows an Egyptian influence. But the Minoan style was less stiff and formal. Look at the flowing shapes of the Minoan figures on the right.

A lot of Minoan art had to do with religious rituals. For example, many statues show gods or worshipers. But some Minoan art – such as animal designs on storage jars – was probably just for decoration. So, for the first time, people were making art for its own sake, just because they liked the way it looked.

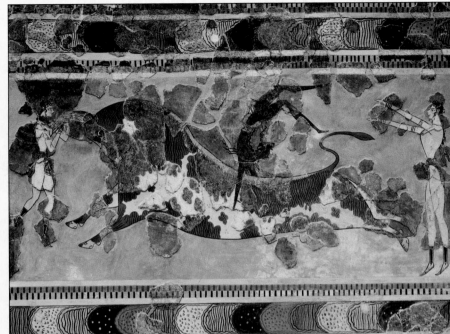

This painting was made on the wall of a Minoan palace in about 1500BC. It shows the Minoan sport of bull jumping, in which athletes would seize a bull by its horns and vault over it. The figures are simplified and their faces are in profile, just like in Egyptian art, but their bodies are more lively.

Artists and warriors

Then, from about 1600-1100BC, a people known as the Mycenaeans dominated most of Greece. They were great warriors and fought many battles, including the Trojan War. You can see their preoccupation with war reflected in their art, which often shows warriors and fight scenes.

The Mycenaeans took over Crete from the Minoans, and were influenced by their art too. But compared with Minoan art, Mycenean paintings seem much less fluid. The difference between the two styles shows how early Greek art developed and changed, unlike Egyptian art, which remained virtually the same for thousands of years.

The Mycenaean vase on the right was made about 1400-1300BC. It shows horse-drawn chariots of the kind the Mycenaeans used in battle.

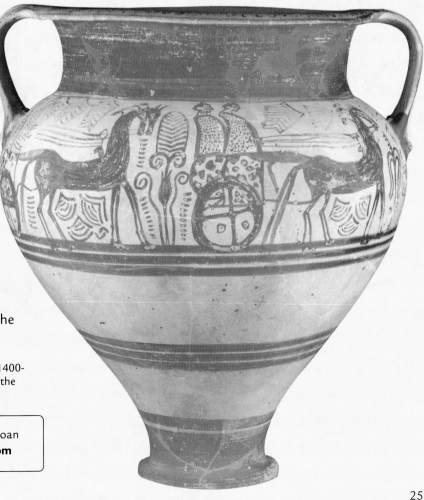

● For links to websites where you can explore Minoan and Egyptian art, go to **www.usborne-quicklinks.com**

Classical art

The brilliant age of what is now called Classical art began in Greece over 2,500 years ago, in the 5th century BC. During Classical times, the ancient Greeks developed amazing new styles of painting, sculpture and architecture, and came up with ideas about politics, law, philosophy and science, which have influenced western civilization ever since.

This Classical statue – a Roman copy of a Greek original – shows a man throwing a discus.

This scene, from a 5th-century Greek cup, shows a dancer and a young man. Their clear profiles show an Egyptian influence, but their poses are more natural.

The art of observation

The ancient Greeks were fascinated by the world around them and studied it closely – and they used their observations of real life in their art. Sculptors of the period tried to show the human body in a realistic, natural-looking way. The standards they set, for both beauty and technical skill, have been admired and imitated for centuries.

Unfortunately, very few ancient Greek paintings have survived. Paintings made on wood rotted away, and wall paintings were lost when buildings were destroyed. But we know quite a lot about Greek painting from ancient writings. And the Greeks were famous for making painted vases and dishes, many of which did survive.

One ancient Greek writer described how a painter named Zeuxis made a picture of grapes that looked so real that birds tried to eat them. But his rival Parrhasius outdid him by painting a curtain which looked so real that Zeuxis tried to pull it.

An ideal world

Although Classical Greek artists created detailed, natural-looking figures, these were not necessarily meant to be real people. Artists wanted to create ideal images of people rather than recording how they really looked.

The statue on the left shows a Greek athlete. His appearance was determined by what the Greeks thought was beautiful. The proportions of his body are perfectly balanced, and his features are calm and regular. These ideals of beauty have had a lasting influence on artists.

This marble figure is a Roman copy of a 5th-century bronze. Sadly the original, made by a Greek sculptor named Myron, was lost centuries ago.

The art of Rome

The Romans dominated Europe for almost 1,000 years, between about 500BC and AD500. But, in art, they were influenced by the Greeks, who were absorbed into their empire. The Romans admired and copied Greek sculptures and techniques. In fact, many Greek sculptures were destroyed or looted at the end of the Classical age, and are now known only from Roman copies which lasted well because they were made of stone.

This portrait bust shows the famous Roman leader Julius Caesar. You can see how lined and careworn his face is compared with the Greek athlete's.

But whereas the Greeks only sculpted idealized or mythical figures, the Romans also wanted to create lifelike portraits of real people. So Roman portraits show faces with expressive features and individual details, such as wrinkles, as you can see on the carved head above.

Buried treasure

In AD79, a volcanic eruption buried the Roman town of Pompeii and, for centuries, it lay hidden under layers of ash. When the town was finally uncovered in 1748, archaeologists discovered houses with walls covered in paintings – portraits, landscapes, mythical scenes and still lifes, painted in a variety of styles.

The paintings from Pompeii show how skilled artists were, over 2,000 years ago, at using texture, shading and some forms of perspective. Roman artists were trying to paint scenes as they would look in real life.

Notice how natural this tree looks compared with the plants in the Eygptian scene on page 24.

Many rooms in Pompeii had no windows, but the false landscapes painted on the walls made it seem as if you could see out.

👁 For links to websites where you can find out more about the art of ancient Greece and Rome, go to www.usborne-quicklinks.com

A wall painting from Pompeii

Patterns and monsters

Just over 1,500 years ago, the Western part of the Roman empire collapsed, plunging most of Europe into a period of chaos, fighting and upheavals, sometimes referred to as 'the Dark Ages.' Without the unifying influence of the empire, many different styles of art began to emerge.

Live and learn

During the Dark Ages, monasteries played a vital role in keeping art and literacy alive. The Church encouraged monks to produce illuminated manuscripts (books written and decorated by hand) of religious texts. This helped them to spread the Christian message.

This is an image of St. Matthew from a manuscript known as *The Book Of Kells*. Notice how the figures are simplified, so they look like parts of the pattern.

Irish illuminations

The Book Of Kells, made around the end of the 8th century, is one of the oldest surviving illuminated manuscripts. It was named after the monastery of Kells, in Ireland, where it was kept until 1007. The book contains the four gospels in Latin, decorated with ornate pictures.

These round, interlacing patterns are known as Celtic knots.

👁 For a link to a website about another 8th-century illuminated manuscript, go to **www.usborne-quicklinks.com**

Making a book

In medieval times, books had to be made and written out laboriously by hand, so they were rare and highly prized possessions. No one in Europe knew how to make paper yet, so books were usually made from animal skin, or 'parchment.' Sheets of parchment were covered with text and pictures drawn using a quill or reed pen dipped in colored ink. Then the sheets were folded, sewn together, and attached to a leather or wooden spine.

Reviving the classics

In the 9th century, there was a revival of art and learning during a period of relative peace in the reign of Charles the Great, or Charlemagne. Charlemagne was King of the Franks, in what is now France. He later came to control most of Europe. He was eager to revive ancient Roman culture and spread Christianity. So he encouraged religious art in a Classical style, which is now known as Carolingian. Unfortunately, few paintings have survived from this time. But some Carolingian art does still exist – mainly illustrations from Classical and Christian manuscripts, made in a natural-looking style inspired by Classical art.

The scene on the left shows Jesus miraculously turning water into wine. It is part of an ivory panel carved in the 9th century, in France, to decorate the cover of a religious book.

Fighting spirit

At the end of the 9th century, Viking raiders from Scandinavia began to attack the lands ruled by Charlemagne's successors. These attacks caused disruption and chaos which largely destroyed Carolingian culture. But the Vikings did bring with them an art of their own. They were expert wood-carvers and metal-workers, who created elaborate animal figures and patterns to decorate their boats, weapons and clothes. They did not share Charlemagne's Christian faith, and may have believed that some of their art – such as the fierce monster heads on their ships – actually had magical powers.

This 11th-century Viking brooch, made of silver and shaped like a dragon, would have been used to fasten a cloak.

Fear of God

In the 11th and 12th centuries, as Europe emerged from the Dark Ages, many new churches and cathedrals were put up. They were built in a grand style based on Roman architecture and known as 'Romanesque,' with stone columns, round arches and vaulted ceilings. These churches were adorned with carvings of people, animals and monstrous devils, designed to put the fear of God into churchgoers. One of the most popular subjects for carvings was the Last Judgement. This was the day when people believed their souls would rise up to Heaven or be sent to Hell.

This carving of a demon from the Last Judgement, at the Abbey of Sainte Foy, in France, was made in about 1115-25. It has a gruesome smile, as if it can't wait to get its hands on a sinner.

Saints and sinners

The Roman empire had been split in two at the end of the 4th century. The eastern part became known as the Byzantine empire, after the old name of its capital, Byzantium (now Istanbul, in Turkey), and its art is known as Byzantine art. This empire outlasted the western empire by a thousand years.

A new religion

Christianity became the official religion of the Roman empire in the 4th century, and Christian themes were common in Byzantine art. Interest in religion made artists more concerned with the spirit and less with what things looked like. They thought it was more important to create symbols of religious experience than to show natural-looking scenes.

This 6th-century mosaic shows a scene from the Bible. Jesus is blessing the loaves and fishes which, according to the story, fed 5,000 people. The artist created natural-looking, shaded figures, but the rich gold background emphasizes the holy and miraculous nature of the scene.

At this time, few people could read, so pictures were used to tell stories and they had to be easy to understand. The scene above has simplified outlines, strong colors, and a plain background to focus attention, a bit like a modern comic strip. The people have big, soulful eyes and contemplative expressions, to show their spiritual nature. But the artist still used realistic techniques such as shading, as the Romans had done.

Marvellous mosaics

Brilliantly colored, shiny mosaics, like the ones on the left, were used to decorate Byzantine churches. Mosaic pictures are made up of tiny pieces of glass or stone; a large mosaic can contain several million pieces. The pieces were all set at slightly different angles, so they would reflect light from different directions and create a shimmering effect.

Mosaics on the ceiling and walls of a 12th-century chapel in Palermo, Sicily

Image-smashers

With the growth of Christianity, richly decorated images of religious figures, known as icons, became popular. But these led to arguments about art among church leaders. Some thought icons could help teach religion. Others believed icons were idols, or false gods, and wanted to destroy them. These people were known as iconoclasts, which means 'image-smashers.'

In the early 8th century, across most of eastern Europe, Turkey and Syria, religious art was banned by the Church. Many early icons were destroyed, so it is rare to see examples of them today. Even when the ban was lifted in the 9th century, there were still restrictions on holy images. Artists could only show saints in certain approved styles and poses, like the one on the left. This is why their pictures often look very similar.

This is a 10th-century Italian icon which shows the Virgin Mary holding the infant Jesus. The figures may look a bit stiff, but their face-on pose was quite conventional.

👁 For a link to a website where you can see Byzantine paintings, carvings and jewels, and find out about them, go to **www.usborne-quicklinks.com**

Saints and symbols

In paintings, saints are often shown with symbols to help identify them. The spear and monster in the picture on the right show it is an icon of St. George, who was said to have killed a dragon with a spear. When a symbol was associated with a particular group of people, the saint would be chosen to be their protector or patron. For example, St. Catherine, who is identified by a wheel, became the patron saint of wheelwrights.

A 15th-century Byzantine icon of St. George, made in Russia

Here are some symbols and what they mean.

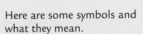

Palm leaf - a martyr (someone who died for their beliefs)

Dove - the holy spirit

Keys - St. Peter, who holds the keys to heaven

Wheel - St. Catherine, who was sentenced to be put to death on a wheel (which broke)

Halo - holiness; most halos are round, but if you spot a square one, it means that the person was alive when the picture was made.

The Wilton Diptych

This precious 14th-century painting shows King Richard II of England kneeling before the Virgin Mary and Jesus, who are surrounded by angels. Richard II is being presented to them by three saints: St. Edmund, St. Edward and St. John the Baptist.

Title: *The Wilton Diptych*
Date: about 1395-99
Artist: Unknown English or French ar
Materials: egg tempera on oak
Size: two panels, each 21 x 15in, joined together by hinges

A portable painting

This picture is made up of two hinged panels, so it can be folded and carried, or unfolded to stand on an altar. A picture with two panels is known as a diptych. Small diptychs like this were usually painted for wealthy patrons. Larger diptychs or triptychs (pictures with three panels) were generally made for churches.

This diptych is known as the Wilton Diptych because it was once kept in Wilton House in Wiltshire, England. Originally, it probably belonged to Richard II himself. It is littered with symbols – if you know where to look for them.

From left to right, the standing men are St. Edmund, St. Edward and St. John the Baptist, Richard II's patron saint. St. Edmund, a former English king, holds the arrow which killed him. St. John holds a lamb, because he called Jesus 'the lamb of God.'

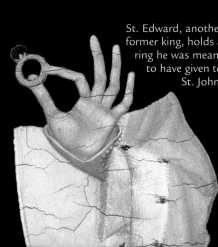

The king wears a gold collar made to look like the seed pods of broom plants. This was the emblem of his family, the Plantagenets, whose name sounded like the Latin for broom, *Planta Genista.*

This white hart (deer) was painted on the back of one panel. It was Richard II's personal emblem. There are white harts on Richard's brooch and robes, too.

St. Edward, anothe former king, holds ring he was mean to have given t St. John

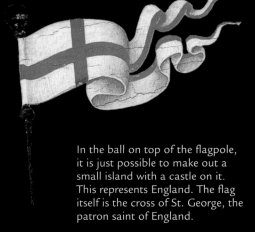

In the ball on top of the flagpole, it is just possible to make out a small island with a castle on it. This represents England. The flag itself is the cross of St. George, the patron saint of England.

Fit for a king

This painting is covered in sumptuous materials, generally used only in small amounts, making it fit for a king. The background is real gold leaf, and the robes worn by Mary and the angels are painted in an expensive blue. To make this rich blue color, the artist used ground lapis lazuli, a semi-precious stone which had to be brought all the way from Afghanistan.

The angels wear collars of broom plants and badges with white harts (the king's emblems) to show their loyalty to the king.

Divine right

The picture was designed to link Richard II's reign with the rule of Heaven. The angels bear the king's emblems, and the infant Jesus holds out his hand toward the king as if to bless him. This illustrates the belief that the king got his authority from God, because he was God's representative on Earth.

A heavenly carpet of flowers contrasts with the bare ground of the ordinary world.

Art and prayer

In the 14th century, most paintings were made for Christian churches and other religious buildings, so the scenes they show are religious too – pictures of saints or stories from the Bible. The few paintings made for private individuals tend to be religious as well, as they were usually designed to help them pray.

Heaven and Earth

The Virgin Mary was an extremely important figure in religious paintings at this time. She was regarded as a link between Heaven and Earth, a channel between us and God – human, like us, but also the mother of Jesus, the son of God. So Mary is at the center of the grand altarpiece on the right. You can see her more clearly in the enlarged detail below.

The Coronation Of The Virgin (1370-71), by Italian artist Jacopo di Cione and his workshop. This was originally made for a church in Florence.

Here, Jesus is crowning Mary the Queen of Heaven.

Dress to impress

The grandest paintings were made to adorn church altars, as the altar was the focus of worshipers' attention. Enormous altarpieces made up of many separate panels were designed to stand directly behind the altar. They were richly colored and often coated in gold leaf. Their huge scale and costly materials were designed to impress people with the glory of God. The pictures themselves were meant to help people who couldn't read to learn stories from the Bible.

Workshops

At this time, artists were seen as craftsmen, whose work depended on their manual skills. They worked together in large workshops, so one picture would be the work of several people. A large altarpiece like the one above would take the workshop about a year to make. It was hard for artists to win individual fame, but successful ones might end up running a workshop.

Donors and devils

Paintings in churches were often paid for by a wealthy individual, or donor, rather than the church itself. The donors were sometimes included in the paintings as well, though they were generally made smaller than the holy figures, to show they were less important. Including donors in religious scenes was a way of advertising the donors' devotion to their religion, as well as their generosity.

Saint Michael And The Devil shows St. Michael (also known as the Archangel Michael) slaying a sharp-toothed little devil. To one side, a much smaller man kneels praying. This is the donor who paid for the picture, Don Antonio Juan. No one knew what St. Michael would have looked like, so he is just made to look handsome and heroic. But Don Antonio has very distinctive features, so this is probably a real portrait. He seems uninvolved with the drama happening in front of him, but prays with a distant expression, perhaps to St. Michael.

You can see the towers of the city of Heaven reflected in St. Michael's armored breastplate.

Saint Michael And The Devil (1468), by Bartolomé Bermejo. This was probably the center of an altarpiece in a church in Spain. The devil combines details from several animals, including snakes, ducks and frogs.

👁 For a link to a website where you can explore a picture of St. George slaying the dragon, go to **www.usborne-quicklinks.com**

Courtly delight

In the rich and glamorous European courts of the 15th century, a new kind of art began to emerge. The princes and their courtiers still wanted art that showed how religious they were. But they also wanted it to reflect their aristocratic lifestyle, or an idealized version of it. So they encouraged an ornamental, richly colored style of art, full of carefully observed details of plants and animals. This is often known as International Gothic.

Beautiful books

The lords and ladies of the courts liked to surround themselves with elegant objects, such as beautifully illustrated books. 'Books of Hours' were especially popular. These were prayer books used at home for private devotions, rather than in church. They contained prayers for different times of day, different days and different seasons, illustrated lavishly. One of the best-known surviving examples, *The Very Rich Hours* (often called by its French title, *Les Très Riches Heures*), was made for a French nobleman, the Duke of Berry. It is full of details of everyday life, such as laborers working on a farm or people celebrating festivals.

An illustration from one page of *The Very Rich Hours: May* (about 1416), by the Limbourg brothers. These riders – some dressed in 'May green' – are taking part in a procession to celebrate the month of May.

My one desire

In those days, large, luxurious tapestries were used as wall-coverings, helping to keep rooms warm as well as giving people something to look at. They often showed hunting scenes or ladies at court, decorated with animals and flowers. Others dealt with love, a popular subject in medieval poetry.

The tapestry on the left is from a famous series known as *The Lady And The Unicorn*. Love is the theme. An elegantly dressed lady stands by a pavilion which is embroidered with the words, in French, 'To my one desire.' A maid is offering her a chest – perhaps it contains a gift from the lady's lover?

To My One Desire (15th century), a tapestry by an unknown artist or artists

Model animals

The Italian artist Antonio Pisano, known as 'Pisanello,' spent most of his career working in the courts of Italian princes. Many of his paintings show hunting and other noble pastimes. He made 'model' books full of detailed drawings of birds and animals, which he could refer to later.

Pisanello probably copied this hare from one of his model books.

If you look at the painting below, you'll see the animals are drawn to different scales, and almost without overlapping. This is because they were copied from model books and preparatory sketches. The animals are all associated with hunting – birds, deer, a hare, and even a bear, as well as the huntsman's own horse and dogs. But the subject is religious too. It tells the story of St. Eustace, the patron saint of hunters. He was out hunting one day and was about to shoot a stag. Then he had a vision of Jesus on the cross between its antlers. This was so powerful it made him convert to Christianity. The story provides a perfect excuse for a decorative and elegant hunting scene. Although Eustace was meant to have been an ancient Roman, Pisanello shows him in the clothes of an Italian courtier of the time.

The Vision Of St. Eustace (about 1438-42) by Antonio Pisano, or 'Pisanello.' Notice how detailed all the animals are.

THE RENAISSANCE

In the 15th and 16th centuries, Europe underwent a cultural revolution. This became known as the Renaissance, which means 'rebirth,' because many people were inspired by a renewed interest in Classical culture. It affected all aspects of life – from art and architecture to science and philosophy. In painting, techniques developed which helped artists create

Detail from *Narcissus* (about 1490-99), by an unknown follower of Renaissance artist Leonardo da Vinci. You can see the whole picture on page 50.

Making it real

In the 15th century, paintings in the Netherlands became much more realistic. For the first time, it became common for artists to use settings and people drawn from life. They paid careful attention to tiny details, especially the effects of light on things, using smooth brushwork and delicate shading to create an almost photographic finish.

Egg and oil

This more realistic way of painting was made possible by the kind of paint these artists used. In Italy, at this time, painters mainly worked in egg tempera – a mixture of colored pigments and egg. But, in the Netherlands, artists began mixing pigments with oil. Unlike egg, oil takes a long time to dry, so artists who used oil paint were able to work more slowly and put in more details.

St. Luke Painting The Virgin (about 1530), by an unknown artist. St. Luke, who lived in the 1st century AD, was the patron saint of painters. Here, he is shown as a 15th-century artist.

15th-century artists had to make their own paints, grinding stones, plants and other things to use as pigments. They couldn't buy ready-made paint.

Light fantastic

The new oil paintings had another important feature – light. They showed the effects of light very accurately, with the light often coming from a source, such as a window, that you could see in the picture itself. Even where the background is dark, as in van Eyck's portrait, it is the light falling across the face that brings it to life. Oil paint was good for representing these effects because it is translucent, which means light can pass through it (unlike egg tempera, which is opaque.)

Man In A Turban (1433), by Jan van Eyck. This is probably a self portrait. The artist signed his work with some lettering on the frame. This reads: 'As I/Eyck can; Jan van Eyck made me, 21 October 1433.'

Setting the scene

At this time, artists often chose up-to-date settings, even for historical scenes. This picture from the Netherlands shows the Virgin Mary nursing the infant Jesus, but it makes her look like a wealthy 15th-century lady. She's wearing a jewel-edged dress and is surrounded by luxuries, including an embroidered cushion and a beautifully illuminated prayer book. To people at the time, this setting would have made her seem closer to them.

The window opens onto a scene of everyday life in the Netherlands, with riders on horseback and a man climbing a ladder.

The picture is very detailed, right down to the hairs on Mary's head – each individual hair was painted separately, using a brush with only one or two bristles. But not all the details are original. The strip on the right, including the goblet and cupboard, was added in the 19th century, to replace a section which had been destroyed.

The Virgin And Child Before A Firescreen (about 1440), by Robert Campin and his workshop, and some anonymous 19th-century picture restorers.

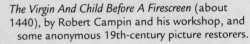

Mary's 'halo' is actually a round wicker firescreen, standing on the floor behind her.

👁 For a link to a website where you can see a collection of beautiful 15th- and 16th-century oil paintings from the Netherlands, go to **www.usborne-quicklinks.com**

Born again

The Renaissance saw an amazing buzz of creativity, especially in Italy, where many leading artists lived. Their discoveries had a profound effect on painting. But although Renaissance artists were inspired by the Classical age, they hadn't actually seen any Classical paintings. Instead, they found out what they could from ancient texts and sculptures.

True to life

Renaissance painters read what Classical writers had to say about the value of making art look lifelike. So they began to study optics (the science of sight) and perspective, in order to make accurate, convincing drawings. Some artists even dissected dead bodies to learn more about anatomy.

Going by the book

In 1436, a writer named Leon Battista Alberti published a book called *On Painting*. It described ways artists could make pictures more realistic by using light, color and perspective. This required a lot of study, especially of the math needed for perspective. Alberti's book was very influential and, as artists adopted his techniques, people began to think of artists more as creative, intellectual types than just skilled craftsmen.

The Virgin And Child (1426), by Tommaso di Giovanni, known as 'Masaccio'

Seeing in 3-D

Since Classical times, painters had used perspective to create an impression of 3-D space on a flat surface. For example, Roman painters made distant objects appear smaller. But, during the Renaissance, artists worked out a system of rules for constructing whole scenes in 'unified' perspective, as if everything was seen from the same viewpoint. This made the illusion of space much more effective.

The Annunciation (1486), by Carlo Crivelli. This painting clearly shows the use of perspective. It is designed to make us feel we are looking through a window rather than at a flat, painted surface.

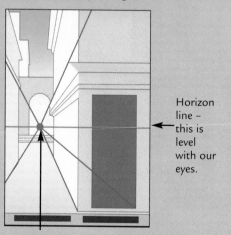

This diagram shows how Crivelli constructed the painting on the left.

Horizon line – this is level with our eyes.

Vanishing point – all the lines pointing into the picture converge at this point.

👁 For a link to a website that shows how to draw in perspective, go to **www.usborne-quicklinks.com**

Art of Florence

The Renaissance spread across Europe, but its earliest champions were Italian, and many of them worked in the same place: Florence, then an independent and wealthy city-state. They included the painter Masaccio, the architect Filippo Brunelleschi and, later, Leonardo da Vinci and Michelangelo Buonarroti.

Patrons of the arts

Most Renaissance artists worked for patrons – rich institutions or individuals who would commission and pay for works of art. Perhaps the most important patrons were the Medici family. They were powerful bankers from Florence, who bought art to decorate their palaces and show off their wealth.

The Battle Of San Romano (probably 1450s), by Florentine artist Paolo Uccello

This painting, which used to hang in a Medici palace, was meant to glorify Florence. It shows a fight between the forces of Florence (on the left) and Siena. This took place in 1432, but in fact was only a minor skirmish – not the great battle shown here.

Uccello was said to have stayed up all night working on the perspective. But he didn't just want to make his picture seem real – he wanted it to look pleasing, too. So there is no blood, and the broken lances and dead bodies are neatly arranged on the flat, pink ground.

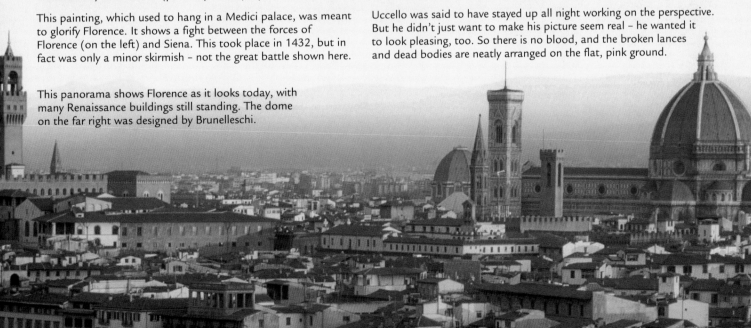

This panorama shows Florence as it looks today, with many Renaissance buildings still standing. The dome on the far right was designed by Brunelleschi.

Renaissance portraits

Portraits became increasingly popular during the Renaissance period. It was no longer just kings and queens who commissioned them, but bankers, merchants, diplomats and scholars – anyone with enough money to pay an artist. The style of portraits changed too, and they became more varied and characterful.

Pictures with a purpose

Renaissance portraits served many purposes. Having your portrait painted was a status symbol, and men's portraits were often designed to show how powerful or rich they were. Women's portraits, on the other hand, tended to emphasize beauty or virtue. Such portraits were sometimes sent to prospective husbands.

A portrait could also be a way of commemorating someone and preserving his or her likeness, even after death. Occasionally, portraits were based on models, or 'death masks,' of dead people's faces.

King Henry VIII of England chose to marry Ann of Cleves after seeing her portrait.

Portrait Of A Lady In Yellow (1465), by Alesso Baldovinetti. The palm leaf pattern on the lady's sleeve is probably a family emblem, but her identity remains a mystery.

Different views

Many early Renaissance portraits show people in profile, just like Classical art. But later portraits often depict three-quarter or full-face views, which were better for capturing facial expressions. They also tend to show more of the person's body and surroundings.

If you compare the *Lady in Yellow* with these portraits by Raphael and Titian, painted about 50 years later, you can see how they use different poses and settings to help show the person's character.

Pope Julius II (1511-12), by Raffaello Sanzio, known as 'Raphael.' Raphael painted many portraits of important church leaders.

Portrait Of A Lady (about 1511), by Tiziano Vecellio, known as 'Titian.' The Classical-style carving on the wall shows the same lady in profile.

The Ambassadors (about 1533), by Hans Holbein the Younger. Try looking at it along the line of the arrows.

Characters, signs and symbols

As portraits got more elaborate, artists began to include symbolic objects to represent aspects of people's characters. A famous example is *The Ambassadors*, a portrait of the French ambassador Jean de Dinteville (on the left), and his friend, Bishop Georges de Selve. It is packed with symbols. The objects on the table represent the men's interests: music (a lute), learning (books and astronomical instruments) and travel (a globe.) Ominously, a distorted skull stretches across the bottom of the picture. It is a *memento mori* – a reminder that death comes to us all. But there is also a tiny crucifix in the top left corner, a symbol of the Christian belief in an afterlife.

Life and death

The skull was distorted using a technique known as 'anamorphosis,' so it can be seen properly from only two angles. To view it, you need to shut one eye and look at it from the direction marked by either of the two arrows. The distortion is meant to grab our attention. And, of course, it shows off the artist's skill.

The Arnolfini Portrait

The *Arnolfini Portrait*, by Dutch artist Jan van Eyck, is one of the best-known portraits of the Renaissance. It shows a wealthy Italian banker, Giovanni Arnolfini, and his wife, standing together in their house in Bruges.

Title: *The Arnolfini Portrait*
Date: 1434
Artist: Jan van Eyck
Materials: oil on oak
Size: 33 x 25in

Play of light

Van Eyck specialized in painting beautifully lit and detailed scenes like this. He was also one of the first and most skilled artists to use oil paint. For a time, he was even credited with inventing it. He built up translucent layers of color, creating subtle variations in light and shade. Light catches and defines everything in the room, from the brassy chandelier to the soft fur and fabric of the couple's clothes.

Notice how individual hairs in the dog's coat shine in the light. Van Eyck may have included the dog as a symbol of love and fidelity.

High fashion

The Arnolfinis are expensively dressed. Giovanni has a fur coat, though the tree blossom outside suggests it isn't very cold. You might think his wife looks pregnant, but she's just wearing the latest fashion: a high-waisted dress with bunched skirts.

Hands up

Giovanni holds up one hand, as if taking a vow, and grasps his wife's hand with the other. Some people think this means the picture shows a marriage ceremony, and refer to it as *The Arnolfini Wedding*. But his gesture is probably just a way of greeting visitors.

Sacred scene

The Arnolfinis must have been very religious, because the picture is full of religious references. A string of glass rosary beads, used to count prayers, hangs on the wall, and the mirror is decorated with scenes from the life of Christ. A carving on the chair shows St. Margaret, along with the dragon she was supposed to have defeated. The single candle flame in the chandelier may be meant to suggest the presence of God. Even the discarded shoes may be significant – it was usual to remove shoes when entering a holy place.

Mirror, mirror

The convex mirror reveals a part of the room we would not otherwise see. As well as reflecting the couple's backs, it shows two figures approaching them through an open door. One of the figures may be the artist himself, who signed his name on the wall above the mirror. Some people think this signature was meant to record the artist's presence as a witness at the Arnolfinis' wedding ceremony, but it is more likely he wanted to sign the picture just to show he had made it.

The lettering above the mirror says (in Latin): 'Jan van Eyck was here 1434'.

Lap of luxury

The room is full of expensive objects which show off the Arnolfinis' wealth. You would only have found the chandelier, carpet, mirror and glass windows in very rich homes. There are also oranges, which were rare and exotic in northern Europe at the time.

👁 For a link to a website where you can see many more paintings by Jan van Eyck, go to **www.usborne-quicklinks.com**

Funny face

Giovanni looks a bit funny, with heavy eyelids, a big nose and a cleft chin. But his wife has more idealized features – her high forehead, small mouth and pale skin all conform to 15th-century ideas of beauty. So van Eyck may have been flattering her, rather than trying to show how she looked in real life.

Van Eyck used tiny brushstrokes, and blended them very smoothly. So you can hardly see any brushmarks, even in these enlarged details.

A fresh look

Religious pictures were very popular in the Renaissance, just as they had been in the Middle Ages. But now when artists painted old, familiar Bible tales, they did it in a very different way. They often moved the stories to their own time and country, and used Renaissance techniques like perspective to make scenes more realistic.

Made to order

Most religious paintings made in the Renaissance were designed for particular churches. The patron paying for the painting would usually tell the artist what to include, but the rest was up to the artist. Different artists adopted very different styles, as you can see from these two pages.

Piero made this scene for a chapel in his hometown, Borgo San Sepolcro, in northern Italy. The chapel was devoted to St. John the Baptist, so he was probably asked to paint St. John baptizing Jesus. In the Bible, this took place in the River Jordan, in the Middle East, but Piero set the event in an Italian landscape. He even included Borgo San Sepolcro in the distance.

Baptism Of Christ (1450s), by Piero della Francesca. This is full of lifelike details, from the reflections in the water to the perspective on the dove.

Divine work

One of the greatest works of the Renaissance was created for the ceiling of the Sistine Chapel in the Vatican, the home of the Pope. It was the work of Michelangelo Buonarroti – the 'divine Michelangelo' to his admirers – and took him four years to complete, lying on his back on a scaffold under the ceiling. Each section had to be painted separately, as the paint was applied to wet plaster and couldn't be altered after it dried. This method is known as 'fresco.' The central part shows the creation of man, as told in the Bible.

Creation Of Adam (1508-12), by Michelangelo Buonarroti

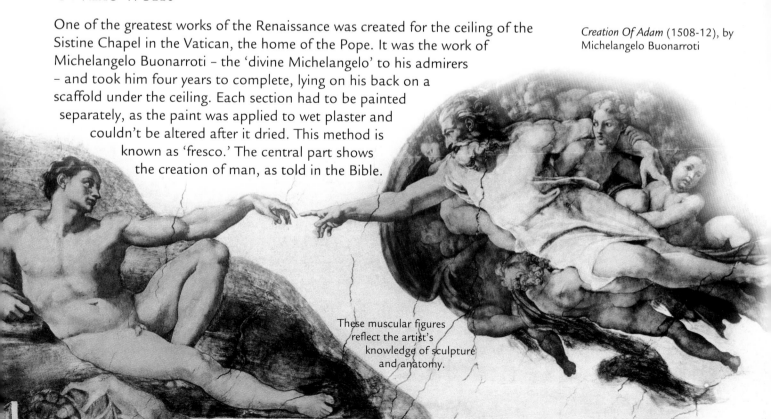

These muscular figures reflect the artist's knowledge of sculpture and anatomy.

On the rocks

Leonardo da Vinci was one of the most sought-after painters of his time – though he was not just an artist, but a scientist and inventor too. He made *The Virgin Of The Rocks* for a church in Milan. It shows the Virgin Mary kneeling in a rocky landscape. Mary is accompanied by an angel and two children, Jesus and St. John the Baptist.

St. John carries a cross made of reeds, one of his traditional symbols. This wasn't painted by Leonardo, but added later, probably to stop people from confusing St. John with Jesus. He also holds a scroll saying, in Latin: "Behold the lamb of God," meaning Jesus.

Leonardo used his knowledge of botany to draw delicate, realistic plants. He had also studied perspective, including 'aerial' perspective – an atmospheric effect which makes colors fade and become bluer in the distance. He imitated this effect by painting the water and rocks in the background in lighter, bluer tones.

The angel's face and veil are beautifully detailed. You can see how Leonardo highlighted individual hairs with bright gold. Her hands, by contrast, were never fully finished, though probably nobody would have noticed this when the painting was lit by candlelight in church.

The Virgin Of The Rocks (about 1508), by Leonardo da Vinci

The Virgin And Child With St. Anne And St. John the Baptist (about 1507-08), by Leonardo da Vinci.

Leonardo used chalk and charcoal to create this delicately shaded drawing. It was meant as a study for a painting which, sadly, he never got around to doing.

Leonardo the cartoonist

Leonardo is known for his drawings as well as his paintings. Before starting a painting, he would make large preparatory drawings like the one on the left. These are known as 'cartoons.' In fact, this was the original meaning of the word – it was only much later that it came to mean comic drawings too. He also sketched designs for many strange machines and inventions.

Leonardo designed a flying machine based on birds' wings, though he never built it.

Telling stories

The Renaissance enthusiasm for the Classical world led many artists to paint scenes from ancient stories, often to satisfy customers who wanted to show off their knowledge of Classical texts. Artists found the stories a rich source of inspiration – and the fictional settings gave them greater freedom to paint nudes, which would otherwise have been considered far too daring.

The moral of the story

Paintings of stories were meant to be entertaining. They often contained lots of detail, so they could be looked at over and over. Some were just meant to tell the story, using dramatic gestures, expressions and compositions to show events unfolding. But others used the story to make a moral point, too. So *Cupid Complaining To Venus* is meant to make us think about the consequences of love, and *Narcissus* (below right) shows the danger of vanity.

Cupid, the god of love, complains to his mother, Venus, that he's been stung by bees while eating honey. The moral of this is that sweet things, like honey or love, are often followed by pain.

Cupid Complaining To Venus (early 1530s), by Lucas Cranach

Local character

Although Renaissance artists loved to paint Classical scenes, that doesn't mean they always made them historically accurate. They were quite happy to change the settings and people's appearances to make them look more familiar to viewers at the time. So Venus and Narcissus have contemporary accessories and clothes and, on the left, Apollo chases Daphne through an Italian landscape.

The scene on the left illustrates a story told by a Roman writer called Ovid. In the story, Daphne was chased by Apollo, and her father turned her into a tree so she could escape him. You can see the city of Florence in the distance.

The picture on the right shows Narcissus, another character described by Ovid. According to myth, he fell in love with his own reflection and gazed at it until he died.

Apollo And Daphne (probably 1470-80), by Antonio del Pollaiuolo

Narcissus (about 1490-99), by a follower of Leonardo da Vinci

Bacchus And Ariadne (1521-23), by Tiziano Vecellio, known as 'Titian.' Notice how Titian divides the picture into two triangles, to emphasize different parts of the story. The top left-hand triangle is blue and empty, containing just the lonely Ariadne and a tiny ship disappearing over the horizon. But the lower right-hand triangle, with Bacchus, is crowded with colorful, unruly figures.

Big and small

In the 15th century, most story paintings were fairly small. They were often made to decorate the furniture people bought to celebrate special occasions, such as weddings. But, by the 16th century, they began to be painted on a bigger scale, sometimes on canvas, sometimes directly onto the walls of grand villas and palaces. This painting by Titian, made for a duke's castle, is many times bigger than any of the ones on the previous page.

Gods and grand schemes

Bacchus And Ariadne was painted for Alfonso d'Este, a learned Italian duke. He wanted to recreate a Greek picture gallery, and asked Titian to work from specific Classical texts to paint this canvas for it. The scene tells several parts of the story. On the left, the princess Ariadne turns, startled, from watching her old lover, Theseus, sail away. Her fearful eyes meet those of Bacchus, the god of wine (you can tell who he is from the vine wreath on his head). He will become her new lover. His passion for her is shown by the way he leaps out of his chariot, his eyes fixed on hers. The stars in the sky are from the story's end, when Bacchus turned Ariadne's crown into a constellation, to make her live forever.

Venus And Mars

The Italian artist Sandro Botticelli is famous for his beautiful paintings based on Classical myths. Here, he shows two lovers reclining in a wooded grove. They are Venus, the goddess of love, and Mars, the god of war. Four young fauns, mythological creatures supposed to be half-human, half-goat, play around them.

Title: *Venus And Mars*
Date: about 1485
Artist: Alessandro Filipepi, known as Sandro 'Botticelli,' or 'little barrel'
Materials: Egg tempera and oil on poplar wood
Size: 27 x 68in

Venus can be identified by her pearl brooch and the myrtle bushes behind her. Pearls were her emblem because, like a pearl, she was meant to have been born from a shell. And myrtles were sacred to her because they are evergreen, so they last as love is meant to last.

You can tell that the man is Mars because of his weapons and armor, even if he isn't actually using them. In fact, he is so fast asleep that not even a conch shell, blown like a trumpet in his ear, can wake him.

In mythology, fauns were meant to be wild and mischievous. But Botticelli painted them as small children, comically dwarfed by Mars' armor, so they won't seem threatening.

Home, sweet home

In Renaissance times, long, rectangular paintings were made to decorate walls or furniture. This one was probably designed for a chest or bed. Paintings like this are known as 'spalliera' panels and usually show scenes from history or myths. Often, several panels were made together, telling a story in stages. They were meant to be fun, but some had a moral too.

Opposites attract

Mars is asleep and vulnerable, while Venus is alert. They embody the opposites of love and war, female and male, and strength and weakness. Venus looks on calmly as the fauns steal Mars's weapons – they may be acting on her orders. So Mars, the warrior, has been disarmed by the goddess of love, proving the moral that love is stronger than war.

Ideal beauty

Venus was meant to be incredibly beautiful. Botticelli painted her according to 15th-century ideals of beauty, with a 15th-century dress and hairstyle. Her features resemble Botticelli's other famous picture of her, *The Birth Of Venus* (about 1483-84). But there is something odd about the way she is lying. If you look closely, her right leg seems to be missing completely.

Deliberate mistakes?

Although the scene is beautifully painted, the bodies of Venus and Mars aren't anatomically correct. As well as Venus' missing leg, Mars' left shoulder juts out too much, and his left leg is shorter than his right. Botticelli may have distorted them by mistake. Or he may have done it deliberately, to make them fit his composition better.

Wasps and wedding bells

Spalliera panels were usually bought when people were married, which seems appropriate for a panel showing the triumph of love. We don't know if it was made for a particular couple, but the wasps buzzing around Mars' head may be a clue. The Italian for wasp is *vespa*. Wasps were the emblem of a rich Italian family named Vespucci that Botticelli had worked for. But there is no record of them commissioning this panel. So perhaps the wasps are only meant to remind us how love may be followed later by a painful 'sting.'

For a link to a website where you can see more paintings by Sandro Botticelli, and find out more about his life and work, go to **www.usborne-quicklinks.com**

Outdoor scenes

Renaissance artists' use of perspective and observation of nature gave them important new tools for creating natural-looking landscapes. At the start of the 15th century, most landscapes were still only painted as backdrops. But, as the century wore on, artists really came to treat landscapes as a subject in their own right. This was helped by the increasing numbers of patrons and collectors who wanted to buy them, after reading about landscape painting in Classical times.

Dawn light

The Italian painter Giovanni Bellini was one of the first to set his figures firmly within a landscape, rather than just using it as a background. *The Agony In The Garden* is a good example of this. It shows Jesus praying as he waits for the soldiers in the distance to come and take him to his death. This landscape is also symbolic, designed to enhance the picture's meaning. The setting is rocky and bare, to suit the bleak subject. But the rising sun is meant to remind us how, in the Bible, Jesus rises from the dead.

The Agony In The Garden (about 1465), by Giovanni Bellini. Notice the glow on the horizon. Bellini used thin layers of translucent oil paints to capture the subtle effects of dawn light.

In the shadows

Flemish artist Joachim Patinir was perhaps the earliest painter to specialize in landscapes. Although he still included religious or mythological figures in his pictures, they seem much less important than the scenery around them. Patinir may have been inspired to focus on landscapes in this way by the new science of 'cartography,' or map-making.

In this painting of St. Jerome, the saint – a religious hermit – is a small figure tucked away at the bottom of the picture. The scene is dominated by a dramatic panorama of rocks and mountains. Patinir used aerial perspective (see page 49) to create the sense of a vast expanse of space, applying cool, blue colors in the distance, while filling the foreground with warm, reddish browns.

Saint Jerome In A Rocky Landscape (probably 1515-24), by Joachim Patinir

Hunters In The Snow (1565), by Pieter Bruegel. The blue-gray color scheme emphasizes the cold.

Ordinary things

The paintings of the Dutch artist Pieter Bruegel were unusual at the time because they had real people in them doing ordinary things, instead of biblical or mythological characters. Many of his pictures reflect the changing seasons. This winter scene includes a range of typical activities: hunters with their dogs, food cooking on a fire and people skating. It's so life-like you can almost feel the cold.

Moody blues

Giorgione was one of the most influential artists of the 16th-century, but he died young and few of his works have survived. His paintings are very moody and atmospheric, but it is hard to say what they are about. *The Sunset* doesn't tell any particular story. A mountainous wasteland stretches back, past glimpses of Italian-style farmhouses, to a startlingly blue horizon. In the foreground are two mysterious figures. One may be St. Roch, who was supposed to have had a bad leg.

The Sunset (1506-10), by Italian artist Giorgio da Castelfranco, known as 'Giorgione'

In the middle distance, you can see St. George and a dragon. They were added by a 19th-century restorer, to cover a damaged area where there seemed to be a dragon. Nobody knows what Giorgione originally painted.

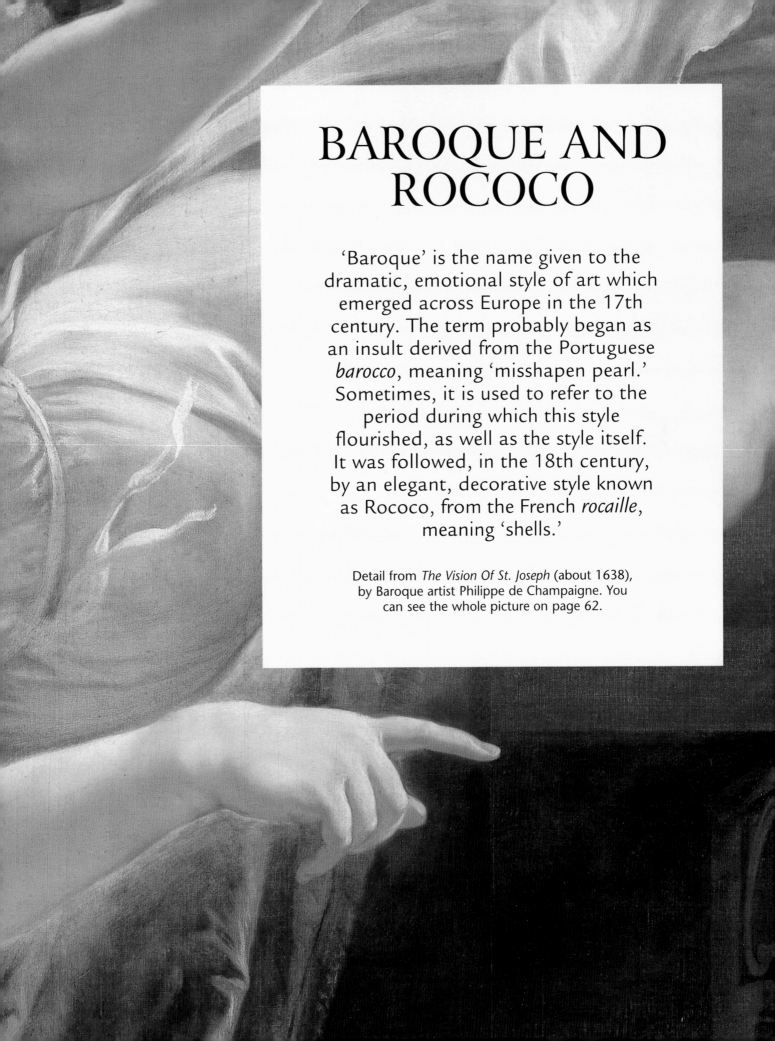

BAROQUE AND ROCOCO

'Baroque' is the name given to the dramatic, emotional style of art which emerged across Europe in the 17th century. The term probably began as an insult derived from the Portuguese *barocco*, meaning 'misshapen pearl.' Sometimes, it is used to refer to the period during which this style flourished, as well as the style itself. It was followed, in the 18th century, by an elegant, decorative style known as Rococo, from the French *rocaille*, meaning 'shells.'

Detail from *The Vision Of St. Joseph* (about 1638), by Baroque artist Philippe de Champaigne. You can see the whole picture on page 62.

Dramatic art

Designed to appeal to the heart rather than the mind, Baroque art was full of drama and movement. It can seem a bit over the top by today's standards, but at the time, it made a lively change from cool, Classical styles.

The Ecstasy Of St. Theresa (1647-52), by Gian Lorenzo Bernini

High drama

Baroque artists had lots of ways of producing dramatic effects. *The Ecstasy Of St. Theresa*, made for a church in Rome, shows St. Theresa seeing an angel in a vision. The scene was cleverly designed to make it look as strange and miraculous as it must have felt to Theresa. The figures are carved in ghostly white marble, and gilded rays of heavenly light mingle with real light from a window above.

Baroque painters used strong lighting to create extreme contrasts between light and shade. Often, scenes are shown close up, so they seem to be happening right in front of you. And many scenes are constructed along diagonal lines. You can see this in the picture below, if you follow the lines of the figures' spears, arms and legs. This emphasizes their movements, making them look more urgent.

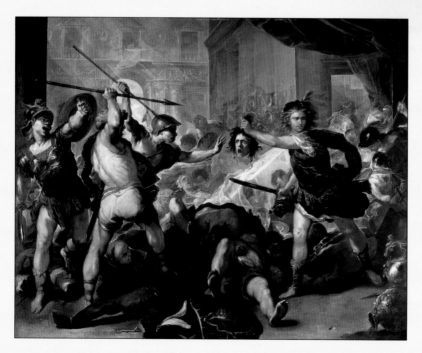

Turned to stone

If you look closely at the scene on the left, you'll see it is built a bit like a stage set. The characters, from a Greek myth about the hero Perseus, are arranged in theatrical poses, and the building in the background looks like a stage backdrop. The spears, arms and rays of light all direct your eye toward the severed head that Perseus is grasping. According to the myth, this head came from a monster named Medusa and turned anyone who saw it into stone. As Perseus holds it up in front of his enemies – careful not to look at it himself – their bodies start to turn an ominous gray.

Perseus Turning Phineas And His Followers Into Stone (about 1680), by Luca Giordano

Breaking out

Baroque artists had ways of creating drama in portraits, too. In this self portrait, the Spanish artist Bartolomé Murillo painted himself, framed by a carved oval. On the ledge beneath the oval are his artist's tools: a preparatory drawing in red chalk, a palette and brushes. But it isn't clear whether the frame is meant to be a mirror or a painting-within-the-painting. He breaks the illusion in a startling and rather creepy way, by showing his hand emerging out of the frame, as if his picture is coming to life. This is known as a *trompe l'oeil* device.

Self Portrait (1670-73), by Bartolomé Murillo. The inscription says: "Bartolomé Murillo portraying himself to fulfil the wishes of his children" – it is to be a portrait they can remember him by after he is dead.

> 👁 For a link to a website where you can view another of Rembrandt van Rijn's most famous history paintings in an interactive exhibition, go to **www.usborne-quicklinks.com**

In extremity

Baroque artists loved extreme situations, such as battles and supernatural tales, which suited dramatic paintings. Both Italian artist Luca Giordano and Dutch painter Rembrandt van Rijn chose scenes of intense drama, such as people being turned into stone (previous page), or a miraculous apparition (below).

Belshazzar's Feast (about 1635), by Rembrandt van Rijn. The writing on the wall is in Hebrew script. Notice how the scene is illuminated by the light blazing out of these letters.

Writing on the wall

According to the Bible, King Belshazzar gave a great feast where he served wine in golden goblets stolen from a temple in Jerusalem. Suddenly, a hand appeared and wrote a mysterious message on the wall. When it was deciphered, the message turned out to be a warning from God: "You have been weighed in the balance and found wanting."

Like Giordano, Rembrandt used extreme gestures and expressions to create the impression of a dramatic split second. But *Belshazzar's Feast* seems more intimate and immediate because it is so close up. We could almost be sitting at the table ourselves, among the astonished guests.

The Supper At Emmaus

Italian painter Caravaggio is famous for his dramatic but realistic paintings, often of religious scenes, such as *The Supper At Emmaus*. It might be hard to imagine now but, at the time, some people found his paintings shocking. They thought he was disrespectful, because he made holy figures look like ordinary, everyday people.

Title: *The Supper At Emmaus*
Date: 1601
Artist: Michelangelo da Merisi, known as 'Caravaggio'
Materials: oil on canvas
Size: 56 x 77in

Back from the dead

This picture tells a Bible story about two of Jesus' disciples. After Jesus had been crucified, they walked to the town of Emmaus. On the way, they met a stranger and invited him to eat with them at an inn. After the inn-keeper had brought the meal, the stranger blessed it in an oddly familiar way – and the disciples realized he was Jesus, miraculously returned from the dead. The painting shows the moment when the shocked disciples recognize their guest.

Living drama

You can see this scene so close up, it is almost as if you are sitting at the table too. There isn't much space around the figures, and the arms of Jesus and the disciples are foreshortened, so they seem to reach right out of the picture toward us. Dynamic poses and strong lighting add to the dramatic tension. Caravaggio's sense of drama may have been influenced by his own colorful lifestyle – he was a fiery character who constantly got into brawls.

Center stage

Jesus sits in the middle of the picture, clearly the center of attention. His red robe makes him stand out from everyone else, and the dark background ensures nothing distracts from his radiant face. He is also clean shaven although, at the time, most paintings showed him with a beard. This made him harder to recognize, so anyone seeing the picture would hesitate – like the disciples – before identifying him.

Here and now

The scene has a gritty realism about it. The disciples are dressed in shabby old clothes, like 17th-century workmen. And the food on the table is what ordinary people might have eaten: bread, fruit and a roast guinea fowl. They look very lifelike – some of the fruit is even beginning to rot. All this helps to make the miracle feel more real, as if it were taking place in front of us and not in the distant past.

Caravaggio turned his realism on himself, too. Experts think this sickly figure is actually a self portrait, painted shortly after he had been in the hospital – which explains his unhealthy color.

Sick Bacchus (1593-94), by Caravaggio

Trick of the light

Although *Supper At Emmaus* looks very real, Caravaggio has twisted reality to suit his purpose. The shadow under the fruit basket forms the shape of a fish, an early Christian symbol. And the shadow of the inn-keeper serving the meal creates a dark halo around Jesus' head. Given where the light is coming from, the shadow should really fall across his face.

Caravaggio used lots of tiny brushstrokes to paint the details.

A violent life

Despite his religious paintings, Caravaggio was a violently argumentative man. He was prosecuted several times, once for throwing a dish of hot artichokes at a waiter's head. In 1605, he was jailed for carrying a sword. And, just a year later, at the height of his success, he killed a man in a dispute over a game of tennis. He had to flee the authorities and spent the rest of his life in exile, dying of fever at the age of 39.

Caravaggio was known for his skill at still lifes. In fact, he began his career painting them in other artists' workshops.

Wars of religion

The 17th century was a time of fierce religious debates, quarrels and even wars. In the end, this made the Christian Church split into two. Northern Europe became largely Protestant, while southern Europe remained Catholic. Religious battles had a huge effect on art. Catholic Church leaders encouraged people to use religious images as an aid to prayer. But in Protestant countries this use of art was frowned on and even considered sinful.

Close to Heaven

If religious paintings were to teach people and inspire their devotion, as the Catholic Church wanted, the artists needed to create clear, compelling images. So they used the Baroque techniques of theatrical lighting and dynamic compositions to convey intense spiritual experiences. Many Catholic paintings illustrated dramatic episodes from the lives of the saints, such as someone having a vision, as in the picture on the right, or being martyred (killed for their beliefs). These were extraordinary scenes, but they were often shown in ordinary, domestic settings, to help people feel closer to the saints.

The Vision of St. Joseph (about 1638), by Philippe de Champaigne. The angel is telling Joseph that his wife's baby is the son of God. Notice Joseph's sandals lying discarded on the floor.

Setting a good example

Protestants believed you should only worship God. But the Catholic Church encouraged people to admire the saints, especially the Virgin Mary, and to address their prayers to God through them. So the Virgin Mary is often featured in Catholic art from this period, and artists such as Sassoferrato painted her time and time again.

The Virgin In Prayer shows Mary praying, perhaps for our salvation. Her calm concentration is designed to set a good example, to encourage people to copy her and pray, as she does. The dark setting, strong lighting and close-up view make her a striking figure. The shadows on her face and robes were painted so delicately that, in a dark church lit only by candles, you could almost mistake this image for a real woman.

The Virgin In Prayer (1640-50), by Giovanni Salvi, known as 'Sassoferrato'

Seeing the light

In Protestant countries, like the Dutch Republic, people thought church services should concentrate on religious readings and prayers. They felt that paintings, statues and other church decorations were a distraction. Some even believed that it was wrong to pray in front of a holy picture – just as the iconoclasts had thought (see page 31). So a lot of religious art was destroyed, and church interiors were stripped bare.

This painting of a church in Utrecht, in the Dutch Republic, was painted not long after the church was 'cleansed' of Catholic imagery. The whitewashed columns and arches appear startlingly bright and clear. Sunshine streams through the plain windows, which until recently would have had stained glass. The grand architecture, bathed in a divine light, is meant to make you think about religion and fill you with awe.

The Interior Of The Buurkerk At Utrecht (1644), by Pieter Saenredam

Homely scenes

Although grand altarpieces and large-scale religious paintings were no longer made for Protestant churches, Protestant art-lovers still bought small religious scenes to hang at home. These usually showed Bible stories, as pictures of saints were taboo outside Catholic countries, and tended to be much less dramatic and imposing than Catholic pictures. Rembrandt's *The Adoration Of The Shepherds* is typical of how Dutch artists painted religious subjects. It shows shepherds praying to the newborn Jesus in a Dutch barn, on a dark winter's night. The scene has a homely, intimate feel, in complete contrast to the grand Baroque style of paintings like *The Vision Of St. Joseph* (above left).

The Adoration Of The Shepherds (1646), by Rembrandt van Rijn. Notice how Rembrandt uses light to draw your eye into the picture.

👁 For a link to a website where you can compare paintings by Sassoferrato and Saenredam, go to **www.usborne-quicklinks.com**

Fit for a king

In the 17th century, kings and queens were much more powerful than today. They lived in grand palaces and paid the best painters to work at their courts. The court painters' main duty was to paint royal portraits. They also created historical and mythological scenes to decorate royal palaces – paintings which were worlds away from the religious images made for the Church.

Spin doctors

Most kings and queens allowed themselves to be painted only by their court painter. Their images were tightly controlled, just as celebrities today try to control how they are portrayed by the media. So court painters were often chosen for their ability to flatter their subjects, as well as their skill in painting – as you can see from the two portraits of kings on this page.

Philip IV In Brown And Silver (1631-32), by Diego Velázquez

Charles I On Horseback (about 1637-38), by Flemish artist Anthony van Dyck

Dress to impress

Diego Velázquez was the court painter of King Philip IV of Spain. In the portrait above, he showed Philip dressed in an impressive, silver-embroidered suit. Philip was supposed to have had a large, jutting-out chin. But Velázquez painted him with his head turned slightly away from us, so it doesn't show too much.

Power and glory

Anthony van Dyck was court painter to the English king, Charles I. In the lifesize portrait on the left, he showed Charles on horseback, towering above the landscape – and the viewer. The painting was so big, van Dyck needed scaffolding to complete it. Charles was really a small, thin man with a narrow face. But van Dyck made him look regal and impressive, by showing him so high above us, in shining armor, and drawing his face from the side.

Risky pictures

Members of the royal courts, or courtiers, would buy historical and mythological scenes for decoration. But they also wanted to show how cultured they were, as only people with a good education would know the stories behind them. The paintings reveal how privileged courtiers were, too. In Spain, the nudity in many of these scenes would simply not have been allowed outside the closed world of the court.

Hidden Venus

The Toilet Of Venus was very unusual, considering when and where it was painted. It shows a female nude – a subject then frowned on by the Spanish Church. Velázquez got away with it because it was made for a royal courtier, but even he probably didn't put it on general display. Nudes were often hung behind curtains and only revealed to select audiences. The winged Cupid identifies the woman as Venus, goddess of love. She is checking her appearance in the mirror – this is the old meaning of 'toilet,' from the French *toilette*. Velázquez plays a game with the reflection: is Venus looking at her own face, or is she watching us in the mirror, coolly returning our gaze?

The Toilet Of Venus (1647-51), by Diego Velázquez. This picture had to be mended after a women's rights protester attacked it with a cleaver in 1914.

Pan pipes

The Triumph Of Pan, by Nicolas Poussin, reflects the educated tastes of 17th-century nobles. It wasn't commissioned by a king, but by someone almost as powerful – Cardinal Richelieu, chief minister of France. His palace had a room full of mythological paintings from the Renaissance. Poussin created this scene to fit in with them. It shows mythical characters celebrating around a statue of Pan, the god of woods and fields. They look quite frenzied, but Poussin turned their wild movements into a highly ordered picture. You can see how their arms and legs are arranged in neat diagonal lines.

The Triumph Of Pan (1636), by the French artist Nicolas Poussin

Peace And War

The Flemish artist Peter Paul Rubens was an important diplomat as well as a prolific painter. In 1630, the Spanish sent him on a mission to England, to try to secure peace between the two countries. As well as putting his case in words, he gave the English king *Peace And War*, a magnificent painting which was meant to be a graphic illustration of the benefits of peace.

Title: *Peace And War (Minerva Protects Pax From Mars)*
Date: 1629-30
Artist: Peter Paul Rubens
Materials: oil on canvas
Size: 80 x 117in

Picture puzzles

This painting is an allegory. This means it holds a hidden message that has to be read by picking up visual clues. The different mythical characters represent abstract ideas. The woman sitting in the middle is Pax, or peace. Around her, everything seems peaceful and contented. But Mars, the god of war, is standing nearby, ready for battle. The painting's structure reinforces the symbolism. It contains three triangles, two bright and happy, the third dark and ominous.

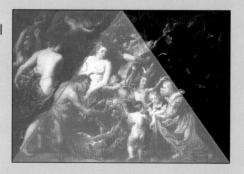

This diagram shows how the picture is made up of triangles. The one on the right has Mars and dark storm clouds; the other two are more colorful. Pax herself sits near the top of the middle one.

Advantages of peace

Around Pax, everything is harmonious. Even the wild creatures have been tamed. The leopard rolls on its back like a kitten. Beside it, there is a satyr – a mythical creature with the body of man and the legs of a goat. Satyrs were meant to be very mischievous, but this one is kindly offering the children fruit from a cornucopia, or horn of plenty. Behind him, there is a woman carrying a basin of gold. The fruit and gold represent the prosperity peace brings. So the children can grow up well-provided-for and happy.

Under threat

But this pleasant scene is threatened. The sky is darkening, and Mars lurks in the background, accompanied by a ghostly Fury, or goddess of vengeance. A woman clad in armor – Minerva, the goddess of wisdom – pushes Mars away. So peace is protected for now. But though Mars is leaving, he is still a threat. He is looking back over his shoulder as if reluctant to depart, and his sword is dangerously close to the girl in the yellow dress.

Reality and myth

The children are actually portraits of the son and daughters of Sir Balthasar Gerbier, the artist's friend and host in London. The boy is dressed as Hymen, the god of marriage, but the two girls are in ordinary 17th-century clothes. By including real children among all the mythical characters, Rubens made his allegory seem more relevant to the time and gave it more impact.

Cherubic mission

The winged cherub hovering above Pax grasps an olive branch, a symbol of peace, in one hand. In the other, he carries a second symbol of peace: a rod with a serpent twined around it. Known as a 'caduceus,' this was supposed to be the staff of Mercury, the messenger of the gods. Perhaps the cherub represents Rubens' own role as a messenger of peace at the English court?

Rubens the diplomat

You can see what Rubens looked like in this self portrait he painted shortly before his death in 1640.

Self Portrait (1638-40), by Peter Paul Rubens

Rubens' mission led England to sign a peace treaty with Spain in 1630. How much this was due to his skill at negotiating, and how much to his talent for painting, it is impossible to say. But the English king, Charles I, was so impressed that he knighted Rubens and commissioned him to paint a ceiling in the royal Banqueting House in London.

Sadly, peace turned out to be short-lived. England and Spain were soon caught up in a long-running European conflict known as the Thirty Years' War. But Rubens was not sent on any more missions. Now in his 50s, he retired to his Flemish country estate, where he devoted himself to painting tranquil scenes of rural life and vast landscapes like the one on page 14.

Rubens' fluid brushwork and strong colors were greatly admired, especially his flesh tones – one critic said they seemed to be painted with milk and blood.

Town and country

Landscapes and townscapes became very popular in the 17th century, as people began to accept they were a suitable subject for paintings. Some artists created beautiful imaginary scenes. But pictures from the newly independent Dutch Republic tended to be about real life instead. The republic's proud citizens wanted paintings that captured the particular character of their countryside and towns.

Heavenly view

French artist Claude was one of the first artists to paint proper landscapes, although they were often disguised as story-telling scenes. This painting is supposed to be about a Biblical character, Hagar, and an angel. But they are just small figures in the foreground. The picture isn't really about them, but the dazzling vista behind them. It's constructed a bit like a theater set: dark trees and shadows neatly frame a sunlit view of a river and hills, which fade into the distance in a dramatic show of aerial perspective (see page 49). The effect is dreamy – quite unlike the down-to-earth Dutch style.

Landscape With Hagar And The Angel (1646), by Claude Gellée, known as Claude Lorrain or Claude

The Avenue At Middelharnis (1689), by Meindert Hobbema

On location

This picture shows a real place: Middelharnis, in southern Holland. It is so accurate that if you went there today, you'd still be able to recognize the spot. As you can see, the land is very flat, but the lines of the trees against the sky give the scene a dramatic perspective. Many Dutch painters paid great attention to skies, because the land was so featureless. The left and right hand sides of the road are very different. On the left, the land is overgrown and wild. But on the right, it has been turned into a neat market garden. This illustrates the Dutch people's success at farming.

Spick and span

The painting on the right, by Dutch artist Pieter de Hooch, shows the courtyard of a house in Delft, a town in Holland where he was living at the time. Later, he moved to Amsterdam and painted pictures of high society, but he is best known for ordinary domestic scenes like this one, which are more typical of Dutch art of the time.

If you look carefully at this picture, you can see how many details de Hooch captured. The inscribed plaque over the doorway still exists today. The patterns created by the tiles and bricks, and the receding view down a corridor inside the house, reveal his skill with perspective. The cleanly swept courtyard and smiling woman and child may be meant to suggest the pleasures of a happy home life.

👁 For a link to a website featuring a Claude glass, and other equipment used by landscape painters, go to **www.usborne-quicklinks.com**

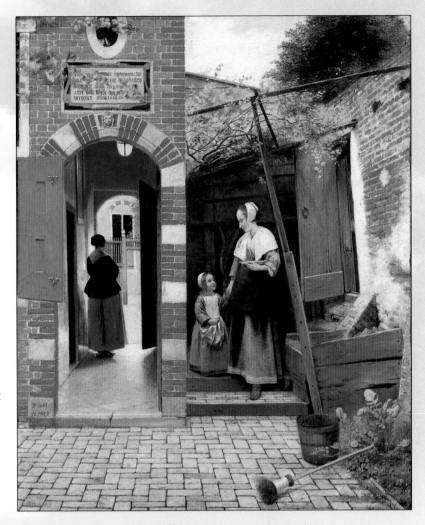

The Courtyard Of A House In Delft (1658), by Pieter de Hooch

Playing tricks

The painting below shows another Delft scene: a view along a street with a musical instrument stall, church and town hall. But the street bends oddly so that, at first sight, everything seems rather unreal. The artist, Carel Fabritius, was interested in optical devices such as the camera obscura (see pages 164-165), which could help him draw more accurately. He was also an expert in perspective. So he deliberately distorted the perspective, as an optical trick. To see it without the distortion, you had to use a special box.

This picture was meant to be inserted into a 'perspective box' and viewed through a peephole, which corrected the distortion.

A View Of Delft, With A Musical Instrument Seller's Stall (1652), by Dutch painter Carel Fabritius

Everyday life

The 17th century saw an enormous increase in paintings of ordinary people in everyday settings, particularly in the Dutch Republic. This wasn't the first time artists had painted scenes of everyday life – but, until now, these had usually only formed a small part of paintings on other, grander themes. Now, everyday life became a subject in itself.

To paint a scene like this requires delicate brushwork. In the detail below, you can see how the artist used touches of pure white to add gleaming highlights to the lady's silk dress and pearls. By contrast, her face is very smoothly shaded.

A Young Woman Standing At A Virginal (about 1670), by Jan Vermeer

Musical moments

A Young Woman Standing At A Virginal pictures a calm, sunlit corner of a wealthy Dutch home. There is nothing special going on and no obvious moral tale, only a beautifully dressed woman standing by a virginal, an old-fashioned instrument similar to a piano. It is a quiet interior scene – a deliberate contrast to the grandeur and drama of Baroque-style art.

The painting in the background shows a cupid holding a playing card. This was sometimes used as a symbol of fidelity. The chair by the virginal is turned inwards, away from the viewer – it is not being offered to the onlooker. So the idea behind the picture may be that the woman is faithfully waiting for the return of her lover or husband, and not seeking out other companions.

The moral of the story

At this time, paintings with moral messages were popular, perhaps because buying them was a way for people to show how virtuous they were. So many everyday scenes show good behavior, such as work or study, that viewers were meant to imitate; or bad behavior, such as drinking too much, they had to avoid. But despite the seriousness, these pictures often tried to be funny, too. They poke fun at bad habits instead of condemning them, to try to entertain their audience as well as teach them.

Books and toys

The painting on the right, by the Dutch painter Caspar Netscher, uses a quiet family scene to contrast hard work and laziness. In the corner of a room, a mother teaches her daughter to read. But her son ignores his lessons, playing idly with a pet dog and his toys instead.

A Lady Teaching A Child To Read (probably 1670s), by Caspar Netscher

The Effects Of Intemperance (about 1663-65), by Jan Steen

Like many Dutch paintings, this illustrates an old Dutch proverb: 'Wine is a mocker' – meaning that wine makes a mockery of those who drink too much of it.

Drunk and disorderly

The Effects Of Intemperance, by Dutch artist Jan Steen, shows the chaos caused by parents behaving badly. The mother is drunk and asleep, while the father is sitting with another woman in the garden. Unwatched, their children misbehave too. One boy picks his mother's purse while another throws roses at the pig. The children on the right feed their dinner to the cat, and the tipsy maid offers her wine to the parrot. Steen hints at the dire consequences which may follow all this. The basket above the mother's head holds a birch rod used to punish petty criminals, a crutch and a kind of rattle carried by beggars.

Making arrangements

In the 17th century, there was a huge demand for still life paintings of flowers, food and other things, especially in the Dutch Republic. Dutch artists specialized in creating amazingly lifelike still lifes on particular themes. But despite the dazzling technical skill they showed, many people considered them less important than other kinds of paintings, because they seemed only to copy how things looked. But there is often more to them than meets the eye.

Flower power

From the early 17th century, flowers became a hugely popular subject for still lifes. At the time, scholars were beginning to learn much more about plants, and this is reflected in the range of species found in paintings. The vase on the right holds at least 14 different flowers, including tulips, which were then so rare and highly prized that some collectors would exchange their life savings for a single tulip bulb.

Flowers In A Terracotta Vase (1736), by Dutch painter Jan van Huysum. Look at the insects on the vase: they are so lifelike, they could almost be crawling over the surface of the painting.

Blooming marvellous

Although *Flowers In A Terracotta Vase* looks extremely lifelike, it isn't as real as it seems. Many of the flowers are larger than life, and the artist, Jan van Huysum, could never have seen them all together like this. Flower artists used to paint one species at a time, as each came into bloom, and gradually build up an imaginary bouquet of flowers from different seasons. Van Huysum took over a year to complete this painting, which includes spring blossom along with summer roses and autumnal fruits.

Lap of luxury

Still Life With Drinking Horn proudly displays the trappings of a luxurious feast. On a table draped with an oriental rug there are glasses of wine, a magnificent drinking horn and a whole lobster on a silver platter, next to a half-peeled lemon. It might seem casually arranged, but everything was carefully chosen to provide contrasting colors and textures.

This painting, like Van Huysum's *Flowers*, was designed to show off expensive luxury items. Even the lemon, which might seem ordinary today, would have been a costly item imported all the way from Italy. The Dutch word for 'show off' is *pronk*. So these arrangements are sometimes called 'pronk' still lifes.

Still Life With Drinking Horn (about 1653), by Willem Kalf. Notice the silver figures supporting the horn. The middle one is St. Sebastian, patron saint of archers – the horn used to belong to an archers' guild.

For a link to a website where you can zoom in on the details of different still lifes, go to **www.usborne-quicklinks.com**

An Allegory Of The Vanities Of Human Life (about 1640), by Dutch painter Harmen Steenwyck. This kind of allegorical still life seems to have been especially popular with scholars, who must have enjoyed deciphering the different symbols.

All in vain

Another popular type of still life was known as a 'vanitas' (*vanitas* is Latin for 'vanity.') These were meant to stop you from being too proud by reminding you that success is only temporary and everyone dies in the end. In this example, a beam of light points to a skull, an obvious symbol of death. It is surrounded by a rare shell and sword, representing wealth and possessions; books, symbolizing knowledge; and musical instruments, which stand for entertainment. But time passes, as shown by the watch and the dying lamp flame, and the shadow of death hangs over everything.

Flights of fancy

In the early 18th century, an elegant new style of art, known as 'Rococo,' appeared in France. Unlike the dramatic, moralizing art of the previous century, Rococo paintings were just meant to be charming and entertaining. They show graceful figures relaxing in dreamy landscapes – scenes which can seem a bit light and frothy by today's standards. The new style was hugely popular with the aristocrats of the French court. But it quickly went out of fashion at the end of the century, when the French Revolution brought a bloody and abrupt end to their privileged lifestyle.

Passing the time

Rococo paintings were basically about aristocrats having a good time, reflecting the life of leisure most of them led. So these scenes show gatherings of fashionably dressed people, playing music, dancing, picnicking and generally enjoying themselves.

These scenes of courtly entertainment are sometimes referred to as *fêtes galantes*. But they are far from lifelike. They always take place in idealized, imaginary settings, painted in soft, pretty colors.

The Scale Of Love (1715-18), by Jean-Antoine Watteau

Love and harmony

One of the earliest and most influential Rococo artists was a French painter named Jean-Antoine Watteau. His paintings often deal with the theme of love. *The Scale Of Love* shows a couple sitting in the woods. The man, wearing a theatrical pink costume, is playing a guitar, while the woman holds a book of music. Watteau matches the angle of the man's guitar to the line of the woman's leg beneath her skirt, creating a strong visual link between them. The title of the painting refers to the traditional association between music and love. The harmonies of the music were supposed to reflect the lovers' harmonious feelings.

Feathery brushstrokes create a hazy effect on the sky and trees.
This technique was influenced by Rubens' style (see pages 66-67).

Time flies

An Allegory With Venus And Time has the delicate colors and light touch of the Rococo style, but shows a mythical scene instead of a *fête galante*. Venus, seated in the heavens, is handing a baby to Old Father Time – you can tell who he is by his hourglass and scythe. The child is Venus' son, Aeneas, who is half human and so must live his life on Earth, subject to the laws of Time.

The painting may have been commissioned to celebrate the birth of a child. It has an unusual shape because it was designed to fit into the ceiling of an Italian palace. As it would have been seen from below, the artist has used aerial perspective to create the impression of looking up to a great height. The tones get lighter and the details become hazier as the things get higher up and farther away, so it is quite hard to make out the faces of the figures at the top.

An Allegory With Venus And Time (1754-58), by Italian artist Giovanni Tiepolo. Notice how the figures are drawn from a steep angle, as if seen from underneath.

👁 For a link to a website where you can visit a virtual exhibition about the Rococo, and see more pictures by Jean-Antoine Watteau, go to **www.usborne-quicklinks.com**

Coffee break

This painting is by one of the most successful Rococo painters, Nicolas Lancret. It shows a family dressed in elegant 18th-century clothes. But, in the fashion of the time, it is an intimate, relaxed scene, rather than a formal family portrait.

There are lots of small details which emphasize the informality of the scene. The mother is offering a spoonful of coffee to one of her daughters. A doll lies abandoned on the ground, and there is a dog digging in the flowerbed. The painting is sometimes referred to as *The Cup Of Chocolate*, but the servant on the left is holding what is definitely a silver coffee pot.

A Lady In A Garden Taking Coffee (probably 1742), by French painter Nicolas Lancret

High society

The 18th century was an important time for art in England. More people began taking an interest in artists' work, and new art societies were established, including the Royal Academy of Arts in 1768. The societies helped artists to study, exhibit and sell their works to a wider public, though many still made their living by painting for rich, upper-class patrons. But there was also a market for satirical pictures criticizing high society.

Mr. And Mrs. Andrews (1750), by Thomas Gainsborough. Gainsborough loved painting landscapes and often included them in his portraits.

Artistic rivals

The leading British portrait artists of the day were Thomas Gainsborough and Joshua Reynolds. Both members of the Royal Academy, they were artistic rivals who took very different approaches to painting, though they respected each other's work.

Reynolds studied Classical art and often based his compositions on what he learned from it. He began his paintings by making careful preparatory drawings, and spent a lot of time working on different paint effects. He even tried mixing his paints with wax and vinegar to create texture. By contrast, Gainsborough painted in a livelier, more spontaneous way, and developed a more personal style.

Wealth and weddings

Gainsborough's *Mr. And Mrs. Andrews* shows a newly wed couple from Suffolk. Robert Andrews, a wealthy landowner, proudly surveys his estate. His wife Frances sits beside him, wearing a fashionable dress with wide skirts. The blank space on her lap was meant to be filled in later, perhaps with a book or an animal. The landscape represents Robert's property, to which his marriage had added. At the time, it was not uncommon for the upper classes to marry for money.

Back in his London studio, Gainsborough painted landscapes from models he made himself, using broccoli for trees and mirrors for lakes.

Fighting man

When he painted people, Reynolds didn't just want to capture how they looked. He also wanted to make his paintings seem important and dignified, to make us take them seriously. So he worked on enormous canvases, and often included allusions to Classical art. For example, the pose of Colonel Banastre Tarleton, the man on the left, was copied from a statue of an ancient Greek god.

Colonel Tarleton commissioned this portrait after fighting in the American War of Independence. It shows him in the middle of a battleground, standing against a cloud of cannon smoke. His pose allowed Reynolds to conceal his fingers, some of which he had lost in battle. But, in spite of his heroic appearance, Tarleton was not a very successful soldier. Some people think Reynolds might have hinted slyly at this in the portrait: amid the debris in the background, there is a cannon aimed at Tarleton's back.

Colonel Banastre Tarleton (1782), by Joshua Reynolds. Notice Tarleton's green coat, the uniform of his cavalry division, which was known as Tarleton's Green Horse.

👁 For a link to a website where you can explore 18th-century London and meet its artists, go to **www.usborne-quicklinks.com**

Making a mockery

The Marriage Settlement, by William Hogarth, mocks high society and the practice of marrying for money or status. Unlike paintings by Reynolds or Gainsborough, it was designed to be the basis for 'engravings,' or printed copies, which were bought in their hundreds by all kinds of people. It shows the arrangements for a marriage between an impoverished earl's son and a rich merchant's daughter. The fathers negotiate the contract, the merchant with a pile of gold coins, and the earl with a copy of his family tree. The young couple waits helplessly, sitting side-by-side, but turning away from each other. They have been forced together, like the chained dogs in the corner.

The Marriage Settlement (about 1743), by William Hogarth. This is one of a series entitled *Fashionable Marriage*. A monster's head looms in the oval frame above the young couple, hinting at trouble ahead. The rest of the series illustrates the dire outcome of their marriage.

Vacation snapshots

In the18th century, it was usual for wealthy gentlemen to complete their education by going on a 'Grand Tour' of Europe, and especially Italy. This was a chance for them to learn about art and culture in other countries, as well as to have some fun away from home. The Tour had a great impact on art. Many 'Grand Tourists' bought paintings and antique sculptures as souvenirs of their travels, creating a profitable line of work for painters and leading to an increased interest in Classical art back home.

Charles Townley's Library At 7, Park Street, Westminster (1782), by Johan Zoffany. This painting shows the extraordinary number of Classical sculptures and replicas collected by one enthusiastic British Grand Tourist, Charles Townley (sitting on the right, wearing a gray jacket), during the course of his travels.

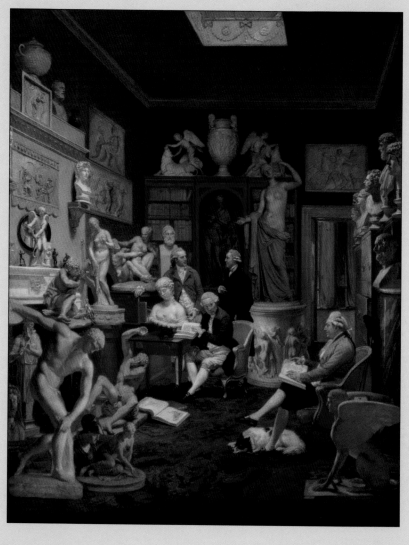

👁 For a link to a website where you can find out more about artists and the Grand Tour, go to **www.usborne-quicklinks.com**

Landscape With Diana And Callisto (about 1757), by Richard Wilson

Humble artists

The Grand Tour was very expensive, so only the wealthiest could afford it. But many artists saw a trip to Rome as an important part of their education. Visiting Rome meant they could study Roman and Italian art, and paint the famous scenery that had inspired Claude, an influential French painter. Many artists found well-paid work there too, making paintings for the Grand Tourists. The painting on the left is a view of Lake Nemi, east of Rome, which the English artist Richard Wilson had visited. The town of Nemi, which you can just see in the distance, was believed to have a shrine to the Roman goddess Diana. Wilson painted Diana and some of her attendants in the foreground.

Interior Of Saint Peter's, Rome (before 1742), by Giovanni Panini

Souvenir scenes

Just as today's tourists buy postcards or take snapshots, 18th-century travelers wanted pictures to remind them of their trip. So some artists specialized in picturesque views of famous sights, like these paintings of Venice and Rome, which they sold to Grand Tourists. The painting on the left shows St. Peter's Basilica, Rome, which would have been on the sightseeing list of any Grand Tourist. The painting below is a view of Venice during a regatta, when there were boat races on the city's canals.

A Regatta On The Grand Canal (about 1740), by Giovanni Canal, or 'Canaletto'

A better view

One Italian painter nicknamed 'Canaletto,' or 'little canal,' became very famous for his detailed scenes of canals in Venice. The picture above is so lifelike, you could almost mistake it for a photo. Canaletto may actually have used a kind of early camera, known as a 'camera obscura,' to help him draw more accurately (see page 165). But he did cheat to improve the scenery, moving buildings to open up the view, and usually showing Venice with sunny skies and sparkling water – just as tourists would want to remember it.

79

REVOLUTION

The 19th century was a time when lots of art movements began to appear. These movements were formed when artists began to work together in groups, sharing ideas and often exhibiting their pictures at the same shows. Many artists began to experiment more widely too, taking advantage of new materials and new scientific theories to create radically different ways of painting the world.

Detail from *A Sunday on La Grande Jatte* (1884-86), by Georges Seurat. You can see the whole picture on page 94.

Making history

The end of the 18th century brought troubled times, with wars all over Europe and a bloody revolution in France. Many artists responded by making big, serious pictures of important events and people of the time, or scenes from the past that seemed to relate to them. Often, these paintings were designed to make viewers take a particular political view of events.

The Oath Of The Horatii (1784), by Jacques-Louis David

New Classicism

After excavations began at Pompeii (see page 27) in 1748, there was a renewed interest in Classical history. French artist Jacques-Louis David was particularly inspired by Classical art. His style, with its clearly drawn, smoothly shaded figures, became known as Neoclassicism ('neo' means new.) In choosing austere, Classical subjects, David was consciously rejecting the more frivolous Rococo style which had gone before.

History lessons

David's *The Oath Of The Horatii* is a history painting (see pages 10-11) in that it illustrates a story. But it was also meant to teach a moral lesson to modern audiences. Set in Roman times, it shows the Horatii brothers swearing loyalty to their father before setting off to battle. Willing to die for the greater good, the brothers represent courage and patriotism – Classical ideals which were very relevant to the artist's own time. This picture was made in 1784, just five years before the violent revolution which overthrew the French king.

David wanted to imitate the polished elegance of Classical sculptures. So he painted very smoothly, hardly leaving any brushmarks that you can see. He also arranged everyone in a row, like the figures in a Classical frieze.

👁 For a link to a website where you can explore a portrait of Napoleon by Jacques-Louis David, go to **www.usborne-quicklinks.com**

Horrors of war

This painting, by Spanish artist Francisco Goya, shows French troops shooting unarmed Spanish civilians. Commissioned by the Spanish king, it commemorates a real incident from the 1808-14 war between France and Spain. It is meant to shock us and make us condemn the shootings. But the painting is not just about one event, it also represents the horrors of every war. Unlike David's picture, which makes fighting and sacrifice seem noble and valiant, Goya doesn't shrink from showing the grim reality of killing.

The Third Of May 1808 (Executions) (1814-15), by Francisco Goya. Notice the lantern by the soldiers' feet. Goya uses its light to focus attention on the victims' terrified faces, the harsh lines of the soldiers' guns, and the gruesome puddles of blood on the ground.

Power and glory

Jean-Auguste-Dominique Ingres studied art under David and, like his teacher, became a successful Neoclassicist. By his early twenties, he was regarded as one of the leading artists in France. He painted the French emperor, Napoleon I, several times. This particular portrait was designed to glorify the newly crowned emperor and show just how powerful he was.

To make Napoleon look important, Ingres concentrated on the trappings of state rather than his character. So the emperor's grand, velvet and ermine robes, and his golden crown, chain and scepters, are painted in beautiful detail. But his face is mask-like, revealing little about him as a man.

Napoleon I On His Imperial Throne (1806), by Ingres. Napoleon's throne, crown, robes and scepters are all traditional symbols of authority. Ingres also added a Roman eagle on the carpet, to make Napoleon seem as mighty as a Roman emperor.

This painting measures a huge 102 x 64in. Its vast size was meant to fill you with awe of Napoleon.

In contrast to the size of his portrait, Napoleon was a small man, only 5ft6in tall. So the painting is much bigger than lifesize.

Sun and storm

Some 19th-century artists were inspired by the power of nature, painting wild landscapes beneath moody, dramatic skies. These scenes were meant to have a powerful emotional or spiritual impact when you looked at them. This approach to art became known as Romanticism.

👁 For a link to a website where you can find out more about painting the weather, and see many pictures, go to **www.usborne-quicklinks.com**

Salisbury Cathedral From The Meadows (1831), by English artist John Constable

Stormy weather

John Constable specialized in painting English landscapes. He created this dramatic scene soon after his wife's death, using the sky – which he described as the 'keynote' of a painting – to set the tone. To the left, it is dark and stormy. But the cathedral's spire rises above the clouds, and the storm is passing, leaving patches of sunlight on the right. The spire may be meant to suggest the consolation of religion,

and the rainbow above it is a traditional symbol of new hope. In this way, Constable made the picture represent both his grief and his faith in the afterlife promised by Christianity.

Constable spent months studying clouds, trying to capture their ever-changing appearance in paint.

Snow and salvation

Caspar David Friedrich was the leading German Romantic painter, and his pictures often have a strong religious symbolism. In *Winter Landscape*, he made a visual link between nature and religion by making the fir trees echo the shape of the distant church. At first sight, the scene seems bleak and cold. But a rosy glow in the sky announces the arrival of a new day. In the foreground, a man has abandoned his crutches and prays in front of a crucifix. The rock he leans on, and the evergreen firs, are meant as symbols of everlasting faith in God.

Winter Landscape (probably 1811), by Caspar David Friedrich. Friedrich based his landscapes on the countryside around Dresden, in northern Germany, where he lived.

Artist in exile

This painting by Eugène Delacroix shows the Roman poet, Ovid, in exile in Scythia, in central Asia. Set apart by his smart, dark blue and white clothes, Ovid watches the Scythians' 'foreign' custom of drinking horses' milk. Delacroix chose this subject because, like Ovid, he felt himself to be a misunderstood artist, isolated among 'barbarians' (by which he meant unsympathetic art critics.) Delacroix used bright, contrasting colors, such as red and green – he said, "color gives the appearance of life."

Ovid Among The Scythians (1859), by Eugène Delacroix. Notice how loose and flowing Delacroix's brushwork seems, compared to the painting by Ingres on page 83, which has a much smoother, more even finish.

Fighting it out

Delacroix was the best-known French Romantic painter, and his vivid, expressive approach is typical of Romanticism. It was very different from the smooth, polished style of the Neoclassicists and Ingres. In the 19th century, art critics argued furiously over the merits of these two styles, often pitting Delacroix's work against that of Ingres. Admirers of Classicism denounced Delacroix's paintings as 'ugly.' But his supporters criticized Ingres' pictures for lacking feeling.

Dreams and legends

Although many 19th-century artists chose to paint the world around them, others found their inspiration elsewhere. Some looked inside their imagination, creating moody, mysterious images of magic and dreams. Others looked back to the past, painting scenes from ancient heroic tales and legends.

Mystery and make-believe

Artists like Gustave Moreau and Odilon Redon in France, and Gustav Klimt in Austria, were preoccupied with dreams and the supernatural, and the mystery of life. But they felt mystery could not be shown directly, so they tried to *suggest* it by using strange, symbolic imagery. This became known as Symbolism. It is hard to say what their symbols mean, they just hint at feelings and impressions.

St. George And The Dragon is Moreau's personal version of the saint's story. Although it is full of details, it is not very realistic. Just look at the way St. George's cloak flies up behind him, defying gravity. Moreau was more interested in exploring his own mind than in creating a lifelike scene, so he painted this picture purely from his imagination. Ideas and feelings were, for him, more important than the world around him – he claimed: *"I believe neither in what I touch nor what I see. I only believe... in what I feel."*

St. George And The Dragon (1889-90), by Gustave Moreau. Notice the saint's halo, copied from earlier religious art.

Flower girl

This pastel drawing by Redon shows a colorful mass of flowers, set against a hazy, mysterious background containing a girl's face. It isn't meant to seem realistic – the girl's features are little more than a blur, and the flowers have oddly blue leaves. Rather, it is a dream-image, more about color and mood than anything else. Redon was said to have been inspired by watching clouds and imagining fantastic figures in the shapes they made.

Ophelia Among The Flowers (about 1905-08), by Odilon Redon

Ophelia (1851-52), by John Everett Millais. Ophelia is surrounded by beautiful plants, all painted from life, many with symbolic meanings. The weeping willow represents sadness, daisies evoke innocence, and poppies and violets are associated with death.

Secret society

Another 19th-century development came from a group of young British painters, including Dante Gabriel Rossetti and John Everett Millais. They admired the spirituality and simplicity of medieval art and disliked the influence that Raphael (see page 44) had had on art for centuries. So they formed a secret society, the 'Pre-Raphaelite Brotherhood,' to promote their ideas, and signed their pictures 'PRB.'

The PRB wanted to make art true to nature, so they always worked from life. They drew people in natural poses, with realistic backgrounds. They also prepared their canvases with white, which made the colors on top look brighter. At first, people criticized their work for looking too bright and awkwardly composed. But eventually their style became very popular.

👁 For a link to a website where you can find out more about Millais' *Ophelia*, go to **www.usborne-quicklinks.com**

Poetic vision

The Pre-Raphaelites often painted scenes from books, especially the Bible and Shakespeare. The painting above shows the death of Ophelia, from Shakespeare's play *Hamlet*. Mad with grief after her father was killed, Ophelia was supposed to have fallen into a stream while picking flowers and drowned.

Millais spent four months working by a river, plagued by mosquitoes and unfriendly landowners, to make his setting as lifelike as possible. For Ophelia, he got his model, Lizzie Siddal, to pose in a bathtub so he could study the effect of the water – making her catch an awful cold in the process. Lizzie married Millais' friend Rossetti. When she died, Rossetti threw a book of his poems into her grave. But he dug them up again later, so that he could publish them.

City life

The 19th century was a time of great changes and upheavals, some of which, like the explosion of cities, the development of new industries and the introduction of railways, changed forever the way people lived their lives. Some artists responded to this by looking beyond the traditional subjects of art, finding their inspiration instead in the hustle and bustle of modern city life.

Paris in the 19th century

Café society

In many ways Paris was at the heart of the new age. The French capital changed rapidly as its old, narrow streets were demolished and replaced by the grand boulevards, designed by Baron Haussmann, that you can see today. New shops, theaters and cafes were built, which form the settings of many paintings by French artists such as Edouard Manet and Edgar Degas, who were born and bred in the city.

Top hats and togas

In painting contemporary scenes, Manet and other artists were influenced by a poet named Charles Baudelaire. He encouraged artists to turn away from the past and paint modern scenes. Top hats, he said, were as interesting as togas, meaning that ordinary modern subjects could be as rewarding as Classical ones. On these two pages you can see examples of some of the kinds of everyday scenes artists chose.

This painting shows a fashionable crowd gathered in a Paris park. The clothes and setting locate the painting firmly in 19th-century Paris. Several of the artist's friends are among the crowd.

Manet included this small portrait of himself on the left.

Music In The Tuileries Gardens (1862), by Edouard Manet. Notice how some parts of this scene are more 'finished' than others. Manet wanted to reflect how we see some things more clearly than others.

A modern style

Many artists looked for new ways to capture the experience of modern life. Rather than trying to create balanced compositions and smoothly painted images, they tried to make their pictures seem spontaneous. They often showed scenes from odd angles, as if glimpsed in passing, or cropped like a snapshot, and they used loose, bold brushstrokes.

At the circus

Miss La-La was a famous circus performer. Here, Degas shows her in the middle of a show, performing a feat of strength. In this part of the show, she hung by her teeth from a rope and spun around. The painting is designed to make us feel we are at the show ourselves, watching from below. The scene is drawn in dramatic perspective and lit from beneath, increasing the sensation of height. But Degas didn't paint it in the circus. He made sketches there, but completed the final painting in his studio.

Miss La-La at the Fernando Circus (1879), by Edgar Degas

👁 For a link to a website that features another picture set in Saint Lazare Station, go to **www.usborne-quicklinks.com**

Saint Lazare Station (1877), by Claude Monet

Light and steam

When Monet painted *Saint Lazare Station*, trains were still a recent invention. This particular station, which is still a working station today, was then one of the newest and busiest stations in Paris.

Monet spent weeks working on a series of pictures of the station. But he was more interested in the light and colors created by steam from the trains than in the trains themselves. He made friends with the station master, who told the train drivers to let off steam specially when Monet was ready to begin painting.

Rain, Steam And Speed

I n 1844, English artist Joseph Turner exhibited a picture of a steam train crossing a river beneath a stormy sky. At the time, this was a startlingly modern subject – the first ever passenger train had run less than 20 years earlier. It was also painted in a very new, blurry and impressionistic style, and created a sensation when it was exhibited.

Title: *Rain, Steam And Speed – The Great Western Railway*
Date: before 1844
Artist: Joseph Mallord William Turner
Materials: oil on canvas
Size: 36 x 48in

Different angles

Turner deliberately contrasted old and new. The train is shown rushing over a modern railroad bridge. To the left, there is an old footbridge. Turner used perspective to emphasize the difference between them. Just compare the lines in the diagram on the right. The old bridge crosses the picture almost horizontally, but the train and the new bridge are drawn at a much steeper angle. It feels as if the train is zooming straight at you.

The shallow angle of the old bridge seems static, while the steep angle of the railroad bridge helps show just how fast the train is moving.

Dashing along

Although it's hard to make out any details, Turner's picture gives a powerful impression of a train racing along. One 19th-century writer was so impressed, he wrote: *"there comes a train... really moving at the rate of 50 miles an hour, and which the reader had best make haste to see, lest it should dash out of the picture, and be away... through the wall opposite."*

Stormy weather

Turner was famous for painting dramatic skies and atmospheric effects. He set the train against a hazy backdrop of clouds and slanting rain, made up of streaks of white paint smeared across the surface of the picture. One critic dismissed this kind of effect as "soapsuds and whitewash." But it was a good way to convey the power of the rainstorm.

Love and hate

Turner loved to travel on trains, and *Rain, Steam And Speed* seems to be a celebration of them. But he wasn't always so positive about the new age of steam. *The 'Fighting Temeraire,'* painted only five years earlier, seems full of nostalgia for the past. It shows a modern tug towing away an old sailing ship for scrap. The setting sun evokes a sense of ending and loss, and the old ship's tall, graceful outline contrasts starkly with the squat modern tug, belching smoke.

The 'Fighting Temeraire' Tugged To Her Last Berth To Be Broken Up, 1838 (1839), by J.M.W. Turner

Finishing touches

Turner was a very fast painter. At the time, artists were generally allowed a small amount of time to retouch and varnish paintings after they had been put up in an exhibition. Turner would submit unfinished pictures, then complete them on the spot in front of an admiring audience. He could transform a whole scene with touches of brilliant color, often making paintings nearby look dull and uninteresting by comparison. The artist John Constable once watched Turner add a patch of red which outshone the reds in his own picture hanging beside it. Constable said, admiringly: "He has been here and fired a gun."

Turner loved watching the weather. He even claimed to have persuaded some sailors to tie him to their ship's mast during a storm, so he could observe its effects.

Self Portrait (about 1799), by J.M.W. Turner. This shows Turner in his 20s – by which point he was already a successful artist.

The great outdoors

In the 1860s-70s, there was a new fashion for painting outdoor scenes *outside*. Painting outside was not in itself new – many 18th-century artists sketched outside – but now, for the first time, artists were finishing entire paintings out of doors.

Portable paints

One of the things that made painting outdoors possible was the invention of new art equipment in the 1850s. Now, artists could buy ready-to-use paints in portable boxes or resealable metal tubes. So they could take them wherever they wanted.

Monet Working On His Boat In Argenteuil (1874), by Edouard Manet. Manet's painting of his friend and fellow-artist, Claude Monet, shows how Monet was prepared to set up studio anywhere.

Fox Hill, Upper Norwood (1870), by Camille Pissarro. Pissarro was interested in the effects of snow. Look at the bright blue he uses in the shadows.

Practical problems

Painting outside brought with it lots of practical problems. It could be bitterly cold, as it was when Camille Pissarro painted *Fox Hill*. Working on a boat, as Claude Monet is doing above, was rocky and unstable. And, when he painted on a beach, the wind blew sand into his paint. But the artists felt it was all worth it for the sense of immediacy and freshness they achieved by working on the spot.

Monet once arranged for some trees' spring leaves to be removed, so he could finish painting a winter scene.

Bold impressions

The new outdoor paintings showed modern subjects in strong colors, with broken brushstrokes leaving an uneven, 'sketchy' finish. Even where artists had worked on paintings for a long time, they wanted them to seem spontaneous, to capture the fleeting effects of sunlight and shadows.

At the time, critics attacked the new style for being 'impressionistic' and crude. Their insults gave rise to the name by which it is now known: 'Impressionism.' Many Impressionist artists went on to be enormously successful, including Auguste Renoir, Berthe Morisot and Alfred Sisley, as well as Monet and Pisarro. But, when they first started, their work was rejected by official exhibitions.

👁 For a link to a web site where you can find out all about Impressionism, go to **www.usborne-quicklinks.com**

The Beach At Trouville (1870), by Claude Monet. Monet painted this while on holiday in northern France. The woman on the left is his wife, Camille.

If you look at this detail, you can see grains of sand got stuck to the wet paint – which Monet applied using big, broad brushstrokes.

Boating On The Seine (about 1879-80), by Auguste Renoir

Bright and sunny

In *Boating On The Seine*, Renoir used bright colors to create the impression of a landscape drenched in sunshine. The effect is exaggerated because he put complementary colors (colors that stand out against each other) together. For example, painting the boat orange made the blue water around it look even brighter.

Blue stands out strongly against orange, its complementary color.

Against other colors, the blue water seems less bright.

Colorful views

Toward the end of the 19th century, some artists thought up startling and original ways of using color. Some wanted to exploit new scientific theories about how we see color. Others began choosing colors for their symbolic or emotional associations, trying to make their pictures bolder and brighter and even more expressive than life.

A Sunday on La Grande Jatte (1884-86), by French artist Georges Seurat; oil on canvas, 81 x 120in

Making a point

In the 1880s, Georges Seurat invented a technique known as "Pointillism," using tiny dots of pure, contrasting colors. The scene above contains about 3.5 million dots. Seen from a distance, the dots blur, so the colors seem to blend together. Seurat was inspired by new research into the science of optics – how we see things, especially color. He thought that letting colors mix in the eye, rather than on his palette, made them appear brighter and richer.

You can see the individual dots more clearly in this enlarged detail.

Contrasts and harmonies

Seurat designed his dots to exploit the way colors are affected by the other colors around them. For example, blue contrasts most strongly with orange, so blue looks brighter next to orange. You can use a "color wheel" to work out these contrasts. In the wheel, each color lies opposite its "complementary" color, the color it contrasts with most intensely. It sits next to its "harmonizing" colors – the colors most similar to it.

The color wheel contains red, yellow and blue, and the colors you get by mixing them.

Expressive colour

Dutch artist Vincent van Gogh believed colors had emotional values. He wrote *"instead of trying to reproduce exactly what I have before my eyes, I use color arbitrarily, in order to express myself more forcibly."*

In 1888, van Gogh moved to Arles, in southern France, and invited his friend Paul Gauguin to stay. Sunflowers grew all around Arles, and van Gogh did a series of sunflower pictures to decorate his house and welcome Gauguin. Van Gogh loved these yellow flowers, which he sketched rapidly in thick, bumpy layers of paint. New "chrome" yellows – bright, chemical-based colors – had recently become available, and van Gogh used them almost undiluted, to dazzling effect. For him, these yellows represented happiness, friendship and harmony.

Sunflowers (1888), by Vincent van Gogh; oil on canvas, 36 x 29in. Notice the tiny touches of blue. They make the orangey-yellows around them look even brighter.

Harvest at Le Pouldu (1890), by Paul Gauguin; oil on canvas, 29 x 36in. Gauguin painted this not long after leaving Arles. Notice how the red dog stands out against the green grass.

Flat shapes

Although Gauguin and van Gogh worked closely together in Arles, their styles were very different. Van Gogh liked painting from life, while Gauguin preferred to follow his imagination. He tended to simplify outlines and create smooth, flat shapes, as you can see on the left. But both artists exaggerated colors, and Gauguin encouraged others to do the same. He claimed color was the most important part of a painting. The friends' partnership lasted until the winter, when they had a violent quarrel and Gauguin fled. Terribly upset, van Gogh – who suffered from mental illness – cut off part of his own ear.

👁 For links to websites where you can find out more about these artists and about how artists use color, go to **www.usborne-quicklinks.com**

Getting away from it all

Although some 19th-century artists were inspired by cities, others rejected city life. They longed for a simpler, more traditional kind of existence – a longing reflected in their paintings, which often show perfect imaginary landscapes or scenes from nature.

Country retreat

French painter Paul Cézanne tried to make a name for himself in Paris, but with little success. So he went home to Provence, in southern France, where he led a quiet country life. Away from his critics, he painted picture after picture inspired by the local landscape, especially the mountain of Sainte-Victoire.

Sainte-Victoire Mountain seen from the Road to Tholonet (1880s), by Paul Cézanne. Cézanne loved painting this mountain because of its solidity, a quality which he sought in his pictures – he said he wanted to create a "solid and durable" art. His style was unpopular to begin with, but he began to win admiration in the 1890s, and had a great influence on younger artists.

Earthly paradise

Paul Gauguin also left Paris to lead a more rural life, first in the village of Pont-Aven and then with van Gogh in Arles. Later, Gauguin travelled to the South Pacific in search of an earthly paradise, raising the money by selling off his pictures.

Gauguin settled on the island of Tahiti. Away from city influences, he developed a deliberately crude style inspired by traditional Pacific art. He simplified shapes and flattened perspective, as you can see in *Faa Iheihe*. Like many of his pictures, this scene is meant to show people living in harmony with nature.

Faa Iheihe (1898), by Paul Gauguin. The name of this picture probably means 'to beautify, adorn or embellish,' in the sense of getting dressed up for a special occasion.

Imaginary voyages

Henri Rousseau was a French customs officer who painted in his spare time. Although he led a quiet life, never traveling far from home, he made imaginary voyages, creating wild scenes based on plants and animals he saw in parks and zoos, or read about in books.

Perhaps because they are imaginary, Rousseau's pictures often have a strange, dreamlike quality. Critics at the time laughed at his simple, self-taught style, and dismissed him as an 'amateur.' But several artists came to admire him, including the Surrealists (see pages 122-123) and Pablo Picasso (see pages 105-107), who organized a grand dinner in his honor.

Tiger In A Tropical Storm – Surprised! (1891), by Henri Rousseau, nicknamed 'Douanier' Rousseau (*douanier* is French for 'customs officer.')

The plants at the bottom of this picture were based on ornamental houseplants. But Rousseau made them much bigger, so they look like exotic jungle plants.

For links to websites where you can find out more about Cézanne and Gauguin, and escape from inside a famous painting in an interactive game, go to **www.usborne-quicklinks.com**

Gauguin used natural, locally available materials for his paintings.

He used pigments like these, made by grinding up dried dirt, to mix his earthy colors.

He painted on rough cloth, or 'hessian,' which was made in Tahiti.

Gauguin loved traditional art, and the shape of this picture was inspired by the sculpted friezes traditionally produced in the Pacific islands. Some of the figures were copied from friezes, too.

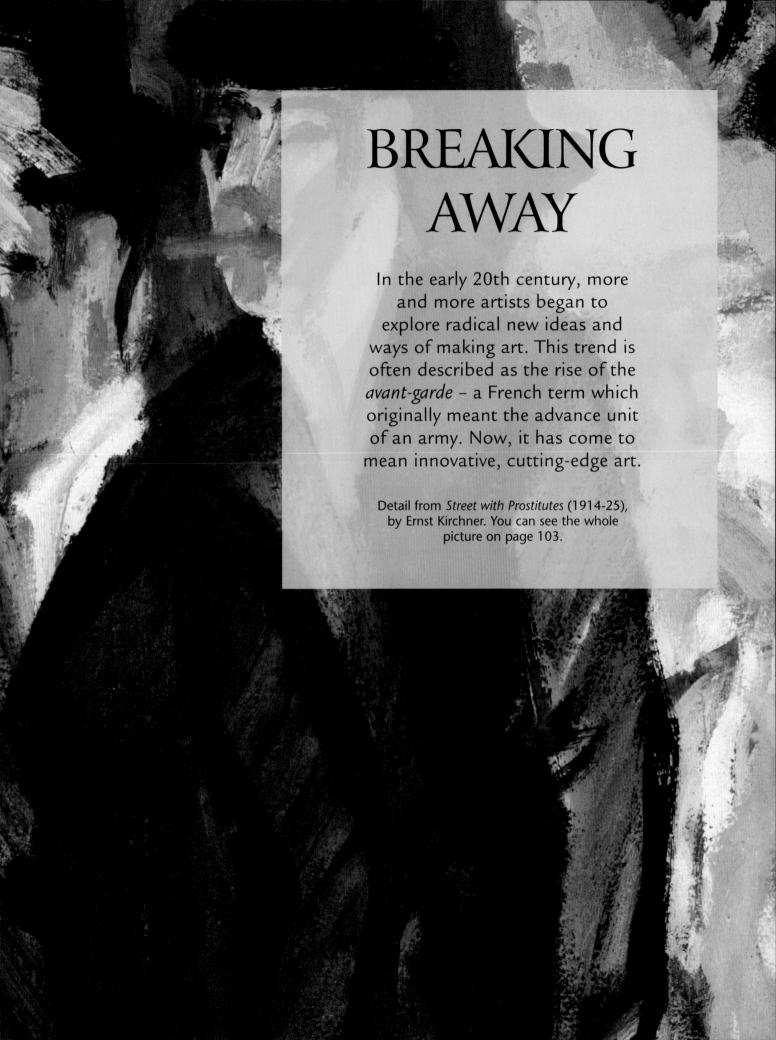

BREAKING AWAY

In the early 20th century, more and more artists began to explore radical new ideas and ways of making art. This trend is often described as the rise of the *avant-garde* – a French term which originally meant the advance unit of an army. Now, it has come to mean innovative, cutting-edge art.

Detail from *Street with Prostitutes* (1914-25), by Ernst Kirchner. You can see the whole picture on page 103.

Running wild

As artists continued to experiment with color, they began to produce paintings that were more vibrant, and less lifelike, than any before. Instead of trying to imitate nature – which seemed less important now photography had been invented – they began to think about what makes a strong picture in its own right. They believed this would help them create more original, imaginative works of art.

Painting lessons

Among the artists exploring new approaches to painting was a group named the Nabis, or "prophets" in Hebrew. They were strongly influenced by Gauguin, who encouraged them to use intense, undiluted colors. Paul Sérusier painted the woodland scene on the right during a lesson with Gauguin. In fact, it looks more like a pattern of colored shapes than a picture of a real wood. It illustrates one of the ideas of the Nabis: "A painting... is essentially a flat surface with colors organized in a certain order."

The Talisman (1888), by Paul Sérusier; oil on wood, 11 x 9in. Can you make out trees with blue trunks?

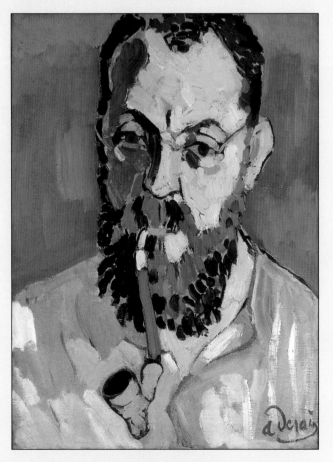

Wild beasts

In 1905, French artists Henri Matisse and André Derain spent the summer at Collioure, a small port in southern France. Here, they painted each other's portraits – you can see Derain's one of Matisse on the left – and other scenes, experimenting with bright, pure colors. Like the Nabis, they didn't think colors had to be lifelike. And they didn't want to weaken the effect by blending them. So they chose the most vivid colors and applied them in solid patches. The result can seem crude, but it is actually a careful balance of complementary colors (see page 94).

When some of the friends' work went on show in Paris that fall, along with similarly colorful pictures by Maurice Vlaminck and a few others, the public greeted it with shock and outrage. One critic thought it looked so wild, he nicknamed the whole group *Fauves*, French for "Wild Beasts." He meant it as an insult, but the name stuck, and it is still how they are known today.

Henri Matisse (1905), by André Derain; oil on canvas, 18 x 14in. Notice how the bluish shadows on the face are offset by patches of orange (the complementary of blue) around the eyes.

Open Window, Collioure (1905), by Henri Matisse; oil on canvas, 22 x 18in. Notice how the wall is a very different color on each side of the window – an effect which could be created by strong sun on one side, and shade on the other.

Matisse thought art should be pleasant and soothing. He said he wanted: "an art of purity and serenity... something like a good armchair that provides relaxation from fatigue."

Sun, sand and sea

The sunny sea view above was painted in Collioure by Matisse. It shows French windows opening onto a little balcony, neatly framing the boats drawn up on the beach beyond. Everything is loosely sketched in dazzling hues, with almost no shading. It is meant to be a celebration of color, not a slavish imitation of real life – though it does give a very real sense of what it is like to look out at such a bright, sunlit landscape.

The open window helps create a sense of space. It also frames the boats like a picture within the picture. Matisse may have meant this to draw attention to the process of picture-making itself, which he was completely revolutionizing.

Warm and cool

Matisse's sea view is built up of colors rather than solid, 3-D shapes. He used the contrast between warm and cool colors to structure his painting, doing the sunny parts in bright, warm reds, pinks and oranges, and the shady areas in cool blues and greens. Matisse said: "When I put a green, it is not grass. When I put a blue, it is not the sky." He was inspired by the intensity and contrasts of the colors themselves as much as by the scene itself.

👁 For links to websites where you can explore a virtual exhibition all about the Fauves or create your own Matisse picture, go to **www.usborne-quicklinks.com**

Express yourself

In the early years of the 20th century, many artists began to search for more expressive ways of painting. Instead of focusing on how things looked, they wanted to explore the vast territory of human emotions. So they began to heighten colors and exaggerate shapes to communicate strong feelings, from joy to despair. This became known as Expressionism.

Screaming out

Expressionism was heavily influenced by the work of two artists: Vincent van Gogh and Norwegian artist, Edvard Munch. Munch made many paintings about sickness, death and loneliness. He said he wanted his work to show "living beings who breathe and feel and love and suffer," as he must have done. His mother and sister died tragically young from TB, and he himself was often ill.

The Scream is one of the most famous Expressionist images. Munch did several versions of it, ranging from bright, jarring oil paintings to bleak, black and white prints, like the one here. It shows a haggard figure standing on a bridge in a swirling landscape. He seems to be clutching his head in pain, as if trapped in a state of anguish, surrounded by a silent but still reverberating scream.

The Scream (1895), by Edvard Munch; lithograph, 14 x 10in. Munch said this image was inspired by a walk he took, when he felt "an endless scream passing through nature."

Reclining Woman with Green Stockings (1917), by Egon Schiele; gouache and black crayon on paper, 12 x 18in. Notice the model's odd, contorted pose and the way she stares directly at us – unlike traditional paintings, which usually show women looking away.

Separate agenda

In Germany and Austria, Expressionism was taken up by groups of rebellious artists who cut themselves off from traditional art academies. Their breakaway movement became known as the Secession. In Vienna, the Secession was led by Gustav Klimt, and he encouraged Egon Schiele to join too. Schiele did many drawings of nude or scantily clad models. Instead of trying to make them appear demure and seductive, as a traditional artist might, he used rough lines and bruised colors to create awkward, tormented images, full of sexual tension and even aggression.

Building bridges

In 1905, four young German artists – Ernst Kirchner, Karl Schmidt-Rottluff, Fritz Bleyl and Eric Heckel – founded a group named *Die Brücke*, which is German for "The Bridge." They wanted to create a bridge to the future, to a new kind of art. Inspired by both African and medieval European art, they used bold, angular shapes and bright, unnatural colors – as in this Berlin street scene by Kirchner.

Kirchner made a series of paintings about the seedy side of life in Berlin. The two women in this picture are probably prostitutes. The men on the sidewalk eye the woman in red, their faces like sickly, green masks. And the odd perspective makes the ground seem to tilt precariously. The effect is to make a busy, everyday street seem strange and unsafe. Kirchner may have been expressing the unease of a nation on the brink of war – he made this painting shortly before the outbreak of the First World War.

Street with Prostitutes (1914-25), by Ernst Kirchner; oil on canvas, 49 x 36in. Notice the blue, watery color of the street, which makes it look more like a river than a roadway.

Horsing around

Another Expressionist group was set up in Germany in 1911, by Franz Marc and Vassily Kandinsky. They named it *Der Blaue Reiter*, German for "The Blue Rider" – which was also the name of a painting by Kandinsky and a journal they published in 1912.

The Blue Rider artists believed art should focus on spiritual ideas. Marc specialized in painting animals, especially horses, because for him they symbolized a better way of life. He thought they were more in harmony with the world around them than people.

Stables (1913), by Franz Marc; oil on canvas, 29 x 62in. The smooth shapes of the horses are broken by the lines of the stables.

Seeing things differently

Ever since the 15th century, most artists had used a system of rules known as perspective to create the illusion of showing people and objects as if in real or 3-D space.

But, in the late 19th and early 20th centuries, some artists began to experiment with different ways of seeing things – with some startling results.

Left: *Still Life with Basket* (1888-90), by French painter Paul Cézanne; oil on canvas, 26 x 32in

Right: *Fruit* (1820), by American still life artist James Peale; oil on canvas, 17 x 27in

Getting it in perspective

Fruit, by James Peale – who specialized in very lifelike still lifes – follows the rules of perspective. Each object is painted with great detail and accuracy, and is the right size and shape in relation to all the others. Everything is seen from a single viewpoint, as if we were standing motionless by the table. By contrast, Paul Cézanne's picture looks roughly painted and full of distortions.

Different angles

To show things in perspective, artists have to draw everything from the same viewpoint. But Cézanne thought that didn't reflect how we really see the world. After all, few people would stare at a table for hours without moving. He wanted to find a new way of representing space. So he began painting scenes from different angles, combining several viewpoints in one picture.

Still Life with Basket shows a clay jar, seen from above, next to a china pot which has been drawn side-on. The left and right-hand sections of the table don't line up, and the basket balances impossibly on the edge. The shifting perspective makes the scene seem disjointed – but perhaps it is closer to how you would see things if you were walking around the room yourself?

Cézanne was obsessed with still lifes like this, painting the same objects over and over again. He would spend hours creating each arrangement, propping things up on piles of coins, and soaking cloths in plaster so they folded just the way he wanted.

Bits and pieces

After Cézanne died, there was a big memorial exhibition of his work in Paris. Its visitors included two young artists, Pablo Picasso and Georges Braque. Inspired by Cézanne, they too began to experiment with perspective. But they went even further and gave up trying to create any illusion of space altogether. Instead, they combined bits and pieces seen from different angles or at different times, and broke up the surfaces of their pictures with geometric shapes. In this way, they hoped to highlight the contradictions involved in trying to paint solid-looking, 3-D objects on a flat, 2-D surface. This new approach became known as Cubism.

Looking for clues

At first glance, it's hard to make out anything in the jumble of shapes on the right. But on closer inspection it's full of clues. Near the top is a rectangular bottle-shape, faintly labeled "RHU" – the beginning of *rhum*, French for "rum." Behind it lies a clarinet, its finger holes seen from the side, but its flared end shown from above. There are also several curly shapes, such as musical clefs, and the word *valse*, French for "waltz," suggesting sheet music. And, near the bottom, can you spot a square fireplace arch and a decorative scroll of the sort you might find carved on a mantelpiece?

Clarinet and Bottle of Rum on a Mantelpiece (1911), by Georges Braque; oil on canvas, 32 x 24in. Can you spot a pin-shape about a third of the way down, slightly to the right of the center? It has a shadow that makes it seem to stick right out of the painting – an ironic 3-D touch in an otherwise flat, 2-D picture.

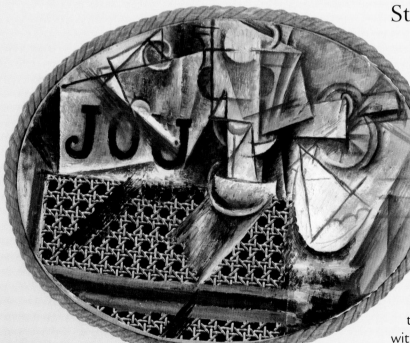

Still Life with Chair Caning (1912), by Pablo Picasso; oil and oilcloth on canvas with rope frame, 11 x 14in. From left to right, the objects shown are: a newspaper with the letters "JOU," a clay pipe, a goblet of beer and a knife slicing a piece of fruit.

Sticky business

From 1912, Picasso and Braque did something no "painter" had done before. They began to glue pieces of paper and cloth onto their pictures. This method became known as collage, from the French *coller,* meaning "to stick." It was the beginning of a new kind of art known as assemblage, where whole works are "assembled" from bits of different materials.

Still Life with Chair Caning shows a group of objects on a cane chair seat, framed with rope. The objects are painted in a fragmentary, Cubist style, but the seat is actually a piece of cloth printed with a canework pattern. The mixture of materials and techniques blurs the boundaries between real objects, such as the cloth, and painted ones, such as the glass. Picasso did this to make us question the relationship between art and reality.

Les Demoiselles

In 1907, Picasso completed his experimental painting *Les Demoiselles d'Avignon* – to the horror of most people who saw it. Even the artist's friends were upset by its crude, harsh style. So he left it rolled up in his studio for years. But it went on display eventually, first in Paris and then New York. Today, it is one of the most famous paintings in the world.

Title: *Les Demoiselles d'Avignon*
Date: 1907
Artist: Pablo Picasso
Materials: oil on canvas
Size: 96 x 92in

Art experiments

Picasso painted *Les Demoiselles d'Avignon* as he and Braque began to experiment with Cubism. They were trying to leave behind traditional ideas about beauty and perspective. So Picasso used glaring colors and jagged shapes, set at odd angles. Everything is fragmented, from the women themselves to the spaces between them, making what should be a 3-D scene appear disjointed and flat.

Ladies of the night

Les Demoiselles d'Avignon is French for "ladies of Avignon." Avignon was the name of a street in the red-light district of Barcelona, where Picasso grew up. So these women are meant to be prostitutes, posing to seduce their clients. But they don't look very attractive. Picasso gave them lopsided, angular bodies, with staring eyes or threatening-looking masks, perhaps reflecting fears of his own about sexuality.

Changing faces

The women on the left of the painting were probably inspired by ancient Spanish statues. They look very different from the women on the right, whose faces resemble African masks. The clash of styles makes the picture feel even more disjointed and disturbing. In fact, Picasso originally gave all the women similar faces. But he was suddenly inspired to repaint the two on the right after seeing displays of African art in Paris. By using non-Western art as a source, he hoped to bypass the history of Western painting and go back to something older and more primitive.

Picasso wrestled with the composition, doing over a hundred preparatory sketches. Early versions included two men, a sailor and a student holding a book or skull. The sailor was probably meant to represent desire, and the student, knowledge. And skulls are a traditional symbol of death. So Picasso may have been thinking of the moral, "the wages of sin are death." But in the end he left out the men and created a less symbolic, more ambiguous composition.

Picasso worked in many different art forms throughout his life. This photograph, taken in 1948, shows him painting a design onto a plate.

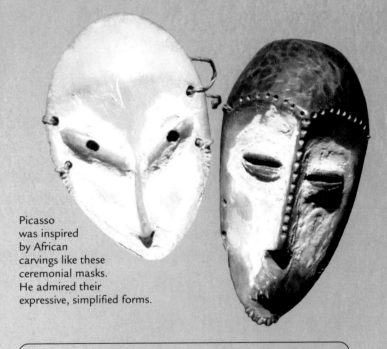

Picasso was inspired by African carvings like these ceremonial masks. He admired their expressive, simplified forms.

👁 Picasso had a long and successful artistic career. For a link to a website where you can explore his life's work, go to **www.usborne-quicklinks.com**

Beyond Cubism

Picasso is probably the most famous modern artist – he was certainly one of the most prolific and varied. He produced an amazing 22,000 works, from portraits, political art, prints and illustrations to sculptures, set designs and ceramics. His early works were atmospheric, delicately colored paintings. Art historians often divide these into a "blue" and a "rose" period, because of the way his use of color changed. Then, he experimented with Cubism and Surrealism. His energy and talent meant he was able to paint in almost any style he wanted.

Bright lights, big city

As the 20th century progressed, cities continued to expand rapidly – and so too did the number of artists who took city life as their subject. But they painted it in very different ways – from shifting Cubist perspectives to a hard-edged precision that seemed well-suited to the new machine age.

City living

French artist Robert Delaunay lived in Paris and did many paintings of the city. Often, he deliberately included symbols of the exciting new age, such as the plane, invented only a few years before, or the Eiffel Tower, then the world's tallest building. *The Red Tower* shows the Eiffel Tower caught between apartment blocks, early high-rise buildings which soon came to symbolize modern urban life. In fact, it is less one view than a series of glances. Delaunay used multiple views to make it feel as if the viewer is actually on the move, caught up in the speed and bustle of the city.

The Red Tower (1911-12), by Robert Delaunay; oil on canvas, 64 x 51in. Shifting angles create a dizzying sense of height.

Caught up in the crowd

As cities grew, so did the crowds of people thronging their streets. British painter and writer Percy Wyndham Lewis was fascinated by the behavior of crowds, and their effect on politics. In *The Crowd*, he shows groups of stick-like figures, gathering in a maze of streets between angular buildings. They seem to be led by men with red Communist flags. There is also a *tricolore*, the French national flag, in one corner. So perhaps the scene is meant to evoke the thrill – or danger – of mass political protests?

It's a blast

Wyndham Lewis helped found a movement known as Vorticism which celebrated modern life, machines and the city. The Vorticists published a magazine called *Blast* to publicize their ideas. In it, they demanded dramatic or even violent changes in British culture, and threatened to blast away everything which seemed old-fashioned.

The Crowd (1914-15), by Percy Wyndham Lewis; oil and pencil on canvas, 79 x 61in. This painting is also sometimes known as *Revolution*.

New York, New York

This atmospheric New York scene is by American painter Georgia O'Keeffe. It shows the 22-story Radiator Building, built just three years earlier and still a landmark in the city today. It was made of black brick with gold trimmings. But O'Keeffe shows it transformed by darkness into a neat pattern of light and dark, with bright white windows and a spotlit summit, and not a person in sight.

The picture is full of sharp lines and smooth shapes. Even the curling smoke on the right has a crisp edge. O'Keeffe liked to paint from life, but she concentrated on shapes so much, her work can seem almost abstract, conveying sensations as much as appearances. O'Keeffe was one of the pioneers of abstract art in America. She said: "One can't paint New York as it is, but rather as it is felt." Here, that feeling seems to be of a grand but rather daunting and impersonal beauty.

Radiator Building – Night, New York (1927), by Georgia O'Keeffe; oil on canvas, 48 x 30in. The word "Stieglitz" is just visible in the red neon sign. This was the name of O'Keeffe's husband, a famous photographer and art dealer.

👁 For links to websites where you can see more works by Delaunay or O'Keeffe, go to
www.usborne-quicklinks.com

The photograph below shows the New York skyline as it looks today. You can see how well O'Keeffe captured the pattern of light in the city's towering buildings.

Into the future

The early 20th century was a time of rapid changes, as more people began to live in bustling cities, work in industries driven by new machines, and travel ever faster by car or plane. In response, many artists began to make art about speed and machines, using experimental methods inspired by Cubism. Others turned their attention to the natural world, using similarly innovative techniques to capture the movement of animals.

Time for a change

Some of the most dramatic changes took place in Italy, where new industries and a new political system were revolutionizing the country. Enthusiastic about modern ideas and the chance to remake their society, a group of Italian artists calling themselves "Futurists" set out to create a new art for the new age.

Futurist leader F.T. Marinetti even wanted to modernize Italian cooking by banning pasta, which he said was "a symbol of... dullness... and fat-bellied conceit."

In 1909, Italian poet F.T. Marinetti wrote a Futurist Manifesto setting out the movement's beliefs and aims. It declared the Futurists' love of fast movement and violent change, saying: "the world's splendor has been enriched by a new beauty, the beauty of speed."

Unique Forms of Continuity in Space (1913), by Futurist artist Umberto Boccioni; bronze, 46 x 35 x 15in. The flowing shapes are meant to convey forceful movement.

For a link to a website where you can find out more about the Futurists and see many of their works, go to **www.usborne-quicklinks.com**

Out with the old

The Futurists wanted to destroy the past completely, saying people should burn down libraries and flood museums. Marinetti even went so far as to praise the destructiveness of war, calling it "the world's only hygiene." But when war actually came in 1914, the movement began to peter out, discredited by the horrors of real warfare and, later, by its links with Fascism.

Man and superman

Unique Forms shows a man striding forward energetically. But his movements have been exaggerated, turning his body into a series of strange, flowing forms. The streamlined edges and overlapping shapes suggest a muscular figure in motion. And the metallic finish makes him look like a powerful machine. The artist may have meant to show a kind of superior, strong man or "superman" described by philosopher Friedrich Nietzsche, and idealized by German and Italian Fascists.

Speeding along

Giacomo Ballà was a leading Futurist painter. Like Marinetti, he idolized the new, fast cars. In fact, their top speed wasn't very impressive by today's standards – only about 30mph – but it was faster than any vehicle had ever gone before. *Abstract Speed + Sound* is meant to show a red car roaring along a white road. The green and blue colors suggest the ground and sky, overlaid by geometric shapes designed to convey the noise and movement of the car. Ballà may have been inspired by the praise of cars in Marinetti's manifesto: "A racing car whose hood is adorned with great pipes, like snakes with explosive breath... is more beautiful than the *Victory of Samothrace*" (the name of a famous classical statue).

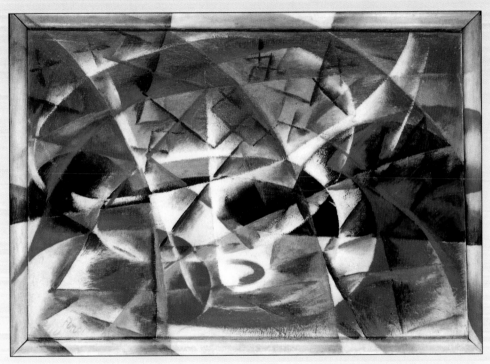

Abstract Speed + Sound (1913-14), by Giacomo Ballà; oil on board, 22 x 30in, including the frame. Notice how the image overflows onto the frame. A frame normally separates off a painting. But Ballà made his frame a continuation of the picture, making it feel closer to you.

Up, up and away

Romanian sculptor Constantin Brancusi was preoccupied by movement and especially flight. He made several abstracted sculptures of birds which he said tried to capture "the essence of flight." The shape on the right may not look like much like a bird. The body is incredibly long and smooth, with no wings or feathers. Even the head is only hinted at by a slanting oval at the top, ending in a beak-like point. But Brancusi wanted to focus on the bird's movement, not its appearance.

Brancusi thought that adding lots of lifelike details, such as wings or feathers, would distract the viewer and make his sculpture look static. So he created an evocative, streamlined shape which rises up from a narrow base, to make it look as if it were soaring up into the air – just like a bird in flight.

Bird in Space (1923), by Constantin Brancusi; brass, 57 x 7in. Brancusi made several versions of this sculpture, some in brass, some in marble, all carefully polished to create a perfectly smooth shape. When U.S. Customs refused to pass one of these *Bird in Space* sculptures as "art," Brancusi took them to court – and won.

Shapes and colors

In about 1910, artists began trying to create pictures which were not images of actual people or places or things, but "things" in their own right. So instead of painting recognizable scenes, they took the elements of painting – colors, lines and shapes – and put them together in expressive or evocative ways. This kind of art is known as abstract art, and many of its earliest pioneers were Russian.

Improvisation No. 26 (Rowing) (1912), by Vassily Kandinsky; oil on canvas, 38 x 43in. This picture is also sometimes known as *Oars*.

Kandinsky said he was inspired to try abstract art by seeing a painting which had fallen on its side. He thought the shapes in it looked more interesting upside down or sideways.

This abstract painting still contains traces of the scene which inspired it. Can you make out two figures in a red boat, grasping long, black lines which might be oars? The boat floats among dramatic splashes of color, suggesting a wild, watery setting. Above, a dark bird-like shape flies through an equally colorful sky.

Music and color

Vassily Kandinsky was a Russian painter who worked in Germany, where he founded the Blue Rider movement. But he was also a pioneer of abstract art, creating early, experimental works like *Rowing*. At first glance, this picture looks like an abstract, colorful pattern. In fact it was loosely based on a scene of two people in a boat. But when you look at it, you are aware of all the lines, shapes and colors as separate elements, rather than as ways of representing a scene. Kandinsky placed special emphasis on his use of color. He thought color could express feelings in the same way as music, claiming: "Color is a power that directly influences the soul... Color is the keyboard... The artist is the hand that plays."

Shaping up

Lyubov Popova was a leading Russian avant-garde artist. She experimented with Cubism and Futurism before going on to develop a more abstract style, setting simple geometric shapes against flat, plain backgrounds. Popova believed artists should not try to copy what they saw, but create their own vision instead. She wrote: "The representation of reality – without artistic deformation and transformation – cannot be the subject of painting."

But by the 1920s, in the aftermath of the Russian Revolution, Popova abandoned painting altogether, having decided that art should have a more practical purpose. So she joined a group known as the Constructivists and began to work on design projects, producing textiles, ceramics and posters.

👁 For links to websites where you can explore another abstract "improvisation" by Kandinksy, view one of Popova's geometric costume designs or discover lots more "Suprematist" compositions by Malevich, go to **www.usborne-quicklinks.com**

Untitled (1910), by Lyubov Popova; oil on canvas. This picture has been reduced to the simplest elements of painting.

Supreme artist

Russian painter Kasimir Malevich believed he could only really create art when he was making things up. He said: "the artist can be a creator only when the forms in his pictures have nothing in common with nature." So he began to create abstract images by painting plain, geometric shapes on square backgrounds. Using squares meant he could avoid traditional "landscape" or "portrait" formats, which might have made his pictures seem more like paintings of things, rather than things in themselves.

Malevich named the new style Suprematism, from the Latin *supremus*, meaning "of the highest order." He meant it to be a purer, more spiritual kind of art. After the Russian Revolution of 1917, he tried to promote abstract art as the right art for the radical new Russia. He didn't really convince the authorities – but he did have a great influence on other artists, including Kandinsky and Popova.

Dynamic Suprematism (1915-16), by Kasimir Malevich; oil on canvas, 31 x 31in. Malevich worried that simple abstract pictures could look static. So he began to use complicated arrangements of shapes, as in this composition, to try to create a sense of energetic or dynamic movement. He called this Dynamic Suprematism.

DREAMS & CONFLICTS

The 20th century was torn apart by two world wars, which had a huge impact on all aspects of life – including art. Artists' work changed, reflecting their shattered faith in new technologies, their distrust of a culture which could allow such things to happen, and the need to rebuild the world afterward.

Detail from *Travoys Arriving with Wounded at a Dressing Station at Smol, Macedonia 1916* (1919), by Stanley Spencer. You can see the whole picture on pages 118-119.

Going to war

Between 1914 and 1918, Europe was engulfed by the First World War. Millions were caught up in the conflict, including many artists – and many of them channeled their experiences into their art.

Often this resulted in striking pictures quite unlike traditional war paintings, which tend to concentrate on heroic battle scenes. The new images revealed a darker, more disturbing side of war.

Grim realities

The First World War was a different kind of conflict from earlier wars, fought with new and deadly weapons, such as planes, machine guns and poison gas. Some artists felt they needed to devise new ways of representing the horrors of mechanized warfare. Others thought only lifelike images could convey the grim realities of war.

Compare the painting on the left, by Mark Gertler, to the print on the right by Otto Dix. They look very different, but they are both about the war. Dix said, "One has to depict war realistically so it will be understood." But Gertler's picture doesn't do this. It uses a spinning carousel, painted in a smooth, almost mechanical-looking style, to symbolize the relentless progress of the war and its new machines.

👁 For a link to a website where you can see a huge selection of war art chosen to commemorate the First World War, go to **www.usborne-quicklinks.com**

Merry-Go-Round (1916), by Mark Gertler; oil on canvas, 75 x 56in. Gertler may have been inspired to paint this scene by a fair for wounded soldiers, held near his home in London.

Fairground horror

Merry-Go-Round shows men and women, some in military uniforms, sitting stiffly on an old-fashioned fairground carousel. They should be having fun. But the claustrophobic composition and bright, jarring colors make everything feel uneasy. And, if you look at the riders' faces, they seem to be screaming.

Gertler protested against the fighting, saying, "I just hate the war." So perhaps he did this painting to express his hatred. But, when the picture was first exhibited, reviewers thought it was just decorative. One even wrote that its style would be "admirably fitted for the adornment of a popular restaurant."

Casualties of war

German artist Otto Dix is famous for his pictures of social problems and war, reflecting his own experience of fighting and disillusionment afterward. The war haunted him, leaving him with recurring nightmares. After it ended, he published a series of 50 prints called *The War* – stark, black and white images of fierce fighting, mutilated bodies and devastated battlegrounds. The series was inspired by perhaps the greatest ever depiction of wartime atrocities, produced a century earlier by Spanish artist Francisco de Goya.

Disasters of War: The Same (1812-13), by Francisco de Goya; engraving, 6 x 9in. This is one of 80 prints Goya did evoking the horrors of the 1808-14 war between Spain and France.

You can see one of Dix's prints below. It shows German troops, their faces hidden by alien-looking gas masks. They seem to be coming straight at us, one with his arm raised to hurl a grenade. The setting is dark and desolate, strewn with barbed wire and broken trees – a reminder of the destructiveness of war. It's a terrifying image. When it was first published, many Germans were shocked; they thought Dix should have made the soldiers look more heroic.

The War: Assault under Gas (1924), by Otto Dix; engraving, 14 x 19in

Travoys Arriving

This painting by British artist Stanley Spencer shows wounded soldiers lying on travoys – stretchers pulled by mules – at a field hospital in Macedonia, in south-eastern Europe, during the First World War. Spencer worked as a medical orderly in Macedonia and later became a famous war artist. He was asked to paint this picture by the British government. It was the first painting he did after returning home from the war.

Title: *Travoys Arriving with Wounded at a Dressing Station at Smol, Macedonia 1916* Date: 1919	Artist: Stanley Spencer Materials: oil on canvas Size: 72 x 86in

Casualties of war

The First World War was a bloody conflict, with huge casualties – over 8 million dead and 20 million wounded by the time it ended. Macedonia, on the war's southern front, saw fighting as bitter as anywhere. Spencer was sent there with the Royal Army Medical Corps in 1916. Years later, he described his experiences in a letter: "there were travoys and limbers crammed full of wounded men. One would have thought that the scene was... sordid... terrible... but I felt there was a grandeur."

Spencer had made sketches in Macedonia, but lost his sketchpad, so this scene was painted entirely from memory. The picture was meant for an official Hall of Remembrance. It doesn't commemorate an actual battle, but the quiet suffering of the wounded and the work of the medics caring for them. Although Spencer gave the picture a specific location, a place called Smol, the men could be any of the thousands caught up in the fighting. Their faces are all hidden, making the scene feel strangely impersonal. It also seems slightly unreal. The perspective has been distorted so things look strangely flat, and the colors and outlines have been simplified. This led critics at the time to compare Spencer with Cézanne and Picasso.

The dull brown and green color scheme makes everything seem bleak and somber. Even the plants in the corner look thorny and uncomfortable.

Religious echoes

The foreground is dominated by stretchers. But they point inward, making the brightly lit operating room the focus of attention. This composition, with the animals' heads silhouetted against the glowing interior, could even remind you of traditional nativity scenes.

Angels in sweaters

Spencer often combined ordinary details and religious imagery – as one critic at the time put it, "even his angels wear jumpers [sweaters]." Some of his best-known works show the Resurrection as described in the Bible, but set in his home village of Cookham. In *Travoys Arriving*, he said he wanted to create a peaceful, religious atmosphere, showing the soldiers like "so many crucified Christs" – reflecting their huge suffering, but also implying a hope that they would, like Christ, come back from the dead.

Salvation or suffering?

Is the painting really as peaceful and religious as Spencer claimed? There are no obvious religious references. Spencer supposedly based the hospital on one that had been set up in a ruined church, but there are no signs of church decor, and the only crosses are the red ones on the medics' armbands.

In fact, there is little hint of salvation – just a growing line of wounded men with no end in sight. More travoys are arriving from the right, and the wheel in the top right corner is a traditional symbol of a never-ending cycle of events. Perhaps Spencer found it hard to create a convincingly optimistic image. In 1919, the tragedy of the war was still fresh in people's minds – and the specter of a second world war was already beginning to loom.

A world gone crazy

During the First World War, some artists began to create deliberately strange, often shocking, works of art. Appalled by the fighting, they wanted to reject utterly the traditional values – cultural as well as political – which had allowed it to happen. So they made art using unconventional materials and methods, relying more on chance than artistic skill. They called this approach Dada – a deliberately meaningless title, chosen by just picking a word at random from a dictionary.

Fountain (1964, a replica of the original which was made in 1917 but later lost), by Marcel Duchamp; ceramic urinal, height 24in. The name "R. Mutt" is a variation of Mott, a French toilet manufacturer. But the signature was added by Duchamp.

Readymade art

One of the most famous Dada artworks ever made is Marcel Duchamp's *Fountain* – a urinal laid on its back and signed "R. Mutt, 1917." Duchamp referred to works which use manufactured objects like this as "readymades." By presenting a factory-made item as a work of art, Duchamp challenged the idea that art should be unique and produced by a skilled artist.

For Duchamp, an artist's ideas mattered more than his actual art. According to him, "Whether Mr. Mutt has made the fountain with his own hands or not is without importance. He chose it... he created a new thought for this object." But not everyone agreed. When Duchamp tried to exhibit *Fountain* at a show held by the Society of Independent Artists, they refused to let him, and he resigned from the society in protest.

👁 For a link to a website where you can explore an interactive timeline to find out about Duchamp's life and art, go to **www.usborne-quicklinks.com**

Putting on a show

Many people took refuge from the war in neutral Switzerland, especially in its biggest city, Zurich. Here, in 1916, Hugo Ball opened the Cabaret Voltaire, an evening show which quickly became an important Dada venue. He said the show's purpose was "to remind the world that there are people of independent minds, beyond war and nationalism" – although the owner of the cafe where it was held simply hoped it would help him sell more beer and sandwiches. At the shows, Ball and his friends staged bizarre acts – a kind of Performance art – in a room decorated with pictures by Hans Arp, Picasso and others. Ball himself dressed up and read "sound poems" composed of nonsense words. He felt he had to use made-up words because ordinary ones had become corrupt and meaningless.

At one Dada show, Hugo Ball put on a bright cardboard costume, with a tall hat, and solemnly chanted a poem full of words like "blago bung" and "ba-umf."

A load of old garbage

German Dada artist Kurt Schwitters made elaborate collages from garbage and the remnants of everyday life. The layers of the collages were a reflection of his own life, incorporating anything from newspapers he had read, to tickets for journeys he had made or shows he had seen. The example on the right includes an old bottle cork, scraps of wood, metal, paper and fabric, and a card with a printed picture of cherries, all carefully arranged into an abstract pattern of shapes and colors.

Schwitters coined the term "Merz" for his collage technique. The name came from one of his pictures where the end of the German word *kommerz*, or "commerce," was visible on a scrap of newspaper. Taking Merz to extremes, Schwitters filled whole rooms with huge, 3-D collages, trying to create a complete environment. He called these constructions *Merzbau*, or "Merz-buildings." While he was working on them, his friends said they would lose small items, such as keys and pencils, only to find them again later, built into his most recent construction.

Merz Picture 32A – Cherry Picture (1921), by Kurt Schwitters; collage of cloth, wood, metal, fabric, paper, cork, gouache, oil and ink on cardboard, 36 x 28in

Picture-traps

Dada had a huge influence on other artists over the following century, especially on a 1960s movement known as New Realism. The New Realists set out to explore modern life and consumer culture, often through works made of discarded items, from torn posters to old coffee grinders. By presenting them as art, these works questioned how things were produced and consumed in modern society. In some examples, known as *tableaux pièges* or "picture-traps," the artist "trapped" a chance collection of objects and hung them on the wall. These also "trap" the viewer by showing the unexpected – real, 3-D objects, instead of the 2-D painting you might expect to see.

Who knows where upstairs and downstairs are? (1964), by Daniel Spoerri; mixed media 3-D collage, 21 x 25 x 6in

In your dreams

In post-war Paris, a group of artists and writers, led by poet André Breton, began to create strange, dream-like works. They wanted to rebel against the rational, everyday world and, by drawing on their imagination and dreams, they hoped to create a new reality, or "surreality." Their movement became known as Surrealism.

More than real

Surrealism is known for its bizarre imagery, but it was not meant to be *un*-real. The name actually means *more* than real, or *sur*-real (*sur* is French for "above"). Breton said the movement rose from the ashes of Dada. It also grew out of a new interest in the workings of the mind, especially the irrational and the unconscious, inspired by turn-of-the-century Viennese psychiatrist Sigmund Freud. He claimed that much of what we do is triggered by unconscious thoughts and desires, and that these can be revealed in dreams.

The Surrealists believed the unconscious was the source of creative genius, and employed some unusual techniques to try to access it. Many tried "automatic" drawing, or drawing without thinking. They created strange, doodle-like pictures, which they believed were really shaped by their unconscious thoughts and impulses. Spanish painter Joan Miró even claimed to have starved himself to bring on hallucinations.

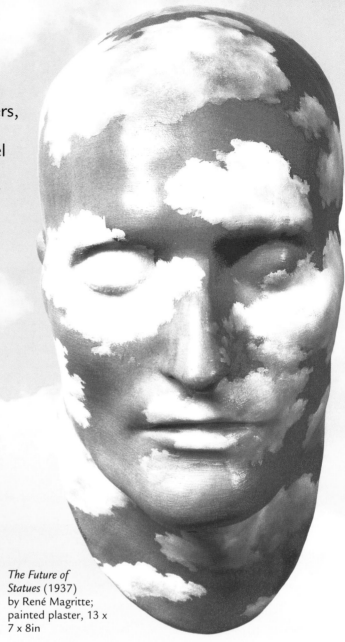

The Future of
Statues (1937)
by René Magritte;
painted plaster, 13 x
7 x 8in

Strange meetings

The Surrealists loved new and startling combinations of things, seeing beauty in images such as "the chance encounter of an umbrella and a sewing machine on an operating table." They thought that these combinations reflected the way the unconscious could form associations and bring unconnected things together, which sometimes happens in dreams. Many bizarre Surrealist sculptures – which they called "objects" – were based on pairing unlikely items.

One of the most famous Surrealist objects was created when Salvador Dalí stuck a plaster lobster over the handset of a telephone.

Light and air

Belgian Surrealist René Magritte often created poetic, disturbing images by painting ordinary things in new and unexpected places. For example, *The Future of Statues* is a human head painted over with a blue sky full of drifting clouds. The sky makes the head seem dreamy and insubstantial, as if it were dissolving into air. Perhaps this dissolving is the "future of statues," which must eventually crumble away?

The head is actually a replica of the Emperor Napoleon's death mask – a cast of his face made after he died. So the sculpture may be meant to refer to human mortality, too. And it is a tribute to the power of the imagination, a visual pun on the idea of a daydreamer with his "head in the clouds."

Dream photography

The Persistence of Memory, by Spanish Surrealist Salvador Dalí, shows a golden landscape dominated by drooping watches and a misshapen, fleshy creature lying on the ground. Three of the watches are melting, while the case of a fourth watch is crawling with ants, as if it is being eaten. The hard, mechanical watches are soft and decaying, no longer able to measure the passage of time. The cliffs in the distance are actually based on the coast of Catalonia, where Dalí grew up – so perhaps the title was meant to refer to the artist's childhood memories. Ants were a childhood phobia of his. And the creature in the middle is actually a distorted version of his own profile, its long-lashed eye shut as if he is asleep or dead, unaware of, or out of, time.

The mysterious, dream-like imagery makes this a very strange scene. But Dalí painted it so realistically that it almost looks photographic – in fact, he called his works "hand-painted dream photographs." By presenting an imaginary scene in such a lifelike way, he intended to blur the boundary between imagination and reality. He said he wanted his paintings to spread confusion, in order to "discredit completely the world of reality."

Dalí was probably the most famous of all the Surrealists. By the end of his life, his face was so well-known that a letter could reach him addressed only with a drawing of his trademark moustache and the word *España* (Spain).

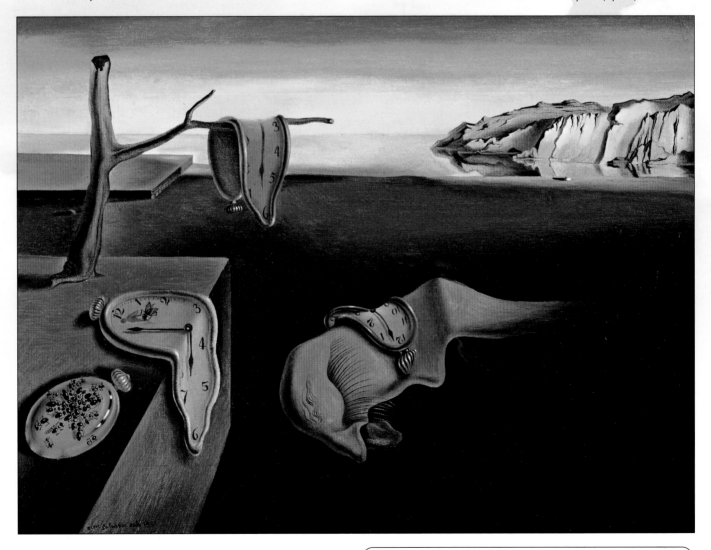

The Persistence of Memory (1931) by Salvador Dalí; oil on canvas, 10 x 13in. This is just one example of what Dalí called his "deceptive, hyper-normal and sickly images of concrete irrationality."

👁 For a link to a website where you can see more of Dalí's paintings, go to **www.usborne-quicklinks.com**

Building the future

In the years following the First World War, there was a need to rebuild countries devastated by conflict, and many artists became involved with architecture and design. By integrating art with their surroundings, they hoped to create a better world for everyone. This resulted in several influential, idealistic art and design movements: Constructivism in Russia, De Stijl in Holland and Bauhaus in Germany.

Constructing art

Constructivism emerged after the Russian Revolution of 1917. The artists who joined the movement wanted to invent a more accessible kind of art for the people of the new Communist state. They tried to develop a fresh approach based on abstract, geometric forms, which they hoped would appeal to everyone, whatever their background.

As their name suggests, the Constructivists also wanted to use their art to build things – although a lot of their ideas never made it off the drawing board. Their slogan was "Art into Life." Many of them worked for the Communist government, designing propaganda posters, clothes, dishes, furniture, buildings and books. But, after Stalin took over, their style fell out of fashion. The leader of the new regime preferred art that showed actual people, generally workers in heroic poses – this style became known as Soviet Socialist Realism. Constructivism was suppressed and many of its most successful artists left Russia.

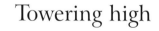

Oval Hanging Construction Number 12 (1920), by Alexander Rodchenko; plywood, aluminum paint and wire, 24 x 33 x 19in. Rodchenko made a series of constructions, but only this one survives. It consists of a flat oval, divided into sections that can be opened up. It was meant to be hung from the ceiling like a mobile.

In 1919-20, Vladimir Tatlin built a huge model showing his plans for a *Monument to the Third International* – a tower to commemorate the Third International Communist Congress, held in Moscow in 1921. But the design never got beyond the model stage.

Towering high

One of the most famous examples of Constructivist design was Vladimir Tatlin's *Monument to the Third International* – even though the monument itself was never actually built. Tatlin wanted it to be the tallest building in the world, a 1,300ft spiraling tower of metal and glass. Inside, there were to be three geometric blocks of office space: a cube at the bottom, a cone in the middle, and a cylinder near the top, all rotating at different speeds. Even with modern engineering, it would probably be impossible to build a structure like this. But the Constructivists wanted to push ideas to their limits.

Setting the style

De Stijl is Dutch for "The Style." This was the title of an art magazine founded in 1917 by Theo van Doesburg, as well as the name of the movement he led with Piet Mondrian. They wanted to create a pure, simple kind of art, using geometric forms and the primary colors – red, yellow and blue. Mondrian made whole pictures based on opposing horizontal and vertical lines, reflecting his belief that the universe was built on opposites. He was so strict about this, he left De Stijl when van Doesburg began to use diagonal lines. The members of De Stijl applied their pared-down style to design and architecture, creating striking, modern-looking furniture, interiors and buildings, as well as abstract paintings. They wanted to combine all the arts to create a harmonious, well-ordered environment. But not everyone liked the results. Van Doesburg's radical designs for the "Café d'Aubette" cinema-dance hall in Strasbourg proved unpopular with visitors and were quickly changed.

Colour Scheme for the Café d'Aubette Ballroom (1927), by Theo van Doesburg; ink and gouache on paper, 21 x 15in. For van Doesburg, the Café was one of the greatest De Stijl achievements and he dedicated a whole issue of his magazine to it.

House of building

De Stijl had a great influence in Germany where, in 1919, architect Walter Gropius set up an art school known as Bauhaus – which means "house of building" in German. Students at the school studied painting and design, along with craft skills such as woodwork and pottery. In this way, Gropius hoped to blur the traditional distinction between arts and crafts. He wanted his students to create objects that were both stylish and practical. He also encouraged them to learn about industrial processes, to help them design items for mass production. Bauhaus designs proved very popular. But its courses were too radical for the Nazis, who feared the school would corrupt its students and forced it to close in 1933. Many of its teachers left Germany, helping to spread Bauhaus ideas abroad – particularly in America, where many of them went on to have successful careers.

👁 For links to websites where you can see pictures of many Constructivist designs and artworks, go to **www.usborne-quicklinks.com**

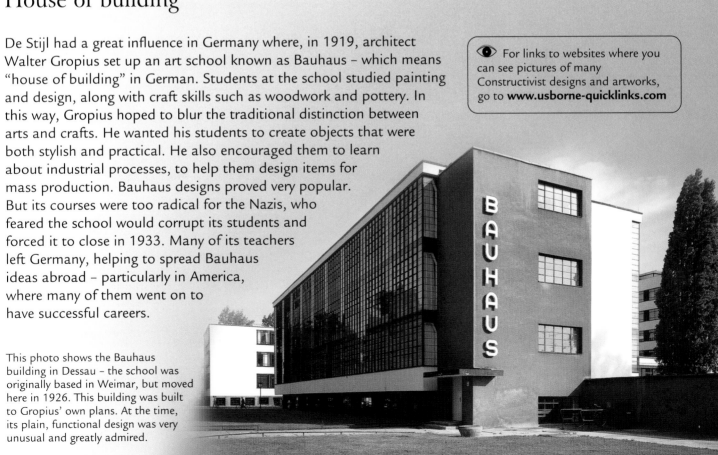

This photo shows the Bauhaus building in Dessau – the school was originally based in Weimar, but moved here in 1926. This building was built to Gropius' own plans. At the time, its plain, functional design was very unusual and greatly admired.

The power of persuasion

For a long time, artists and governments have used art as a form of protest or propaganda, to try to shape people's ideas. Especially potent images were created in the 1930s, as the Nazi party rose to power in Germany. Anti-Nazi artists attacked the new regime, while the Nazis tried to suppress this art and promote their own instead.

Happy families

In the 1930s, the Nazis mounted a huge campaign against what they called "degenerate" art, by which they meant all radical art, because they thought it was subversive. Nazi leader Adolf Hitler, himself a failed artist, hated a lot of art, particularly Expressionism. He wanted art to be "the messenger of noble and beautiful things" – not to examine difficult emotions or social problems. *Family Portrait* is an example of the kind of art he liked.

At first sight, this painting looks like an innocent family scene. But it was designed to promote Nazi ideas. The blond, blue-eyed figures represent Hitler's ideal Aryan, or pure-blooded, Germans. The nursing mother reinforces Nazi ideas about the proper role of women. And the pretty setting, with the family surrounded by the produce of a well-tended garden, reflects the Nazis' belief in the importance of land. They used a need for land as an excuse to invade neighboring countries.

Family Portrait (c.1939), by Wolf Willrich; oil painting, further details unavailable as, like much Nazi art, it was later destroyed.

One man's war

Some of the most memorable anti-Nazi works of art were made by German artist and pacifist John Heartfield. (He was actually born Helmut Herzfelde, but changed his name in 1916 to protest against German nationalism.) He developed a technique known as photomontage, combining sections of different photos. The results could be both savagely satirical and startlingly lifelike.

Adolf, the Superman shows Adolf Hitler making a speech. But an "X-ray" view of his insides shows he has been swallowing gold, and there is a Nazi swastika where his heart should be. Heartfield wanted to imply that Hitler was in the pay of rich industrialists and didn't really care about the people he claimed to represent. The Nazis retaliated by banning Heartfield's work and threatening to arrest him, and he was forced to leave Germany in 1933.

Adolf, the Superman: Swallows Gold and Spouts Junk (1932), by John Heartfield; photomontage, 14 x 10in. This image was designed as an anti-Hitler election poster.

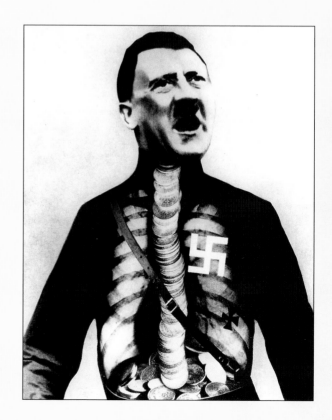

The awful truth

Marc Chagall was a Russian Jew whose art tended to focus on mystical feelings rather than politics. But, in *White Crucifixion*, he set out to tell people the truth about Nazi Germany. The year he painted it, the Nazis attacked Jewish property and deported thousands of Jews or sent them to death camps. Chagall shows Jesus as a Jewish martyr, surrounded by scenes of mayhem and persecution. By combining all these different elements, Chagall linked the suffering of Jesus with the suffering of the Jews in his own time.

White Crucifixion (1938), by Marc Chagall; oil on canvas, 61 x 55in

Jesus is draped in a Jewish prayer shawl, and there is a Jewish candlestick at his feet. The lettering above his head calls him the "King of the Jews." Although Jesus was a Jew, he is rarely painted in this way.

On the left, a mob is advancing toward burning houses, waving red Communist flags. Topsy-turvy houses suggest a world turned upside down.

On the right, a German soldier is setting light to a synagogue, its contents ransacked and scattered on the ground.

Refugees flee left and right. One man clutches a sacred Jewish scroll, glancing back at flames billowing from another scroll. Beside him, a man wears a white placard like the ones German Jews were forced to wear, to show their religion.

Overhead, a group of biblical characters look on in tears.

Degenerate Art Exhibition

In their campaign against "degenerate" art, the Nazis confiscated over 17,000 artworks, including pieces by Munch, Picasso and Chagall, and used them to stage a "Degenerate Art Exhibition." This was designed to ridicule the art. The paintings were shown crowded together, with mocking labels. One Nazi critic called them "the crippled products of madness, impertinence and lack of talent." But ironically the exhibition proved very popular with the public, and attracted thousands of visitors each day. After the show closed, most of the art was sold to other countries to raise money for the Nazis. Anything left unsold was burned.

Aftermath

The Second World War saw many horrors, from ruthless fighting and the bombing of civilians to the systematic slaughter of millions in Nazi concentration camps. Shocked and disillusioned by events, a lot of people struggled to come to terms with what had happened, even years later, and this has been reflected in much of the art made since the war.

Human frailty

After the war, Alberto Giacometti began to draw and sculpt frail, stick-like people standing alone in space. *Man Pointing* is an early example. It shows a lone figure, as tall as a real man, but painfully thin. He is frozen in an unexplained gesture, pointing to something unseen. Such fragile, isolated figures expressed the anguish and uncertainty of the post-war period. Their thinness also evoked the suffering of the concentration camp victims, many of whom had starved to death.

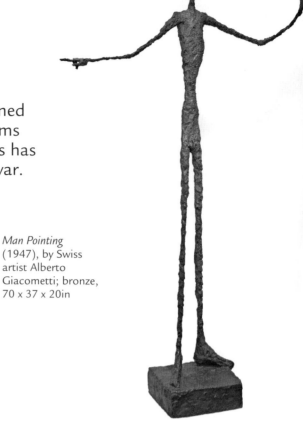

Man Pointing (1947), by Swiss artist Alberto Giacometti; bronze, 70 x 37 x 20in

Horror show

Francis Bacon's *Three Studies for Figures at the Base of a Crucifixion* is filled with horror at the human condition. The three panels show deformed, tortured bodies, set against a blood-red background. The three-panel or "triptych" format was often used in Christian art and the title suggests the Christian theme of crucifixion.

You might expect it to refer to Jesus, whose death was meant to save mankind. But there is no sign of a savior in these pictures, and Bacon, who was an atheist, said he didn't intend the imagery to be Christian. According to him, the three figures are actually Furies – Greek goddesses of vengeance.

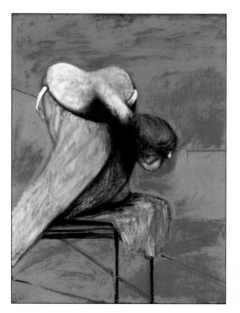

Three Studies for Figures at the Base of a Crucifixion (c.1944), by British painter Francis Bacon; oil on board, three panels, each 37 x 29in. Notice the intense red background color. It might suggest blood or fierce heat – or perhaps the fires of Hell?

Nameless Library (2000), by Rachel Whiteread; room-sized concrete cast. The red cylinders are candles left by visitors, to honor the dead.

In remembrance

In 2000, a new memorial designed by British artist Rachel Whiteread was unveiled in the Austrian capital, Vienna. Entitled *Nameless Library*, it commemorates the 65,000 Austrian Jews killed by the Nazis between 1938 and 1945. It was actually cast from real bookshelves, lined with thousands of books. Around the base are the names of the concentration camps to which Austria's Jewish population was deported.

Set in concrete, the library becomes a sealed chamber, with doors that can't be opened, full of books that can't be read – symbolizing the untold stories of all the victims' lives. It is a room turned inside out, a method which Whiteread said was meant to "invert people's perception of the world and to reveal the unexpected."

👁 For links to websites where you can look at more paintings by Francis Bacon, or find out about another famous memorial, Maya Lin's *Wall*, which commemorates those who died in the Vietnam War, go to **www.usborne-quicklinks.com**

Public art

Memorials are one of the most common forms of public art. Until the first public art galleries and museums were built, around the beginning of the 19th century, public art – outdoor monuments and statues, and religious art in churches – was the only art that many people had ever seen. This kind of art has been a familiar part of our towns and cities for a long time. And it can still arouse strong feelings. *Nameless Library* is no exception.

When the *Library* was first planned, local residents complained its bunker-like design was ugly and out of keeping with the square where it was to be built. Then, construction was almost abandoned when workers uncovered the ruins of a medieval synagogue on the site. It had been burned in 1421, in an earlier wave of anti-Jewish attacks. Many Austrian Jews felt that the ruins would be a better memorial, but eventually a compromise was reached. The ruins were preserved beneath the modern monument, and today you can visit both.

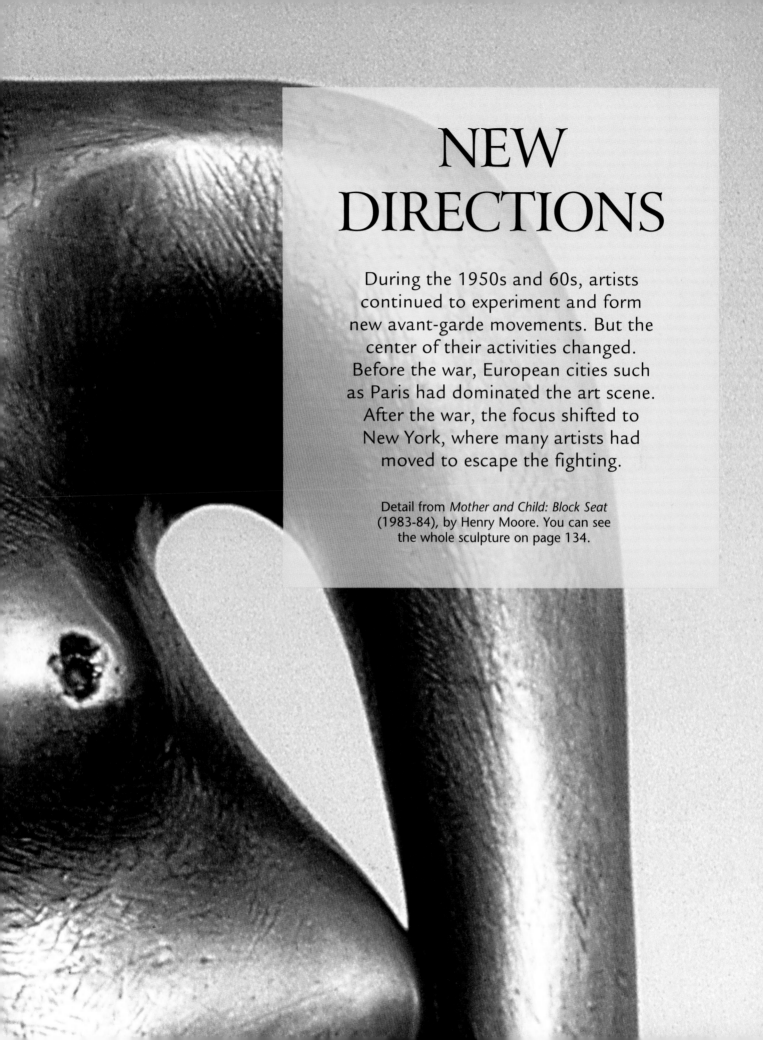

NEW DIRECTIONS

During the 1950s and 60s, artists
continued to experiment and form
new avant-garde movements. But the
center of their activities changed.
Before the war, European cities such
as Paris had dominated the art scene.
After the war, the focus shifted to
New York, where many artists had
moved to escape the fighting.

Detail from *Mother and Child: Block Seat*
(1983-84), by Henry Moore. You can see
the whole sculpture on page 134.

New York, New York

In the 1940s-50s, a group of New York painters became world famous for a new kind of art called Abstract Expressionism. They weren't united by any particular style, but by the ambition and scale of their work. They created vast, abstract paintings meant to awe viewers and provoke deep emotional or spiritual responses. Their work had a huge impact, helping to turn New York into a major center for avant-garde art. And the city remained a focus for later movements such as Minimalism (see below right).

Number 1 (1948), by Jackson Pollock – probably the most famous Abstract Expressionist; oil and enamel on canvas, 68 x 104in

Action man

The Abstract Expressionists believed art should be a form of spontaneous personal expression. So they all developed their own, very individual ways of working. One artist, Jackson Pollock, specialized in densely textured paintings like *Number 1* – a canvas covered in a rich, tangled mass of splashes and streaks, with occasional splotches of color. Pollock made it by laying the canvas flat on the floor and splattering it with a brush. He also punctured paint cans and swung them over the surface with the paint pouring out. For thick, ridged lines, he squeezed oil paint directly from the tube. The drips, lines and splashes draw attention to the physical process of painting. And the boldness and density of the marks create an impression of restless energy and spontaneous rhythms. This method came to be known as Action Painting. For Pollock, it was so absorbing it was almost like a trance. He said, "When I am *in* my painting, I'm not aware of what I'm doing. It's only after a sort of 'get acquainted' period that I see what I have been about. I have no fears about making changes... because the painting has a life of its own."

Fields of color

Another New York artist, Mark Rothko, developed a style known as Color Field Painting, based on huge blocks of color. He painted with brushes and rags, giving the blocks such soft, hazy edges that they seem to float and shimmer, and almost come alive. His pictures are meant to absorb you in colors, shapes and textures. Some are like doorways or windows opening onto other worlds; others are like bars, locking you in.

Rothko hated the label "Abstract Expressionism," but he did admit that he wanted his art to communicate a particular feeling or state of mind. He said: "I'm interested only in expressing basic human emotions... The people who weep before my pictures are having the same religious experience I had when I painted them."

Right: *Number 8* (1952), by Mark Rothko; oil on canvas. The horizontal bands in this image create a sense of space, as if they were really sky and earth, separated by a yellow horizon.

Ursula's One and Two Picture 1/3 (1964), by Dan Flavin; fluorescent light fittings of various dimensions

Minimalism

Unlike the Abstract Expressionists, the Minimalists didn't want to make self-consciously "expressive" art. In fact, their ideas developed partly as a reaction against Abstract Expressionism. Their work was about reducing things to their simplest forms, exploring their physical qualities without trying to give them deeper meanings. For example, Frank Stella painted neat gray and black lines, while Carl Andre and Dan Flavin built plain, geometric shapes out of industrial materials such as bricks and lights.

Minimalism presents things just as they are, plain and unadorned. Flavin said of his work, "It is what it is and it ain't nothing else..." People have often criticized this approach for not being very "artistic," but it has had a great influence on modern art. But although Minimalism is a commonly used term, it was never an official movement and many so-called Minimalists have rejected the name.

Fierce arguments sprang up when the Tate Gallery in London bought a set of bricks named *Equivalent VIII*, by Carl Andre. Supporters said the work revealed the beauty of manufactured objects. But others said it was just a load of bricks.

133

Shaping up

In the 1930s and 40s, a new kind of sculpture emerged in Europe. At the forefront of the new style were two young British artists: Henry Moore and Barbara Hepworth. They created smooth, organic-looking sculptures, inspired by the natural world and their belief in being true to materials. This meant they tried to respond to the different qualities of wood or stone, or whatever they were working with at the time.

Natural rhythms

Henry Moore wanted to be a sculptor from the age of 11, when a teacher told him about the famous 16th-century sculptor Michelangelo. But he didn't want to imitate Michelangelo's detailed, lifelike style. Instead, Moore found his inspiration in the landscape, in the bodies of people and animals, and in ancient sculptures from around the world. Based on these, he created powerful, simplified figures like the one on the left. He wanted his works to be displayed outdoors, to help viewers see the connection between the sculptures and their surroundings.

Mother and Child: Block Seat is one of the last sculptures Moore ever made, and illustrates one of his favorite themes: maternity. It shows a woman sitting on a block-shaped seat, cradling her child. The sheltering, protective shape of the mother is enhanced by the sheltering trees which surround the work. Moore said he wanted his art to show "universal shapes to which everybody... can respond." The relationship between mother and child is one of the most basic, widespread human experiences, so it made an ideal universal subject. For Moore, it may also have been a reflection of his own creativity, since an artist gives life to art as a mother gives life to her child.

👁 For a link to a website where you can find out more about Henry Moore, see lots of his sculptures or explore 3-D panoramic views of his studio, go to **www.usborne-quicklinks.com**

Mother and Child: Block Seat (1983-84), by Henry Moore; bronze, height 96in. Notice how the mother's body curves protectively around her child.

Strings attached

Barbara Hepworth was friends with Henry Moore, and shared many of his ideas about art. But, while Moore achieved international recognition for his huge, bronze works – many of which are on display in public spaces in cities around the world – Hepworth tended to work on a smaller scale, using wood or stone. She spent much of her life by the sea, and often, her art seems to echo the shapes of waves, shells and sea-rounded pebbles.

Hepworth liked to follow the natural properties of her materials and let her sculptures evolve, rather than just carving them into set shapes. She was interested in the contrasts between different textures, and inner and outer surfaces. For example, she painted the inside of *Wave* a very pale blue, to contrast with the rich, polished wood of the sculpture itself. The pale hollow forms a delicate inner world, linked to its curving wooden shell by a series of taut threads.

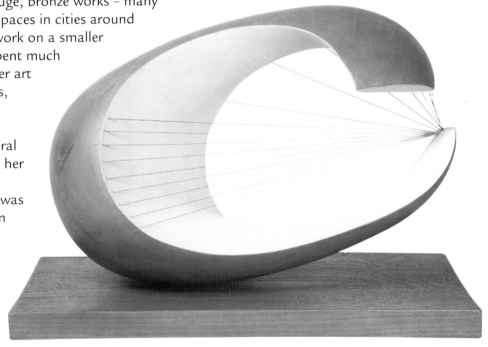

Wave (1943-44), by Barbara Hepworth; wood, paint and string, 12 x 18 x 8in. Does the curved shape remind you of the way a wave rolls and crashes onto a beach?

Distant echoes

Moore and Hepworth had a huge influence on modern sculpture, partly because of the way they worked with abstract shapes, but also because they made pieces that interact with the world around them. This is something that sculptors are still doing today.

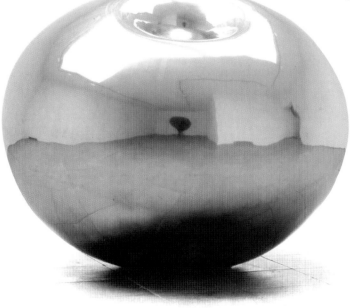

This dimpled steel sphere was created fairly recently by British sculptor Anish Kapoor. Its shiny, rounded shape makes it look a bit like an enormous drop of water. It is an interesting shape in itself. But its mirrored surface makes it even more interesting. When you look at the sculpture, you see yourself and your surroundings reflected in it. But the curved shape distorts appearances and makes everything look different – which may be why Kapoor called the piece *Turning the World Inside Out*.

Turning the World Inside Out (1995), by Anish Kapoor; stainless steel, 58 x 72 x 74in

On the streets

As the 20th century wore on, people's attitudes to cities changed. The early enthusiasm of groups like the Futurists was quelled by economic decline and the effects of two world wars. Increasingly, artists began to make art about urban decay or loneliness. Some artists built sculptures out of junk they found in the streets, while others found inspiration in urban graffiti.

👁 For links to websites where you can see lots more street scenes by Edward Hopper, discover an unusual fountain designed by Jean Tinguely, or find out more about Jean-Michel Basquiat, go to
www.usborne-quicklinks.com

Nighthawks (1942), by Edward Hopper; oil on canvas, 33 x 60in. Nighthawks are nocturnal birds – and so also a nickname for people who do things at night. Notice the strong contrasts between light and dark. They create a moody, almost cinematic effect, like the lighting used in *film noir* – movies about urban crime and corruption popular in the 1930s-40s. The picture is shaped like a movie screen, too.

Lonely nights

American artist Edward Hopper became known for painting atmospheric scenes of urban life – empty streets, lonely buildings and roads going nowhere. *Nighthawks* shows a late-night diner overlooking a deserted street corner. According to Hopper, the picture was based on a real restaurant in New York. But there is nothing to identify it – the picture could be set in any one of hundreds of U.S. cities. Hopper claimed he didn't set out to paint symbols of isolation or emptiness. But he did admit that in this painting, "unconsciously, probably, I was painting the loneliness of a large city."

Much of the effect comes from the way Hopper painted light. The harsh glare in the diner is probably due to fluorescent lights, which began to be used in the 1930s-40s. The light spills out onto the street, creating an eerie glow on the pavement and leaving deep, menacing shadows in the corners. It makes the brightly lit interior seem like a refuge. But there is no sign of an entrance, just an unbroken wall of glass separating the viewer from the people inside. And those people seem to be cut off from each other, too. They aren't talking to one another, just sitting there absorbed in their own thoughts.

Urban junk

Swiss sculptor Jean Tinguely made "Kinetic" (meaning "moving") sculptures out of urban junk. Their movements were generally chaotic and sometimes destructive. So perhaps Tinguely meant to criticize the power of machines – unlike the Futurists, who celebrated them. One of his most famous constructions, entitled *Homage to New York*, self-destructed in 1960, outside the Museum of Modern Art in New York. It included a painting machine, a device which billowed out clouds of white smoke, and a piano that played while going up in flames.

Surviving fragment of *Homage to New York* (1960), by Jean Tinguely. The original sculpture was 26ft high. It was built out of bottles, bicycle and buggy wheels, a bathtub, a balloon, a bell, a car horn, a radio, playing cards, fire extinguishers, scraps of the U.S. flag, a hammer and a saw – all powered by 15 engines.

Homage to New York ran for 27 minutes, creating a huge racket, until it destroyed itself.

Graffiti art

The art of New York painter Jean-Michel Basquiat is often related to graffiti, although he hated being labeled as a "graffiti artist." And the idea of graffiti as "art" is itself controversial, since it is illegal to deface other people's property. But Basquiat began his career doing just that, scrawling pictures and slogans signed "SAMO" on walls around New York. Even after Basquiat began painting on canvases instead of walls, his pictures still had many graffiti-like qualities. They are built up out of overlapping layers and fragments, using simple, spiky shapes, often with scrawled words. Some were done on canvas stretched over frames made from junk found in the streets. The images are vivid and expressive, based on Basquiat's feelings and experiences as a young Black man growing up in the U.S. Some of them celebrate Black American history or street culture. But others seem to be about anger or violence.

Gas Truck (1985), by Hispanic-African-American artist Jean-Michel Basquiat; acrylic and oil on canvas, 50 x 165in

Being popular

The post-war era saw a huge boom in mass-produced goods and mass entertainment. This gave rise to a new popular – or "pop" – culture. Many artists responded by borrowing elements of pop culture to create something now known as Pop art. This emerged in England but soon spread to New York, and many of the most famous Pop artists were American.

Pop rebellion

People often distinguish "high culture," such as paintings – which are expensive and often seen only by a small elite – from pop culture, which is available to everybody. But Pop art defied this distinction, by taking images from magazines, television and other mass media, and by copying commercial mass-production techniques. The Pop artists were also rebelling against the success of Abstract Expressionism, which they thought was too pretentious and inward-looking.

Whaam! (1963), by Roy Lichtenstein; acrylic on canvas, 68 x 160in. This painting imitates the style of printed comic books. If you look closely, you can see dots like the ones produced by some printing presses. What you can't see is the scale – in real life, this picture covers a whole wall.

Just what is it...?

This 1956 collage by British artist Richard Hamilton is sometimes called the first Pop picture. It shows a modern-looking room with a photograph of the moon looming overhead – perhaps a reference to the race between the U.S. and the U.S.S.R. to put a man on the moon. On the left, a body-builder grasps a huge red lollipop labeled "POP." On the right, a woman poses provocatively beneath a poster celebrating romance. Together, they form a kind of "ideal" couple – or a parody of one. They are surrounded by assorted consumer items, including an extendable vacuum cleaner, a reel-to-reel tape recorder and a can of ham, cut from magazines and catalogs. It is a ridiculous combination, making a mockery of advertising and the picture-perfect life it tries to sell us.

Just What Is It That Makes Today's Homes So Different, So Appealing? (1956), by Richard Hamilton; collage, 10 x 10in. Even the title of this picture parodies the language of adverts.

Mass-produced art

Roy Lichtenstein and Andy Warhol were among the best-known American Pop artists. Lichtenstein painted huge comic-book pictures such as *Whaam!* Was he suggesting that comics deserve to be considered "art," or trying to make us take a critical look at comic-book values? According to him, comics "express violent emotion in a completely mechanical and removed style." He imitated them so closely, he even copied the colored dots used in cheap printing.

Warhol went a step further, making prints of everything from soup cans to movie stars. (You can see an example on pages 142-143.) For him, art was no longer about creating something unique. He even named his studio "The Factory," comparing his work to mass production.

Questions of taste

Pop art was very successful very quickly, perhaps because people found it amusing and easy to understand. Hamilton ironically defined it as: "Popular (designed for a mass audience), Transient (short term solution), Expendable (easily forgotten), Low cost, Mass-produced, Young (aimed at youth), Witty, Sexy, Gimmicky, Glamorous, Big business." Compared to the serious abstract works artists had done in the 1950s, Pop seemed light-hearted and fun. And the commercial images and techniques it imitated were designed to have a broad appeal. But not everyone liked it. Some critics referred to Pop art as "New Vulgarism," because they felt Pop artists had lost sight of art's more serious goals.

Staying popular

Pop has had a lasting influence, even today, in the work of artists like Jeff Koons. Like the Pop artists, he turns everyday objects into art. For example, he took a rabbit-shaped balloon – deliberately selecting a trashy or "kitsch" object – and made it into a polished steel sculpture. It might look amusing, but do you think it was meant to have a serious message? Perhaps Koons meant to celebrate consumer culture, or comment on the throwaway nature of society, by making a throwaway item such as a balloon into something more permanent.

Rabbit (1986), by Jeff Koons; cast stainless steel, 41 x 19 x 12in. Koons has made several works based on novelty balloons like this.

A Bigger Splash

British artist David Hockney moved to California in the 1960s, drawn by the sunny Californian climate and relaxed way of life. It inspired him to create many colorful, idealized paintings of life there. *A Bigger Splash* captures the moment as a diver enters a cool, blue pool beneath a luminous turquoise sky.

Title: *A Bigger Splash*
Date: 1967
Artist: David Hockney
Materials: acrylic on canvas
Size: 96 x 96in

Real and imagined

Although this scene looks very realistic, Hockney actually made it up. He based the pool on a photograph he had seen in a book about swimming pools. The background, with its low-slung, 1960s-style house, he took from a drawing he had done of buildings in California.

The clear horizontal lines of the house and pool contrast strongly with the diagonal diving board and the spindly, vertical palm trees. It is a curiously empty picture – the only sign of life is the splash itself. The house windows reflect other buildings, suggesting this is an urban scene. But, oddly – or perhaps because this is an imaginary picture – there are no buildings visible behind the house, giving the impression of vast open space beyond.

Plastic paint

The bold colors stress the intensity of the Californian sunlight. The yellow diving board stands out dramatically against the cool blue of the water, and the pink house contrasts with the bright blue sky. Hockney had recently begun to use acrylic paints instead of traditional oils. Acrylic paints are based on plastics and were only invented in the 1950s. They give very strong colors and dry much faster than oils, so they were good for the sunny colors and sharp outlines of Hockney's painting.

Hockney was always ready to experiment with new techniques, even making art out of fax-machine printouts.

Rolled and brushed

Hockney emphasized the way the splash breaks the stillness of the pool by the way he applied his paints. He did the main blocks of color first, using rollers to get a very smooth surface. Then he painted in the details with brushes. For the splash itself, he used deliberately rough, textured brushstrokes, to contrast with the smooth blue water and the flat surfaces in the background.

Hockney chose to leave a border of unpainted canvas around the scene, to frame it. (The canvas is the background color of these pages.)

Frozen moments

Although the splash would have lasted only moments, this painting took Hockney about two weeks to finish. He compared this with the way a photograph "freezes" a moment, saying: "I realize that a splash could never be seen this way in real life, it happens too quickly. And I was amused by this, so I painted it in a very, very slow way."

Everyday pop

Hockney's work became famous at about the same time as Pop art. People often associate him with that movement, although he has always rejected the label. But he was painting ordinary, everyday things in a straightforward way – something many Pop artists were doing too.

For a link to a website where you can take an online tour of one of the biggest collections of Hockney's work, go to **www.usborne-quicklinks.com**

Famous faces

Pop art drew heavily on pop culture, so it is not surprising that it often featured famous faces from movies and pop music. But the relationship between artists and celebrities got even closer, with some movie and pop stars commissioning or making art, and some artists becoming famous in their own right.

Famous for 15 minutes

Andy Warhol was fascinated by fame. He held celebrity parties in his studio and made sure his own image, complete with artificial white wig, became well known. Much of his art dealt with fame, too. He made colorful prints of movie stars like Marilyn Monroe and Liz Taylor. *Elvis I & II* shows the singer Elvis Presley, posing with a gun for a movie called *Flaming Star*, repeated four times. The mechanical repetition makes it impersonal, reminding you that this is a screen image, not a personal portrait. And, as you look across the canvas, the image blurs and fades into black and white. Perhaps this was about the short-lived nature of fame? Warhol once predicted fame would become briefer and briefer. He said, "In the future everyone will be world-famous for 15 minutes."

Elvis I & II (1964), by Andy Warhol; synthetic polymer paint, aluminum paint and silkscreen ink on canvas, two panels, each 82 x 82in – just over lifesize. Notice how each Elvis is slightly different from the others. Though they are printed, they are not exact copies. How they look depends partly on chance.

Album cover: *Sgt. Pepper's Lonely Hearts Club Band* (1967), by Peter Blake; photograph, 12 x 12in

Art and commerce

Although Pop art was originally inspired by commercial art, it soon became a two-way relationship, with many Pop artists also working in advertising or design. For example, Warhol's art grew out of his experience of drawing advertisements and designing shop windows. As the pop music industry boomed, some artists began to design record covers. This led to one of the most famous pieces of commercial Pop art – the cover for The Beatles' album, *Sgt. Pepper's Lonely Hearts Club Band* (1967). Its distinctive collage-style look was created by British artist Peter Blake. It shows the band among a crowd of lifesize cardboard cutouts and models. The colorful figures in the middle are the real Beatles; they appear again as wax models on the left, this time in dark suits. The other figures are well-known actors, singers, artists, writers, spiritual leaders and sports stars, meant to represent the band's ideal audience.

Celebrity art

As the world today seems obsessed with fame, it is perhaps only natural that art reflects this. Now, art and celebrity appear closer than ever. Stars such as the singer Madonna are known as art collectors, while others, such as former Beatle Paul McCartney, have turned to painting. In fact, many musicians, including David Bowie and the pop group Blur, began their careers at art school. The idea of the celebrity-artist cultivated by Warhol continues with artists like Damien Hirst, who is often in the news. Artists still work with pop music – Blake recently did a cover for singer Robbie Williams. And artists continue to explore the nature of fame, too. For example, Michael Jackson has featured in paintings by Gary Hume. And Sam Taylor-Wood (see page 152) filmed pop star Kylie Minogue miming naked to opera to create a work entitled *The Misfit*.

For links to websites where you can read about the making of the *Sgt. Pepper* album cover and discover who all the people in the crowd are, or view lots more prints by Andy Warhol, go to **www.usborne-quicklinks.com**

Faces in the crowd

Among the artists sampling the pop culture of today is Black British painter Chris Ofili. He uses pictures from magazines, along with brightly colored pins and deliberately rough-looking lumps of elephant dung, to create works like *Afrodizzia*. This features hundreds of black faces, including famous musicians James Brown, Louis Armstrong and Michael Jackson, set in a swirling mass of color. The picture captures the energy and excitement of their music, as well as paying tribute to black musical traditions.

Ofili compared painting to writing a song, saying, "you want to get the right rhythm and base line." He builds up his pictures in layers, borrowing bits of other images, rather like music sampling. His unusual techniques were also inspired by his sense of his African heritage. The bead-like dots of paint were influenced by African cave paintings. He started using elephant dung after bringing some back from Africa – though he now gets supplies from London Zoo.

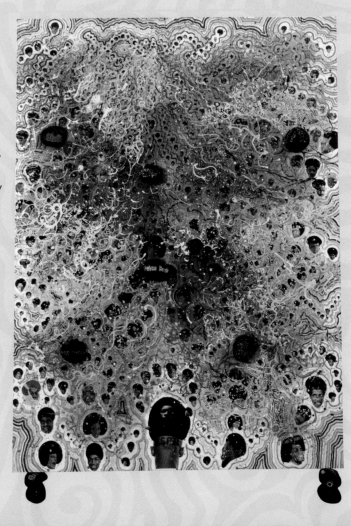

Afrodizzia (1996), by Chris Ofili; acrylic, oil, resin, paper collage, glitter, map pins and elephant dung on canvas, 96 x 72in. This painting rests on elephant-dung feet.

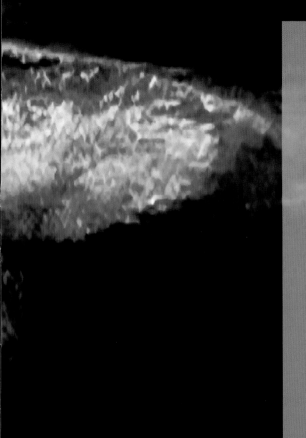

ANYTHING GOES

Art can mean almost anything nowadays, with artists using everything from traditional oil paints to the latest medical imaging technology. Artists have taken art outside galleries too, creating works outdoors and in some startlingly unexpected places and ways.

Detail of *Departing Angel* from *Five Angels for the Millennium* (2001), by Bill Viola. You can find out more about this video and sound installation on page 153.

Beyond the frame

To many artists in the 1960s-70s, traditional painting and sculpture felt too limited. They wanted to make art that would stretch the definition of what "art" really was – and perhaps change people's ideas about the world, too. So they began to create a different kind of art, by recording ideas, staging performances or building things. These works had no frame to keep them separate from their audience, so they couldn't be looked at in a traditional way.

> 👁 For a link to a website where you can read about a Conceptual work entitled *Pharmacy* by Damien Hirst, and see photographs showing how it changed as it was installed in different art galleries around the world, go to **www.usborne-quicklinks.com**

What's the big idea?

The term "Conceptual art" began to be used in the 1960s. It describes art where the concept or idea behind the work is more important than anything the artist actually makes. In fact, there is often no artwork at all, only written notes or photographs explaining the artist's idea. For example, how many chairs do you see on the right? There is only one actual chair – but there is also a photograph of it and the text of a dictionary entry for "chair." So, as the title says, there are both "One and Three Chairs." In this way, the piece explores the nature of reality and how it can be represented in pictures or words.

One and Three Chairs (1965), by Joseph Kosuth; photograph of a chair, wooden chair and dictionary entry for "chair"

Acting up

Some of Yves Klein's art was created by live models. He called them "living brushes."

Performance art – also sometimes known as "Happenings" – was designed to blur the boundaries between art, theater and real life. In a series of performances known as *Anthropometries*, Yves Klein got nude models to smear themselves with paint and roll on paper in front of an audience, accompanied by live music. The finished paintings were mounted and framed, but the process of creating them was considered as important as the end result.

Explaining away

In a 1965 Happening, *How to explain paintings to a dead hare*, Joseph Beuys covered his head with honey and gold leaf, tied a length of iron to one foot, and went around a Düsseldorf gallery with a dead hare, explaining the pictures on display. Although Beuys must have looked very odd, he wouldn't have minded. To him, the piece was "about the problems of thought [and] consciousness." To act it out, he had to express his thoughts. But, because the hare could not listen or understand, Beuys also showed how we may fail to communicate our ideas to others.

Beuys described his work as "anti-art," because he wanted to reject art's traditional values and uses. He didn't want to make beautiful things. Instead, he believed that art could change society – and that "Everyone is an artist."

Installing art

An installation is the name given to a 3-D work that takes over a whole room or field or other space, and creates a new environment of its own. Probably the biggest example is Robert Rauschenberg's ¼ *Mile or 2 Furlong Piece*. This includes hundreds of elements, from street signs and stacks of books and boxes, to collages and prints, and even sounds such as traffic or a baby crying. It is about trying to show the structure within seemingly random arrangements – what Rauschenberg called "Random Order."

¼ *Mile or 2 Furlong Piece* (1981-present), by Robert Rauschenberg; mixed media, variable dimensions. Rauschenberg is still adding to this. When it's finished, he wants it to stretch the full length of its title. Its progress records the artist's life and art as it has developed over time.

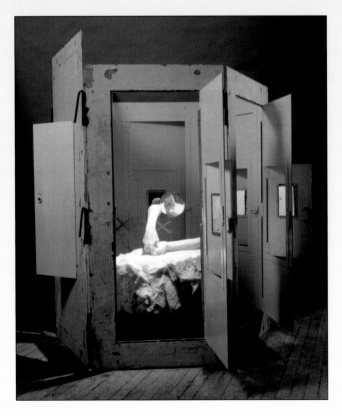

In the cells

French-American sculptor Louise Bourgeois made a series of installations that she called "cells." As the name suggests, they are small, enclosed spaces, which viewers peer into through shuttered windows or half-open doors, creating an uneasy, claustrophobic feeling. The cell on the left contains a shaving mirror and a pair of hands on a block of stone, the fingers knotted together as if in pain. According to Bourgeois, the cells represent different types of pain: "the physical, the emotional and the psychological, and the mental and intellectual." Some of her cells use broken glass and menacing industrial machines to suggest suffering. Perhaps here, the pain is meant to be the lack of privacy – the mirror and open shutters invite us to look at the hands from every angle. The shape of the cell is important too. The walls form a circle, so there is no beginning or end point – just a continuous cycle.

Cell (Hands and Mirror) (1995), by Louise Bourgeois; marble, painted metal and mirror, 63 x 48 x 45in

Cold Dark Matter

The installation *Cold Dark Matter*, by British artist Cornelia Parker, is a mass of debris suspended on invisible wires in a darkened room. A single light bulb shines in the middle, so all the bits and pieces cast eerie shadows on the walls. They are actually the charred remains of a garden shed packed with old junk and plastic explosive, and blown up by the British Army.

> Title: *Cold Dark Matter: An Exploded View*
> Artist: Cornelia Parker   Date: 1991
> Size: approx. 157 x 197 x 197in
> Materials: a garden shed and contents blown up for the artist by the British army, the fragments suspended around a light bulb

What is the matter?

The splintered pieces of wood around the outside are the fragments of the shed itself. Hanging between them is an odd assortment of junk, including old books, letters, shoes, toys, garden tools, bicycle parts and a twisted bucket. "I like to take man-made objects and push them... so that they become something else," explained Parker. Here, she has taken ordinary, everyday items discarded by other people and turned them into art.

The title works on several levels. Sheds are often cold, dark places. "Cold dark matter" is also a term from astronomy. According to Parker, it is "the material within the universe that we cannot see and we cannot quantify. We know it exists but we can't measure it." So the title suggests a link with science and outer space. Many scientists believe the universe was formed by a huge explosion known as the "Big Bang." Perhaps this installation is meant to be a kind of small-scale version of that cosmic event?

> 👁 For a link to a website where you can see more works by Parker, including one named *Mass (Colder Darker Matter)*, go to **www.usborne-quicklinks.com**

Right: *Breathless*
(2001), by Cornelia
Parker; brass musical
instruments flattened and
suspended, seen against a round ceiling

The art of destruction

Parker makes art in very unconventional ways. As well as blowing things up, she has run over coins with a train and crushed pieces of silver – plates, candlesticks, spoons, boxes and trophies – with a steamroller. For *Breathless,* she created an arrangement of squashed brass instruments. Although their shapes are instantly recognizable, the flattened instruments really did become "breathless" and unplayable – to the anger of some musicians.

For one installation, Parker steamrollered more than 1,000 silver objects and arranged them into 30 neat, round piles. She called it *30 Pieces of Silver*, referring to the Bible story about Judas, who betrayed Jesus for 30 pieces of silver.

Parker described what she does to her objects as "cartoon deaths" – and there is something comic about the way she destroys them. But there is also something touching about the way she selects broken, discarded items and resurrects them through art. But she avoids pinning down the meaning of her work, saying, "All I try to do... is to make something that makes the hairs on the back of my neck stand up, and then I hope that it might do that for someone else."

Outside the gallery

A lot of modern art takes art out of galleries and into places that you wouldn't normally think of – from remote country landscapes to busy urban environments. Some artists have chosen to do this because they are trying to make people aware of environmental issues. Others want to make art that cannot be bought and sold, and to make people look at the world in new ways.

👁 For links to websites where you can see many examples of Land and Environmental art, go to **www.usborne-quicklinks.com**

Mud Hand Circles (1989), by Richard Long; circles of mud handprints, about 126in across. Long made this painting on a wall in Jesus College, Cambridge, using mud he brought back from the River Avon.

Working the land

Landscapes have always been a traditional subject for paintings. But in the 1960s and 70s, some artists began to work directly with the land, making art out in the open and then documenting it. They used natural materials and allowed changes in the weather and light to add to the result. This approach is known as Land art, or Earthworks. It can range from huge mounds made with bulldozers to something as small and short-lived as a line of crushed grass.

British artist Richard Long became known for making Land art based on walks in wild, remote places, which he records with maps, poems and photos. On some walks, he builds simple arrangements of stones or driftwood. Sometimes, he collects natural materials to make similar pieces back in the gallery. *Mud Hand Circles* is one example. Like much of Long's work, it explores the relationship between people – represented by the handprints – and nature. With large-scale Earthworks, probably the best-known examples are American. One artist, Robert Smithson, built a huge spiral jetty in the Great Salt Lake, Utah, using vast quantities of rock and earth.

U.S. artist Walter De Maria covered an enormous field with a grid of steel poles designed to attract lightning.

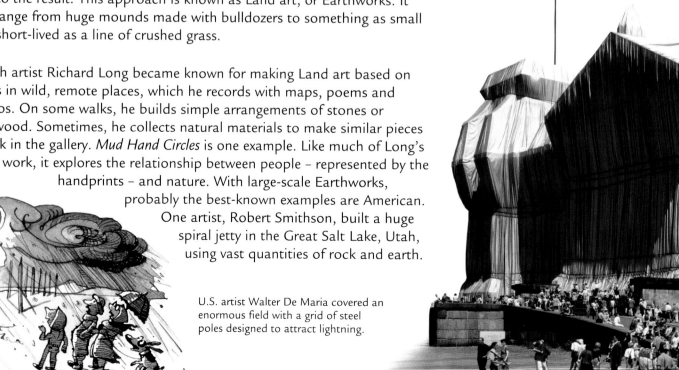

Snow and ice

British artist Andy Goldsworthy makes art inspired by specific landscapes, from English woodland to the Arctic wastes. He gathers natural materials, such as leaves and feathers, and arranges them in simple shapes. He has even worked with snow and ice, creating giant snowballs and delicate sculptures such as *Icicle Star*. His art is designed to interact with its setting and often doesn't last long, reflecting the changes that occur in nature. Like Long, he is interested in exploring the relationship between people and the world around them.

Icicle Star (1987), by Andy Goldsworthy. This was made of icicles stuck together with frozen water. But it has long since melted and now exists only in photographs.

All wrapped up

For two weeks in 1995, the *Reichstag*, the German parliament building in Berlin, was swathed in silvery fabric held in place by blue ropes. This project was planned by two artists who call themselves Christo and Jeanne-Claude. They describe their work as Environmental art (not Land art) because they do it in many different places, not just out in the wild.

Wrapped Reichstag, Berlin (1971-95), by Christo and Jeanne-Claude. This required special permission from the German government, and a huge team of workers and professional climbers.

Under cover

The fabric transformed the Reichstag, hiding its usual appearance but revealing its basic shape. The project also had a political meaning. As the seat of the German parliament, the building is also a symbol of German democracy. So for many people *Wrapped Reichstag* was a reminder of the difficult struggle Germany had to achieve democracy.

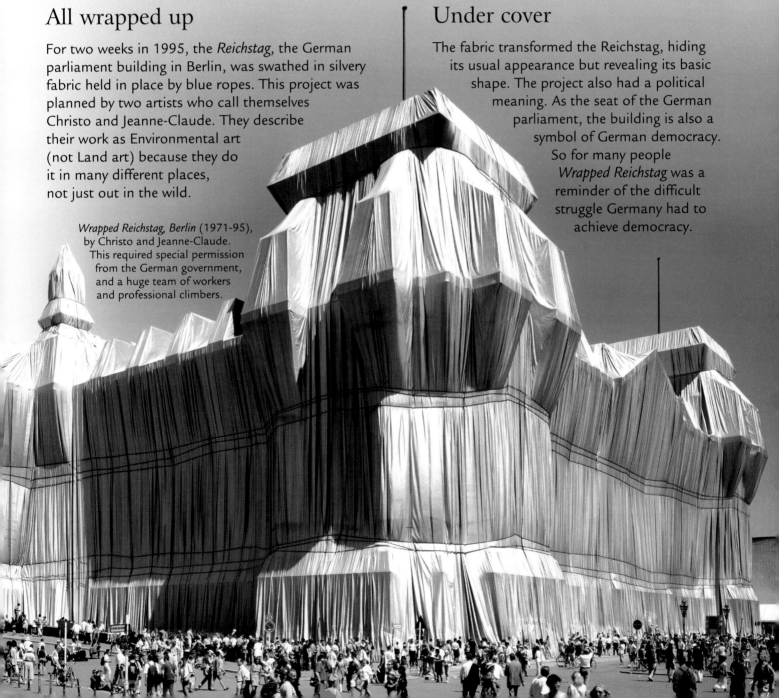

Religious visions

Although many artists now use materials and techniques that weren't available in the past, their art often deals with the same issues. Since about the 5th century, Christianity has been one of the main subjects of western art – a lot of art was made to tell Bible stories or provide a focus for prayer. For a time, modern art pushed religion to the margins. But, over the past decade, it has re-emerged as a major theme.

Pieta (2001), by Sam Taylor-Wood; 35mm film/DVD, duration: 1 minute 57 seconds. The film runs in a loop, with no sound and almost no movement. The pose of the two figures in the film was inspired by a marble sculpture made five centuries earlier, by famous Italian artist Michelangelo Buonarroti.

Moving pictures

Sam Taylor-Wood's *Pieta* takes an old Christian theme and gives it a modern twist by turning it into a film. *Pieta* is Italian for "pity." In art, it usually means a painting or statue of the Virgin Mary with the body of her dead son, Jesus. Taylor-Wood's film shows a woman cradling a man's lifeless body. It is an awkward pose – the woman's muscles strain to take the weight, and the man's arm dangles stiffly. But the result is a striking image of sadness and dignity in the face of death. Taylor-Wood assumes the role of Mary, and actor Robert Downey Jr. takes the part of Jesus. This has led some critics to link the film's concern with suffering to the artist's own fight against cancer, and Downey's struggle with addiction.

Small angel

Ron Mueck is known for creating incredibly lifelike figures – in fact, he started out making models for television and movies. His work is painstakingly crafted, down to each individual hair. The results are so convincing, they are often dubbed "hyperreal." But they are also unreal, because Mueck plays with sizes in startling ways. For example, *Angel* is a tiny figure slumped on a stool and dwarfed by his own wings, which seem to weigh heavily on his shoulders. Despite his name, he looks far from angelic. His face is set in a sulky scowl, and his head is propped sadly in his hands. Being good, this sculpture seems to suggest, isn't necessarily fun.

Angel (1997), by Australian artist Ron Mueck; silicon rubber and mixed media, 43 x 34 x 32in. The body was modeled in clay before being cast out of rubber. The wings are made of white goose feathers.

Man to man

When British artist Mark Wallinger was asked to do a new artwork for an empty plinth in London's Trafalgar Square, he decided to make a statue of Jesus. He named it *Ecce Homo*, which is Latin for "Behold the man." According to the Bible, this is what was said as Jesus was shown to the crowd just before his crucifixion. So it was appropriate for this work to be displayed in a busy city square. The statue shows Jesus as he would have looked at that moment, wearing a loin-cloth and a crown of thorns, with his hands tied behind his back.

Wallinger modeled the statue on a real man. It looked tiny on the plinth, which was designed for a much grander monument. But Wallinger didn't want to make his statue any larger than life. He said his aim was to show Jesus "as an ordinary human being." But he cast the statue out of pale white marble resin, which gives it a ghostly effect. So it seems both lifelike and other-worldly at the same time.

Ecce Homo (1999), by Mark Wallinger; marble resin, lifesize. This photograph shows the statue as it appeared in Trafalgar Square, the first in a series of temporary displays on the plinth.

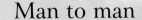 For a link to a website where you can see other artworks which have been displayed on Trafalgar Square's empty plinth, go to **www.usborne-quicklinks.com**

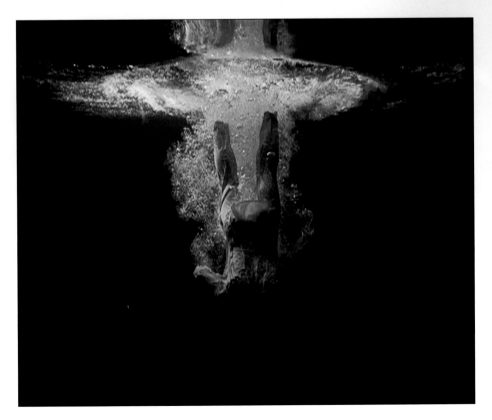

Millennium angels

American artist Bill Viola uses video to explore spirituality and basic life experiences such as birth and death. *Five Angels for the Millennium* is a set of five simultaneous video projections. They show an underwater world which is sometimes sky blue, sometimes fiery red – the colors of Heaven and Hell. Periodically, a human figure appears in a burst of noise and light, rising up out of the water or plunging down into it. But the movement is slowed down, so it seems strange and mystical, like the arrival or departure of an angel.

Departing Angel from *Five Angels for the Millennium* (2001), by Bill Viola; video and sound installation

Model relationships

For some artists and critics, especially feminists who are concerned with women's rights, the role of women in art has been a troubled and neglected political issue.

In the past, a lot of art was made by men for men, and many women felt it failed to represent their point of view. But recently, women artists have set out to challenge this.

Left: *Dancing Ostriches from Walt Disney's Fantasia* (1995), by Portuguese-born artist Paula Rego; pastel on paper mounted on aluminum, 59 x 59in. This picture was inspired by cartoon ostriches similar to the ones below.

When Rego was asked to create art based on movies, she did a series of pastel drawings inspired by Disney cartoons. The women on the left are her version of the dancing ostriches in *Fantasia*.

Telling stories

Paula Rego often creates pictures based on stories, especially ones with strong female characters. Here, she drew three women in ballet costumes and poses taken from Walt Disney's *Fantasia*. Disney's artists sketched real dancers, and then turned them into ostriches. Rego reversed this and turned the birds back into real women. She said, "I always want to turn things on their heads, to upset the established order."

Surprisingly, though, the women in Rego's drawing aren't actually dancing. Two are propped on cushions, while the third hitches up her skirt. Despite their ribbons and tutus, they don't look much like ballerinas – their bodies are too heavy and middle-aged. But the picture isn't really about ballet. It's about the women themselves, and the conflict between their dreams and their aging bodies.

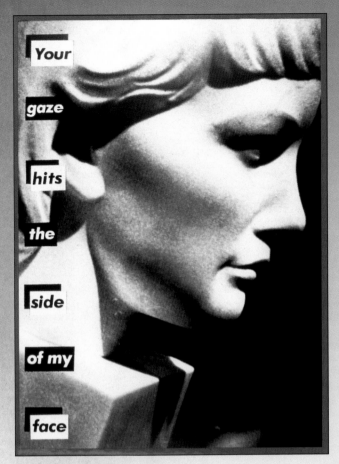

Packing a punch

American artist Barbara Kruger began her career designing magazines and often uses magazine pictures in her art, combined with short, punchy phrases. The effect is meant to challenge people's ideas about power and identity. She says she works with pictures and words because they have "the ability to determine who we are."

Your Gaze Hits the Side of My Face is a stark, black and white photo of a woman's head, sculpted in a fairly traditional-looking style. The woman's face is turned modestly away. But the words on the left make it seem as if she is speaking out, accusing viewers of not seeing below the surface/side of her face. Kruger wanted to illustrate the feminist belief that traditional art shows women only as objects to be looked at, rather than as the people doing the looking.

Untitled (Your Gaze Hits the Side of My Face) (1981), by Barbara Kruger; lithograph, 55 x 41in. Notice how Kruger uses slogan-like text and stylish photography to create something which resembles an advertisement.

Guerilla tactics

There has been a lot of feminist criticism of the art of the past, especially of female nudes such as *Odalisque* by 19th-century French artist Ingres. It is a beautiful painting, but the politics behind it may be less attractive. An "odalisque" was a female slave, so this woman is being shown in a powerless, submissive role. She would have been meant to appeal to male viewers. Nearly two centuries later, Ingres' painting appeared in a very different way, on a poster designed by the "Guerilla Girls" – an anonymous group of women artists who campaign on political issues. The poster compared the number of female nudes with the number of works by women artists in the prestigious Metropolitan Museum in New York. The Guerilla Girls wanted to draw attention to what they saw as an unfair, if unconscious, bias in the art world, where the majority of critics and curators are men.

👁 For links to websites where you can find out more about the artists on these pages, go to **www.usborne-quicklinks.com**

Odalisque (1814), by Jean-Auguste-Dominique Ingres; oil on canvas, 36 x 64in. This painting hangs in the Louvre Museum in Paris.

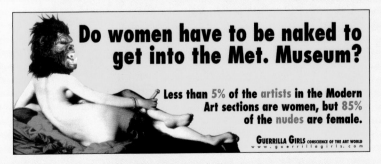

Do women... (1989), by the Guerilla Girls; billboard poster. This was created for the Public Art Fund in New York – who refused to display it.

155

Taking pictures

Many people wonder if photography is really art – partly because it depends on chemical processes rather than skill with a paintbrush. But photographs still have to be composed and printed. They aren't always about recording how things look, either. The artists here used photographs to create imaginary characters and experiment with the whole idea of image-making.

For links to websites where you can see more of Cindy Sherman's *Untitled Film Stills* or another photomontage by David Hockney, go to **www.usborne-quicklinks.com**

Moving pictures

In the late 1970s and early 80s, American artist Cindy Sherman made a series of photographs called *Untitled Film Stills*. They weren't really taken from films, but are lit and framed in a cinematic way. Sherman said they were inspired by movie publicity shots.

Sherman herself appears in each photograph, dressed up like a Hollywood actress playing a clichéd role, such as a runaway lover or a young housewife. Many people think the images are meant to draw attention to film stereotypes about women. But, unlike real film stills, there are no fixed stories behind these pictures, so it is up to the viewer to decide how to interpret them.

Untitled Film Still #48 (1979), by Cindy Sherman; photograph on paper, 30 x 40in

Happy days

Like Sherman, British artists Gilbert and George made themselves the subjects of their art. In 1970, they began to call themselves "living sculptures." Then they started taking pictures of themselves. They became known for creating huge, bright, grid-like arrangements of photos, which look rather like modern stained glass windows.

Happy is from a series entitled "Modern Fears," made at the start of the 1980s. The series dealt with the artists' everyday life, including their fears, fantasies and moods. Here, they are making grotesque faces – despite the title, they seem anything but happy. The yellow face appears worried or scared, and the red one looks like a creature from a horror movie. The lighting adds to the horror-movie effect – both faces are lit from below, casting sinister shadows. But many people enjoy being scared by horror movies, so perhaps the picture is meant to make viewers happy by giving them a similar thrill?

Happy (1980), by Gilbert and George; photographs on paper, 95 x 79in

My Mother, Los Angeles, Dec. 1982 (1982), by David Hockney; photographic collage, 53 x 39in

Notice the jumps in colors and angles where one photo overlaps the next. The carpet varies from mustard to reddish-brown or beige, showing how much the appearance of something can vary in different photographs.

Multiple views

David Hockney has made large photographic collages, which he dubbed "multiples," made up of dozens or even hundreds of individual photos. He combined the photos in a deliberately disjointed way, sometimes overlapping, sometimes with gaps – like this portrait of his mother. Each photograph offers a slightly different glimpse of the scene, so there are strange jumps and distortions, and abrupt changes of color. Hockney linked this technique to Cubism.

Like a Cubist painting, it shows everything from multiple viewpoints, so you see an array of separate details, rather than a unified whole. It also shows just how incomplete each individual photograph really is. But Hockney overcame this limitation by combining multiple views. For example, in the collage above, you can see both the artist's feet at the bottom and the ceiling at the top – a far wider view than you could get in a single shot.

Me, myself and I

Self portraits have been popular with artists for at least 500 years, ever since good mirrors became available. But, now photographic portraits are so widespread, artists are no longer as concerned with capturing a likeness. Some of them have chosen to explore very unusual techniques instead.

👁 For a link to a website where you can see another self portrait by Chuck Close and find out more about his painting methods, go to **www.usborne-quicklinks.com**

Flesh and blood

Marc Quinn has made a lot of sculptures based on his own body. Probably the best known is *Self* – a model of his head made from his own blood. It took Quinn five months to have enough blood extracted. The blood was then poured into a mold and frozen. Its reddish color gives the face an unexpected, almost sinister look. It makes the head seem both familiar and strange, like Quinn's view of his "self." "The self is what one knows best and least at the same time," he said. The features look frost-bitten, creating a frightening sense of decay. But the calm expression gives the head a peaceful look. The eyes are shut as if in death, like a traditional death mask – a cast of a dead person's face taken to preserve his or her memory. The fragility of the sculpture (it has to be kept in a refrigerated case) also adds to its meaning, by reminding you just how fragile life is.

Self (1991), by Marc Quinn; blood, stainless steel, perspex and refrigeration equipment, case 82 x 25 x 25in. This artwork contains almost as much blood as an average human body.

Photorealistic

American artist Chuck Close specializes in huge portraits, done in a detailed, almost photographic style known as Photorealism. Close actually starts by projecting a photograph onto a gridded canvas. Then he fills in the grid, square by square. To begin with, he used an airbrush to get a flat, even finish. But, in 1988, a blood clot in his neck left him badly paralyzed. This made him develop a new, more expressive technique using brushes strapped to his wrists.

The self portrait on the left was done with brushes. Although it looks very realistic, if you stand very close to it, it dissolves into a near-abstract pattern of shapes and colors. Close described his pictures as "paintings first and portraits second." They are designed to challenge our assumption that photos are "real."

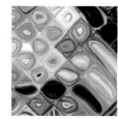

Self Portrait (1997) by Chuck Close; oil on canvas, 102 x 84in. The enlarged detail on the right shows Close's colorful, looping brushstrokes.

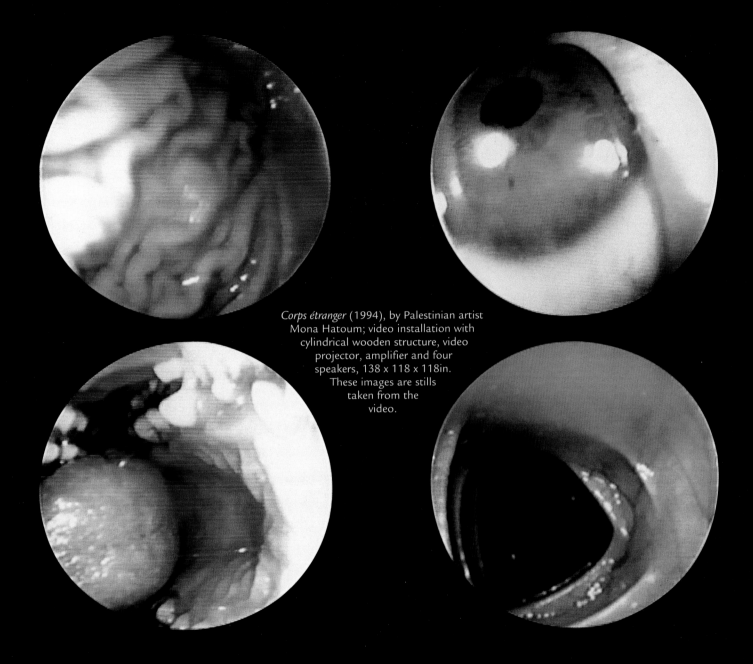

Corps étranger (1994), by Palestinian artist Mona Hatoum; video installation with cylindrical wooden structure, video projector, amplifier and four speakers, 138 x 118 x 118in. These images are stills taken from the video.

Inner self

Much of Mona Hatoum's art is about bodies, both her own and that of the viewer. Corps étranger is a film of a journey through her body, projected onto the floor of a tall white cylinder, which you enter through a narrow doorway. The filming itself was done by a surgeon using a miniature fiber optic camera. The film begins by showing the outside of Hatoum's body in extreme close-up, revealing tiny details such as the pores in her skin or the veins in her eyes. Then the camera plunges right inside her body, down her throat and into moist, pulsating tunnels, accompanied by the sound of her breathing and heartbeats.

The film magnifies everything to an impossible size, revealing things you couldn't normally see. It makes bodies seem strange, both attractive and repulsive at the same time. It is a kind of self portrait, but you couldn't recognize Hatoum from these images. Corps étranger is French for "foreign body." Some people think this title is meant to refer to Hatoum's own flesh, made "foreign" or unfamiliar by being shown in this way. But for others, the "foreign bodies" are actually those of the viewers themselves, intruding into an intimate, enclosed space where they don't really belong.

BEHIND THE SCENES

This section explains some of what happens behind the scenes in artists' studios and art museums. You can find out how paintings are made, including artists' materials, technical tricks and famous forgeries, and discover how museums preserve old, fragile pictures. You can also read about how art is sold. At the end, there is a reference section with a timeline, artists' biographies and a glossary explaining useful art terms.

These pages show a sample of acrylic paintwork, produced for this book by Antonia Miller.

Artists' materials

Artists' materials and techniques have changed greatly over the centuries, from laboriously hand-prepared colors to modern paints squeezed straight from a tube. These pages look at the most common methods of painting, from egg tempera to modern acrylics.

These colored powders, or pigments, were usually made by grinding up colored stones, plants or metals. More unusual ingredients included Egyptian mummies, used to make 'mummy' brown.

Breaking eggs

In the Middle Ages, most paintings were produced by large workshops. The head of the workshop would design each picture and oversee its production. The paint used was known as egg tempera, a fast-drying mixture of colored pigments and egg, which had to be applied very carefully and methodically in stages.

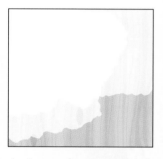

1. A panel was cut and shaped from wood. This was then covered in 'gesso,' a chalky paste which created a smooth surface for painting on.

2. Any gilded areas were painted red and then covered in a thin layer of gold leaf. The gold was polished and, sometimes, patterns were scratched into it.

3. The 'underpainting,' or first layer of colors, was applied next. Some surprising colors were used. Skin was painted green, to balance the pink used later.

4. The top layers of paint were filled in slowly. Artists had to mix their paint in small amounts and use tiny brushstrokes, as egg tempera dries so fast.

The Virgin And Child With St. John And Angels (probably about 1495), by Michelangelo Buonarroti, usually known just as 'Michelangelo.' This egg tempera painting was never completed. You can see the grayish-green underpainting on the unfinished figures.

Oil and canvas

During the Renaissance, artists began to experiment with oil paints – mixtures of pigments and oil that dried much more slowly than egg tempera. Soon, most people were working in oils. At first, oil paintings were done on wood. But, from the early 16th century, artists began painting on canvas. Unlike wood, canvases don't split, they are easier to join together for large paintings, and are lighter and easier to carry.

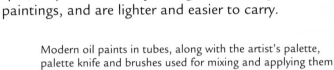

Modern oil paints in tubes, along with the artist's palette, palette knife and brushes used for mixing and applying them

1. Canvas is stretched over a wooden frame, or 'stretcher,' and tacked into place. Nowadays, many artists buy their canvases ready-stretched.

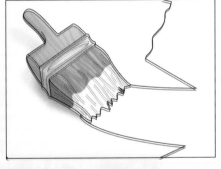

2. The canvas is 'primed,' or coated with a plain layer of paint. This is usually white, but other colors can be used to give different tones to the final picture.

3. Some artists sketch in their design. Then they apply the paint. Oil paints are slow-drying and translucent, so colors can be built up gradually, in layers.

4. Oil paint can be applied smoothly, or thickly so that it retains visible brushmarks. It holds its shape so well, you can even scrape patterns into it.

Modern materials

In the 19th century, developments in the chemical industry gave rise to brighter, more varied colors based on chemical, rather than natural, pigments. Ready-made canvases, ready-mixed paints and new kinds of brushes also became available. In the past, most brushes had been bunched and tied with thread. But the new brushes were bound with metal, so they could have flat tips, which made flatter, squarer marks.

Lots of new techniques have been developed in the last hundred years. Collage, where fabric, newspaper and other materials are stuck onto pictures, was introduced in the early 20th century. Then a completely new kind of paint, acrylic, was invented in the 1950s. Acrylic paintings look similar to oils, but dry much faster. Today, artists continue to experiment, using everything from fluorescent lights and film to waste paper and elephant dung.

Tricks of the trade

Over the centuries, artists have invented many tools to help them design and plan compositions, and solve the difficult problem of representing 3-D subjects on a flat, 2-D surface. Some have used mathematical rules to work out the effects of perspective and the proportions of the human body. Others have experimented with contraptions containing glass, lenses or mirrors to help them draw more accurately.

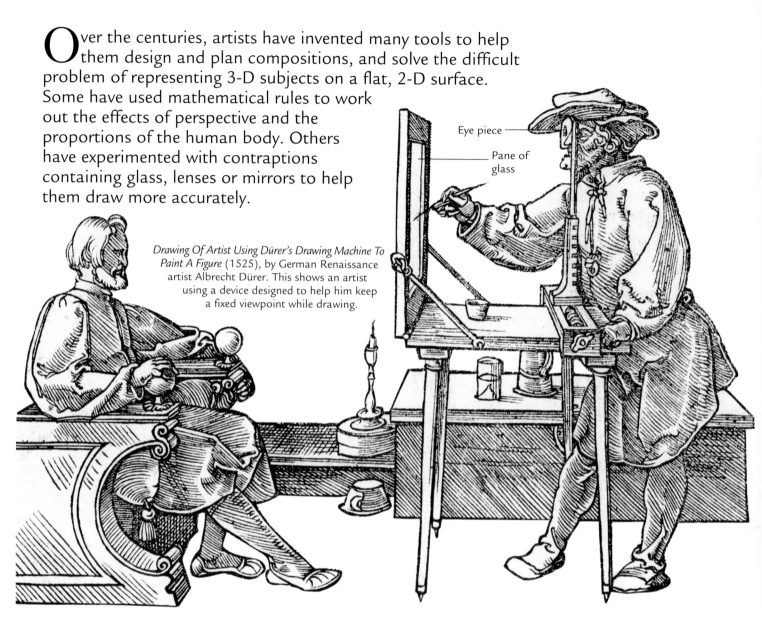

Eye piece

Pane of glass

Drawing Of Artist Using Dürer's Drawing Machine To Paint A Figure (1525), by German Renaissance artist Albrecht Dürer. This shows an artist using a device designed to help him keep a fixed viewpoint while drawing.

Keeping an eye on things

The most lifelike way of drawing a 3-D scene is to show it from one particular viewpoint, at one particular moment, like a snapshot. So the artist and subject have to stay very still – which is difficult when the artist is constantly glancing between the subject and his sketch.

The illustration above shows a 'drawing machine' designed to help. The machine is made up of a fixed eyepiece and a sheet of glass. The eyepiece keeps one of the artist's eyes steady at a fixed point. (His other eye is closed, as it will have a slightly different viewpoint.) He can see his model through the glass, so he can trace the model's outlines without having to move his head. But to turn the sketch into a finished painting, the artist would still have to transfer it to canvas and fill in all the details.

Mirrors and magic

16th-century artists such as Dürer were happy to publish pictures of simple optical aids to help their fellow artists. But they were very secretive about more complex instruments involving lenses and mirrors. These had been invented by this time, but many people believed they worked by witchcraft, which was punishable by death. So anyone using them had to keep very quiet, and we don't know how many artists had them.

Drawing in the dark

One complex device which artists did use is known as a *camera obscura*, which is Latin for 'dark room.' At first, it really was a darkened room, with a tiny hole in one wall. The hole let a small beam of light inside. When the beam fell on a flat surface, it projected an image of whatever was outside in the light. Inside the dark room, the artist placed a piece of paper in the beam and traced the projected image. Lenses could be used to make the image stronger and sharper. Over time, people realized they could make the device much smaller. Eventually, it became a small viewing box, rather like a modern camera.

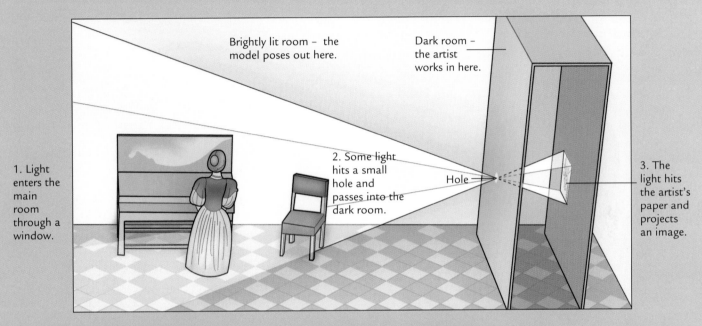

Brightly lit room – the model poses out here.

Dark room – the artist works in here.

1. Light enters the main room through a window.

2. Some light hits a small hole and passes into the dark room.

Hole

3. The light hits the artist's paper and projects an image.

This diagram shows how an artist could set up an early camera obscura.

Who used cameras?

There is a lot of evidence to suggest that two of the artists in this book, Jan Vermeer (see page 70) and Canaletto (see page 79), sketched scenes with the aid of a camera obscura. Joshua Reynolds (see pages 76-77) also owned a portable version, which could be folded away into a case designed to look like a large, leather-bound book. Reynolds may have wanted to hide the fact that he used a drawing aid. Other artists may have had similar contraptions, but the evidence is often very controversial.

Trickery or talent?

A camera obscura helped artists translate 3-D scenes into 2-D pictures more accurately. But it had many disadvantages. The early, room-sized version was awkward to set up. The image it projected was upside down, so the artist had to right it by tracing it or using complex arrangements of mirrors. And it was too dark to see colors properly inside the camera, so it could only be used for initial sketches. Mirrors and lenses could help improve the projected image, but they were expensive and difficult to make. And even then the apparatus could distort things, for example by blurring bright highlights. So artists still needed a huge amount of skill to paint a convincing image.

A Young Woman Standing At A Virginal (about 1670), by Jan Vermeer. You can see a larger reproduction on page 70.

This painting is so accurate, it is possible to reconstruct the room it shows exactly. A 3-D model of the room was used to draw the diagram above.

Preserving pictures

Most things deteriorate gradually with age, and paintings are no exception. The materials they are made from can warp, crack and discolor, completely changing how the paintings look, and eventually destroying them. So museums and galleries have 'conservators,' who look after paintings. They use the latest techniques to preserve and repair pictures and their frames – sometimes making some surprising discoveries in the process.

Changing tastes

Ideas about how paintings should look have changed over time. Nowadays, conservators try to keep pictures as the artists intended. But, in the past, restorers would sometimes paint over part of a picture, if it was damaged, or if they thought their changes would 'improve' it. They even covered paintings in brown varnish, to tone down colors they thought looked too bright.

Now, when a picture is restored, this kind of overpainting and varnish are usually removed, revealing how the picture was originally meant to look. But occasionally old repainting work is left, if the paint beneath has been lost completely. This was the case with the picture on the right, where a whole section had been destroyed.

The Virgin And Child Before A Firescreen (see page 41) dates from the 15th century. But a large strip on the right, including the goblet and Mary's elbow, was actually painted in the 19th century, when restorers reconstructed a missing section. Look for where the varnish changes color – this marks the join.

In the frame

Many pictures have elaborate frames which also need looking after. Often, these have ornate carvings covered in gold leaf, or paper-thin pieces of real gold. Conservators repair damaged sections of frames and, if necessary, replace parts with carefully matched carvings. These are then gilded (coated with gold) by hand, as shown here.

A conservator working on a gilded frame. It can take weeks to restore a large frame like this.

True colors

Over centuries, paintings become very dirty, particularly if they have spent years in smoky, candlelit churches. Some old paintings were varnished to protect them, but varnish turns yellow over time. Conservators can clean off dirt and old varnish to reveal a picture's true colors. But this has to be done very gently, with mild solvents, so as not to damage the paint underneath. Often, old paint cracks, blisters or flakes away, especially if the wood or canvas behind it has warped. Loose flakes of paint are stuck down with special glues and, sometimes, small areas are repaired with touches of carefully matched paint (see below). If the wood or canvas is very warped, conservators can even separate the whole painted layer and attach it to a new backing – a painstaking process that may take years.

A badly discolored painting, before restoration

The same painting, after restoration

These details from Titian's *Bacchus And Ariadne* (see page 51) show the startling difference cleaning and repairs can make. After this picture was cleaned in the 1960s, some people complained that the colors revealed by the process were too bright. But experts today say that these are the original colors and that they match recent discoveries about Titian's techniques and use of pigments.

Making a match

Before repairing damaged paint, conservators examine paint samples and analyze pigments. They try to match an artist's original materials and techniques as closely as possible, to make their repairs blend in.

A conservator repairs damage on Holbein's *The Ambassadors*. You can see the fully restored painting on page 45.

Air-conditioning

Conservators also work to prevent more damage from happening. Warping is caused by heat and dampness, and strong light and air pollution make certain pigments fade or change color. So, in museums and galleries, light levels are controlled and air quality is monitored. Especially fragile pictures can be put behind glass or 'lined' – given extra backing to strengthen them.

Fame and fortune

Works of art often sell for vast sums, a fact that puzzles or even angers many people. It can be difficult to justify the high prices. Art – especially modern art – covers such a broad range of ideas and approaches that it is impossible to get everyone to agree on what things are worth. This spread looks at the awkward question of how art is valued and sold.

> 👁 For a link to a website where you can see details of the top ten most expensive paintings, go to **www.usborne-quicklinks.com**

What's it worth?

The price of a work of art depends on the artist's reputation, current fashion and the state of the art market, as well as the cost of making that work. Rare works are more valuable, so prices often rise after an artist's death. Today, most art is sold by dealers or at auctions. Dealers set their own prices, keeping a percentage of the cost to cover their expenses. If art is auctioned, the price is decided by what people are prepared to bid at the sale.

The record for the most expensive painting is held by Pablo Picasso's *Boy with a Pipe*. In May 2004, it fetched $104 million at auction, beating the previous record-holder, Vincent van Gogh's *Portrait of Dr. Gachet*, which raised $82.5 million in 1990. But records like these reflect only what has come up for sale. A lot of art in museums has never been auctioned and is considered priceless.

Art and money

Some artists have fought against the way they see money dominating art. For example, some 1960s artists chose to make Environmental or Performance art, precisely because it couldn't be bought and sold. Ironically, though, it often had to be financed by art market sales of photographs showing the finished work, or drawings of the artists' plans.

In 2001, British artist Michael Landy created a radical performance piece entitled *Break Down*. He wanted to protest about contemporary values and the emphasis society puts on owning and consuming things. So he organized a team of workers to destroy everything he possessed, from his car to a favorite sheepskin coat. After two weeks, he was left with just the clothes he was wearing and his pet cat. The event was paid for by sponsors, who were meant to receive the debris afterward. But Landy decided to bury it instead – perhaps to ensure it could never be sold.

The auction of Picasso's *Boy with a Pipe* at Sotheby's in New York attracted some of the highest ever bids. Picasso painted this picture when he was only 24 and still struggling to make ends meet.

Sotheby's

SOTHEBYS

Collector's items

Bunny (1997), by Sarah Lucas; tights, chair, clamp, stuffing and wire, 40 x 35 x 25in. This provocative figure is one of the works in the Saatchi Gallery, London. The half-woman, half-rabbit, headless body mocks the idea of attractive women posing as "playboy bunnies."

In the past, wealthy patrons and collectors had a huge influence on art. Most artists worked for patrons, who commissioned them to make paintings or sculptures to order. But, during the 19th century, more art came to be sold through dealers, who sell uncommissioned art directly to the public. This gave artists more creative freedom – though they still needed to sell their work to earn a living.

Most art continues to be sold through dealers today. But individual collectors can have a big impact, setting fashions and creating new museums. American heiress Peggy Guggenheim founded the Guggenheim Museum in Venice, and advertising millionaire Charles Saatchi set up the Saatchi Gallery in London. Saatchi has also done a lot to promote young British artists, such as Damien Hirst and Sarah Lucas. His critics say that he deliberately selects controversial art in order to make headlines. Once the art is better known, it fetches a higher price, so he can sell it on at a profit. But Saatchi himself claims big museums neglect young artists and says he is trying to fill a gap.

Award winners

Another way for artists to gain recognition is through contemporary art prizes. There are several European awards, but the Turner Prize in Britain is perhaps the best known. This prize has often been the focus of fierce protests, including egg-throwing, graffiti and demonstrators in clown suits. In 1993, two millionaire musicians known as the "K Foundation" decided to award a prize to Britain's worst artist, to be chosen from the real Turner Prize shortlist. Sculptor Rachel Whiteread won both prizes, and gave the K Foundation prize money to charity.

In 2003, the media circus which has grown up around the Turner Prize had a field day. The prize went to Grayson Perry, who calls himself a "transvestite potter from Essex". He creates delicately crafted vases with titles such as *Boring Cool People* or *We Are What We Buy*, blurring the distinction between arts and crafts. Despite his unusual dress sense, the judges felt he was a serious artist who bought a radical edge to a traditional medium.

Here, the potter Grayson Perry (who is a man, but likes to wear women's clothes) poses with one of his award-winning vases at the Turner Prize ceremony.

For links to websites where you can see more works from The Saatchi Gallery, London, or find out all about Britain's Turner Prize, go to **www.usborne-quicklinks.com**

169

Faking it

There is a lot of money in art. Paintings by famous artists regularly sell for millions. Some of the most expensive are works by van Gogh; his *Portrait of Dr. Gachet* held the record for over a decade, fetching $82.5 million. With wealthy art lovers willing to pay such vast sums, it is hardly surprising some unscrupulous painters have been tempted to produce fakes. These two pages describe some of the most notorious cases, but there must be hundreds more – many still undiscovered.

Portrait Of Dr. Gachet (1890), by Vincent van Gogh. In 1990, this painting – a genuine van Gogh – sold for a record-breaking sum. But experts say up to 100 drawings and paintings, supposedly by the artist, may in fact be fakes. Limited sales records (van Gogh sold only one painting in his lifetime) and his habit of making copies of his own work make it hard to check the origin of his pictures.

Mona Lisa (1505-14), by Italian artist Leonardo da Vinci. This picture was stolen and its whereabouts unknown for two years. When it was finally recovered, experts examined the pattern of cracks in the varnish and other tiny details to check it was the genuine painting, not a forgery.

MONA LISA GONE! Daring theft of famous painting

One of the most daring art crimes involved the *Mona Lisa* portrait. For years it hung in the Louvre Museum, Paris. But on August 21, 1911, while the Louvre was shut, a workman took it down and quietly disappeared. The police searched the country in vain. Meanwhile, six wealthy Americans were fooled into paying about $300,000 each for fake *Mona Lisas*, in a scam which may have been the real reason for the theft.

Then, in 1913, Vincenzo Perugia told a Florentine antique dealer that he had the real *Mona Lisa*. Doubtful, the dealer asked to see it. So Perugia took him to a hotel and showed him the painting, hidden in a secret compartment in his trunk. The dealer alerted the police and Perugia, who had been hoping for a reward, was arrested. He admitted stealing the portrait after working at the Louvre. But he got off lightly, claiming he had only wanted to return it to Italy. He was given the minimum sentence. As for the painting, it was returned to the Louvre, where it still hangs today.

"I made it!"

Dealer's astonishing claim about valuable Vermeer

After the end of World War Two, a Dutch art dealer named Han van Meegeren was put on trial for collaborating with the Nazis. His crime? Selling them a prized painting by 17th-century Dutch artist, Jan Vermeer. To defend himself, van Meegeren made a startling confession: he had painted the picture himself. To prove it, he created another 'Vermeer' in front of witnesses, completing it in just two months.

As it turned out, van Meegeren had been forging pictures for years.

He had fooled experts by using real 17th-century canvases and carefully replicating old pigments. He had also developed a way of baking his pictures, to 'age' them. But, perhaps most importantly, he was a gifted painter. His fakes were much admired before the con was revealed. At the end of the trial, he was acquitted of collaboration. But he was given a prison sentence for forgery.

Woman Reading A Letter (1935-36), a 'Vermeer' fake by Han van Meegeren. (You can see a genuine Vermeer on page 70.)

Han van Meegeren, in front of the forgery which proved him innocent of Nazi collaboration

Speaking at his trial, Han van Meegeren said:

"Yesterday this picture was worth millions... experts and art lovers would come from all over the world and pay money to see it. Today, it is worth nothing, and nobody would cross the street to see it for free. But the picture has not changed. What has?"

Pictures and their provenances

To check if a painting is genuine, collectors don't just look at the picture itself. They also check its history or 'provenance,' inspecting details of former owners and sales. One of the most successful art crimes of recent times depended on the forgery, not of paintings, but of their provenances.

Together, John Myatt and John Drewe passed off more than 200 pictures in various styles before they were caught and sent to prison. Less than half of these have been recovered. Myatt forged paintings by several artists, including Georges Braque and Henri Matisse. Technically, the fakes weren't very good. Myatt used a mixture of decorator's paint and lubricant gel quite unlike the real artists' paints. But many people were taken in because Drewe, an accomplished document forger, provided them with false sales receipts, and stamps and certificates of authenticity. He even doctored museum records of artists' works.

Passing judgment

Fakes are often interesting pictures in their own right. Forgers might start out copying others, but some build up reputations of their own. For example, Hungarian forger Elmyr de Hory is so well known, other forgers now sign his name on their fakes. So does it matter who made a picture? Many early artists didn't sign their work, and would not have understood our idea of a 'fake.' They judged a picture on its own merits, rather than the fame of the artist. Perhaps collectors today should do the same?

Timeline

These two pages list many of the important dates in history, and in the history of art, so you can compare what happened when.

For links to websites where you can see timelines of the history of art, and find out more about different periods and styles, go to **www.usborne-quicklinks.com**

Pre-1400: ancient and medieval times

ABOUT 35,000BC earliest cave paintings made in France and Spain.

FROM 2628BC pharaohs rule Egypt; great pyramids built in Giza.

ABOUT 2000-1450BC Minoan civilization on Crete.

ABOUT 1600-1200BC Mycenaeans dominate Greece.

ABOUT 1350BC hunting scene painted in nobleman's tomb in Thebes, Egypt.

ABOUT 1000BC Rome founded.

ABOUT 500-338BC Classical age of Greek culture.

146BC Romans conquer Greece.

ABOUT 100BC paper invented in China.

FROM 312 rise of Christianity in Europe.

395 Roman empire is split into two: the eastern Byzantine empire and a western empire centred on Rome.

476 western Roman empire collapses.

726-843 controversy over religious art: 'iconoclasts' destroy pictures, and new religious icons are banned for years.

800 Charlemagne crowned emperor of much of Europe.

ABOUT 800 Book of Kells illuminated.

ABOUT 1150 first European papermill.

1200s Gothic art and architecture flourishes across Europe.

ABOUT 1395-99 Wilton Diptych painted.

About 1400: the Renaissance

1400s oil paints pioneered in northern Europe.

1410-16 Limbourg brothers make The Very Rich Hours for the Duke of Berry.

1434-1737 Medici family control Florence, Italy.

1434 Van Eyck paints the Arnolfini Portrait using oil paints.

1436 Alberti publishes On Painting.

1450 beginning of book printing in Europe; paper widely used.

1453 Byzantine empire collapses.

ABOUT 1485 Botticelli paints Venus and Mars.

ABOUT 1505-14 Leonardo paints the Mona Lisa.

1508-12 Michelangelo paints the Sistine Chapel ceiling for the Pope.

1517 Martin Luther proposes changes to Catholic church, eventually leading to the creation of Protestant religions.

1533 Hans Holbein the Younger paints The Ambassadors.

About 1600: start of the Baroque period

1601 Caravaggio paints The Supper at Emmaus.

1618-48 Thirty Years' War in Europe.

1629-30 Rubens paints Peace and War, to show the benefits of peace.

1648 Dutch Republic founded.

1650s camera obscura in use in Europe.

ABOUT 1700-1800 Grand Tour of Europe at its most popular.

1715-18 Watteau paints The Scale of Love.

ABOUT 1730 height of popularity of ornate Rococo art in Europe.

1754-58 Giovanni Tiepolo paints An Allegory with Venus and Time.

1775-83 American War of Independence.

1777 Scottish engineer James Watt designs a successful steam engine.

1789 an angry mob storms the Bastille Prison in Paris, sparking off the French Revolution.

About 1800 on: era of revolutions

1804-15 Napoleon Bonaparte rules France.

1808-14 'Peninsular War' between France and Spain; in **1814-15** Francisco Goya paints The Third of May 1808 (Executions) showing French soldiers shooting Spanish civilians.

1838 Louis Daguerre invents early photographs, or 'daguerreotypes'.

1841 Metal paint tubes patented.

1844 Turner exhibits Rain, Steam and Speed.

1848 the Pre-Raphaelite Brotherhood is founded; 'Year of Revolution' sees uprisings across Europe; the Communist Manifesto is published.

1870s-80s: Impressionism

1870 Monet paints The Beach at Trouville.

1874 The first Impressionist exhibition is held in Paris.

1878 James Whistler sues critic John Ruskin for libel over comments on Nocturne in Black and Gold (1875).

1880s Cézanne experiments with perspective.

1884-86 Seurat paints A Sunday on La Grande Jatte.

1885 Karl Benz builds the first motor car.

1888 George Eastman mass markets 'Kodak' cameras; van Gogh moves to Arles and begins painting sunflowers; Gauguin helps Sérusier create The Talisman.

1895 Munch creates The Scream.

1897 The Tate Gallery is founded.

1900 Psychiatrist Sigmund Freud publishes 'The Interpretation of Dreams;' his theories about the unconscious inspire the Surrealists.

1903 Wright brothers make the first successful powered flight in America.

1905-20s: Expressionism

1905 Matisse and Derain spend the summer painting at Collioure, France, and earn the nickname *Fauves*; *Die Brücke* art movement forms in Germany.

1906 Cézanne memorial exhibition in Paris; visitors include Picasso and Braque.

1907 Picasso paints *Les Demoiselles d'Avignon*.

1908 Braque paints *Houses at L'Estaque*, described as resembling "a pile of little cubes," giving rise to the name Cubism.

1909 First Futurist Manifesto issued.

1910: Abstract art begins

1910 Kandinsky begins experimenting with abstract art.

1911 Kandinsky and Marc found *Der Blaue Reiter* movement in Germany.

1912 Picasso creates *Still Life with Chair Caning*, one of the first collages.

1913 Malevich begins to work on Suprematism; Duchamp attaches a bicycle wheel to a kitchen stool to create *Bicycle Wheel*, the first readymade.

1914 Wyndham Lewis founds the Vorticist movement in Britain.

1914-18 World War One – 17 million die.

1916 Dada movement founded by artists and writers protesting against the war; first performances at the Cabaret Voltaire.

1917 Russian Revolution; Society of Independent Artists refuse to exhibit Duchamp's readymade *Fountain*; van Doesburg founds *De Stijl* magazine in Holland.

1919 Bauhaus art and design school founded in Weimar, Germany; Spencer paints *Travoys Arriving with Wounded*.

1920 First Constructivist group forms in Russia; its members create many designs for the new Russian government during the early 1920s.

1921 Third International Communist Congress held in Moscow; Tatlin designs a monument to commemorate it.

late 1920s Stalin's government suppresses Constructivism and promotes Soviet Socialist Realism instead.

1924-40s: Surrealism

1925 First Surrealist exhibition is held.

1926-28 Van Doesburg designs the interior of the Café d'Aubette in Strasbourg.

1929 start of the Great Depression; the Museum of Modern Art is founded in New York.

1931 Dali paints *The Persistence of Memory.*

1933 Adolf Hitler comes to power in Germany.

1936-39 Spanish Civil War.

1937 Nazi exhibition of 'degenerate' art in Munich; after it closes, the art is sold abroad or burned.

1938 Chagall paints *White Crucifixion*; Dali creates *Lobster Telephone*.

1939-45 World War Two.

1940-50s: Abstract Expressionism

1943-44 Hepworth creates *Wave.*

1944 Bacon paints *Three Studies for Figures at the Base of a Crucifixion.*

late 1940s Pollock develops Action painting; Rothko begins to create Color Field paintings.

1950-60s: Minimalism, Conceptual art and Pop art

1950s acrylic paints invented.

1956 Hamilton makes *Just What Is It That Make's Today's Homes So Different...?*

1957 Klein patents an intense blue color called "International Klein Blue".

1960 Tinguely's Kinetic sculpture *Homage to New York* self-destructs.

1960s First exhibitions of Minimalist art.

1961 Yuri Gagarin is the first man in space.

1963 Lichtenstein paints *Whaam!*

1964 Warhol creates *Elvis I & II.*

1965 Joseph Beuys performs *How to explain paintings to a dead hare*; Kosuth creates *One and Three Chairs.*

1967 Pop artist Peter Blake designs the cover for Beatles' *Sgt. Pepper* album; Hockney paints *A Bigger Splash.*

1969 Neil Armstrong walks on the moon.

1970s-80s Sherman produces her series of *Untitled Film Stills.*

1977 De Maria creates *The Lightning Field*; the Pompidou Centre opens in Paris, displaying an important collection of modern art.

1980s Hockney begins to work with photomontage.

1981 Kruger creates *Your Gaze Hits the Side of My Face.*

1983 Turner Prize is founded in Britain.

1984 The Saatchi Gallery opens in London, displaying a controversial collection of modern art.

1985 Protest group the Guerilla Girls form in New York; Basquiat paints *Gas Truck.*

1987 Goldsworthy makes *Icicle Star.*

1990s: Britart

1991 Parker makes *Cold Dark Matter*; Quinn sculpts *Self*; Hirst makes *The Impossibility of Death...*

1993 Whiteread creates *House*, a sculpture cast from the inside of a real house.

1994 Hatoum creates *Corps Étranger.*

1995 Kapoor creates *Turning the World Inside Out*; Christo and Jeanne-Claude complete their project *Wrapped Reichstag.*

1996 Ofili creates *Afrodizzia.*

1997 The "Sensation" exhibition of young British artists opens in London, causing a storm of controversy; Mueck creates *Angel.*

1999 Bourgeois creates *Maman*; Wallinger's *Ecce Homo* is displayed in London; Emin's *My Bed* is nominated for the Turner Prize.

2001 Viola creates *Five Angels for the Millennium.*

2004 Picasso's *Boy with a Pipe* sells for a record U.S. $104 million at auction.

About the artists

If you want to find out more about the artists in this book, you can read short biographies of them here.

For even more information, go to **www.usborne-quicklinks.com**, where you will find links to some useful websites.

Leon Battista ALBERTI (1404-72)
Italian artist, architect and writer. He wrote *On Painting* (1436), describing how to use light, color and perspective to make pictures look more realistic.

Carl ANDRE (Born 1935)
American sculptor. Associated with Minimalism. Started out working on railways, which gave him the idea of using standard, repeated elements, such as bricks.

Hans ARP (1887-1966)
German-born painter and sculptor. Joined the Dada group in Zurich during the First World War. Later developed his own abstract, geometric style. Worked with **van Doesburg** on the Café d'Aubette.

Francis BACON (1909-92)
Irish-born British painter. Friend of **Freud**. Worked as an interior designer before turning to painting. Developed a dramatic, Expressionist style. Many of his paintings feature distorted human figures, often based on portraits of friends.

Alesso BALDOVINETTI (about 1426-99)
Italian painter. Also made stained glass and mosaics. Studied in Florence.

Hugo BALL (1886-1927)
German writer. Founded the Cabaret Voltaire in Zurich in 1916 and took part in Dada performances there.

Giacomo BALLA (1871-1958)
Italian artist. First worked as an illustrator, caricaturist and portrait painter. Founded Futurism with **Marinetti**. He also designed Futurist furniture and clothing.

Jean-Michel BASQUIAT (1960-1988)
Hispanic-African-American painter. Became famous as a graffiti artist in New York, going by the tag 'Samo.' Later worked with **Warhol**. His exuberant, aggressive style had great commercial success. Died from a drugs overdose at the age of only 28.

Giovanni BELLINI (about 1430-1516)
Italian painter. His father and brother were also artists. Worked in oil paint, then more common in the Netherlands, and developed techniques which revolutionized Venetian painting. Influenced **Giorgione** and **Titian**.

Bartolomé BERMEJO (worked 1460-98)
Spanish painter. Known for his religious scenes. Influenced by Netherlandish art.

Gian Lorenzo BERNINI (1598-1680)
Italian sculptor and architect. Helped establish the Baroque style. Designed many large buildings in Rome, including the square and buildings in front of St. Peter's. Made busts of important people.

Joseph BEUYS (1921-86)
German artist. Studied medicine, then joined the air force in 1940. After WWII, dedicated his life to art. Made professor of sculpture at Düsseldorf Academy in 1961. Dismissed for allowing 50 rejected students to attend class. Became more and more involved in politics. Believed that art could change society, and that "everyone is an artist."

Peter BLAKE (born 1932)
British artist. Member of the Pop Art movement. Uses comics and magazines to make collages, often showing cult figures such as Marilyn Monroe. Has also designed record covers.

Fritz BLEYL (1880-1966)
German architect. One of the founders of the Expressionist group, *Die Brücke*, with his friends **Kirchner, Heckel** and **Schmidt-Rottluff**.

Umberto BOCCIONI (1882-1916)
Italian painter and sculptor. Knew **Marinetti** and helped write the Futurists' *Technical Manifesto*. Pioneered Futurist sculpture, sometimes in mixed media. Enlisted in the army in WWI and was killed falling from a horse.

Sandro BOTTICELLI (about 1445-1510)
Italian painter. Real name Alessandro Filipepi. Born in Florence. Renowned for his paintings of classical myths such as *Venus and Mars* and *The Birth of Venus*. Also made just as many religious works.

Louise BOURGEOIS (born 1911)
French-American sculptor. Studied in Paris with **Brancusi** and **Giacometti**. Creates sculptures and installations using many different media including metal, wood and fabric. Much of her work explores the body, power and surveillance.

Constantin BRANCUSI (1876-1957)
Romanian-French sculptor. Moved to Paris in 1904, where he became friends with **Matisse** and **Picasso**. Known for his strikingly original, modern-looking works such as *Bird in Space*.

Georges BRAQUE (1882-1963)
French artist. Was a decorator before studying art in Paris. Influenced by the Impressionists and Fauves. From 1907-14 (when he was called up), worked closely with **Picasso** developing Cubism.

André BRETON (1896-1966)
French poet and leader of the Surrealists. Argued Surrealism should include art when many of its supporters believed it should be a strictly literary movement.

Pieter BRUEGEL (1564-1638)
Flemish artist. His sons and grandsons also became painters. Became known for his landscapes and often humorous scenes of country life.

Filippo BRUNELLESCHI (1377-1446)
Italian sculptor and architect. Trained as a goldsmith. Designed many buildings in Florence, including the cathedral dome.

Robert CAMPIN (about 1378-1444)
Dutch painter. Also known as the Master of Flémalle. Painted religious works in a natural-looking way.

CANALETTO (1697-1768)
Italian painter. Real name Giovanni Antonio Canal. 'Canaletto' means 'little canal' in Italian. Famous for his pictures of Venice, which he sold to tourists. Came to London in the 1740s, but his English pictures were less popular.

CARAVAGGIO (1571-1610)
Italian painter. Real name Michelangelo Merisi, or Amerighi. Known as 'Caravaggio' after his birthplace. His work was sensational and innovative, breaking from tradition by showing religious figures as ordinary people. Helped develop the dramatic Baroque style, specializing in light and shade. Had many fights and had to flee Rome after killing a man.

Paul CEZANNE (1839-1906)
French painter. Abandoned legal studies to become a painter. Worked in Paris where he met **Pissarro**, **Monet** and **Renoir**. Then moved back to southern France and turned his attention to landscapes, developing an almost geometric way of working. Greatly influenced the Cubists.

Marc CHAGALL (1887-1985)
Russian-born painter. Influenced by Expressionism and Cubism, as well as his own Jewish background. Many of his works celebrate Russian-Jewish culture or reflect personal feelings.

Philippe de CHAMPAIGNE (1602-74)
Flemish painter. Worked in Paris. Trained as a landscape artist, but made his name painting portraits and religious subjects.

Jean Baptiste Siméon CHARDIN (1699-1779)
French painter. Son of a craftsman. Worked as a restorer. Became known for his still lifes and scenes of everyday life, though these were not fashionable subjects at the time. Later became president of the French Academy of Arts. Influenced **Manet**.

CHRISTO (born 1935)
Bulgarian sculptor. Works largely in the U.S. Has become famous, with his wife Jeanne-Claude, for creating large-scale outdoor works by wrapping things, or using fencing or umbrellas.

Jacopo di CIONE (about 1325-99)
Italian painter. The youngest of four brothers, all artists. Completed many large commissions in Florence.

CLAUDE Lorrain (1600-82)
French painter (actually born in the independent Duchy of Lorraine). Real name Claude Gellée. May have begun his career as a pastry cook in Rome. Painted atmospheric landscapes, often with biblical or mythological themes. Recorded all his drawings in a portfolio, the *Liber Veritatis*, to prevent forgeries.

Chuck CLOSE (born 1940)
American painter. Associated with Photorealism and known for his incredibly lifelike, detailed pictures of family and friends. Had to adapt his methods after he was badly disabled in 1988, and developed a looser, more colorful style.

John CONSTABLE (1776-1837)
British painter. Worked in his father's windmills in Suffolk, where he said he learned to study the sky. Then went to London to become a painter. Did portraits before committing himself to landscapes. Taught himself to reproduce the effects of light and weather. Was often compared to **Turner** (whose work was more popular at the time in England). Much admired in France and an influence on **Delacroix**.

Lucas CRANACH (1472-1553)
German painter, engraver and illustrator. A Protestant, and friend of the religious reformer Martin Luther. Made pro-Protestant woodcuts. Known for his portraits and scenes with the Virgin Mary.

Carlo CRIVELLI (about 1430-94)
Italian painter. Developed a decorative style using gold leaf. Very skilled in the use of perspective. Made many religious works, including *The Annunciation* (1486).

Salvador DALI (1904-89)
Spanish artist, designer and writer. Expelled from the Madrid Academy of Art. Moved to Paris and met **Picasso** and **Miró**. Became a leading Surrealist, making films and paintings illustrating the world of the unconscious. Went to the U.S. to avoid WWII. Flamboyant and eccentric, he once gave a lecture in an old-fashioned diving suit, accompanied by two wolf hounds. He claimed, "The only difference between me and a madman is that I am not mad!"

Jaques-Louis DAVID (1748-1825)
French painter. Leading figure of Neoclassical painting. Dominated art in France from the outbreak of the French Revolution to the fall of Napoleon, making successful political paintings for very different regimes.

Edgar DEGAS (1834-1917)
French artist. Studied law then art. Known for his paintings of dancers, racehorses and city life. Also made pastels and sculptures exploring movement. Exhibited with the Impressionists but didn't share all their ideas. Became a recluse in old age, suffering ill health.

Eugène DELACROIX (1798-1863)
French painter. Successful history painter and a leading figure of the Romantic movement. His loose, colorful style is often contrasted with the stricter, Classical work of **David** and **Ingres**.

Robert DELAUNAY (1885-1941)
French painter. Made stage sets, then turned to art. Interested in color theory and Cubism. Known for his almost abstract pictures of colored circles.

Walter DE MARIA (born 1935)
American sculptor. Associated with Land Art. His works include filling a gallery with soil up to waist height, and *Lightning Field*, an installation of 400 steel poles arranged in a grid in a field in New Mexico.

André DERAIN (1880-1954)
French painter. Studied alongside **Matisse**. In his youth, known as one of the Fauves. Later experimented with Cubism, and knew **Picasso** and **Braque**.

Otto DIX (1891-1970)
German painter and graphic artist. Influenced by **van Gogh** and the Futurists. Fought in WWI. Afterwards, war became a dominant theme in his work. Like **Grosz**, known for his satirical paintings about social corruption. After WWII he turned to painting religious subjects.

DUCCIO di Buoninsegna (about 1260-1319)
Italian painter. Influenced by Byzantine art. Clashed with authority, but rose to a position of power and wealth, becoming a leading master of the Sienese style. Known for his religious works.

Marcel DUCHAMP (1887-1968)
French artist. Worked as a librarian while studying art. Early paintings were  influenced by Cubism. Became a leader of the Dada and Surrealist movements in New York. His 'readymades' changed people's views about what constitutes art. Also a professional chess player.

Albrecht DURER (1471-1528)
German artist. Son of a goldsmith. Famous for his engravings and woodcuts, which were widely reproduced. Studied Italian painting in Italy, and combined the innovations of the Renaissance there with northern artistic traditions.

Tracey EMIN (born 1963)
British artist. Associated with Britart. Works include paintings, prints and sculptures, as well as installations. Much of her work is autobiographical.

Carel FABRITIUS (1622-54)
Dutch painter. Real name Carel Pietersz. Pupil of **Rembrandt** and teacher of **Vermeer**. Killed in the explosion of a gunpowder warehouse in Delft. Fewer than a dozen of his paintings are known.

Dan FLAVIN (born 1933)
American artist. Associated with Minimalism, but said the label was "objectionable." Specializes in sculptures using fluorescent light tubes.

Lucian FREUD (born 1922)
British painter. Grandson of Sigmund Freud and friend of **Bacon**. His subjects are often people in his life, such as friends, relatives and lovers.

Caspar David FRIEDRICH (1774-1840)
German painter. Leader of the German Romantic movement. Known for his symbolic, atmospheric landscapes.

Thomas GAINSBOROUGH (1727-88)
British painter. Influenced by **Watteau**, Dutch and Rococo art. Born in Suffolk, but made his  name in Bath, a fashionable spa town, where his flattering portraits were very popular. Later moved to London. Loved painting landscapes, sometimes basing them on models made from broccoli and other materials.

Paul GAUGUIN (1848-1903)
French painter and sculptor. A sailor and then a stockbroker, he gave up his job to become an artist, but found it hard to make ends meet. He developed a flat, colorful style which influenced the Nabis. Worked in rural France, at one point living with **van Gogh**, then went to the South Seas, where he died.

Théodore GERICAULT (1791-1824)
French painter and sculptor. Became a leading figure of the Romantic movement in France. Often painted horses, but also darker subjects such as *The Raft of the 'Medusa'* (1819). Worked with Ingres and **Delacroix** in Italy. Later visited England.

Mark GERTLER (1891-1939)
British painter. Son of Polish-Jewish immigrants. Studied in London along with **Spencer**. Painted *Merry-Go-Round*, considered by many critics to be the most important painting of WWI. Depressed by ill health and inability to sell paintings, he tragically committed suicide in 1939.

Alberto GIACOMETTI (1901-66)
Swiss sculptor and painter. Son of a painter. Known for his sculptures of eerily thin figures. Friend of **Picasso** and writers Simone de Beauvoir, Jean-Paul Sartre and Samuel Beckett.

GILBERT and GEORGE
Two artists, Gilbert (Proesch, born in Italy in 1943) and George (Passmore, born in Britain in 1942). Initially known as performance artists, always wearing identical suits. Many early works featured them as 'living sculptures.' Later works include films, installations and large, colorful photomontages, often using shocking images.

Luca GIORDANO (1634-1705)
Italian painter. An important decorative artist who introduced the Baroque style to southern Italy. Completed many commissions in Italy and Spain, working so fast that he was nicknamed *Luca Fa Presto* ('Luca does it quickly').

GIORGIONE (about 1478-1510)
Italian painter. Born Giorgio, or Zorzi, da Castelfranco. Greatly influenced **Titian**. Died young, leaving several unfinished works. These were then completed by other artists, especially **Titian**.

GIOTTO di Bondone (about 1266-1337)
Italian painter and architect. Very successful early Renaissance artist, admired by **Michelangelo**. Designed many important buildings in Italy. Also famous for his frescoes.

GIOVANNI di Paolo (about 1403-82)
Italian painter. Trained in Siena and influenced by other Sienese artists, but developed a very personal style. Produced many works over his long career.

Andy GOLDSWORTHY (born 1956)
British artist. Worked on a farm as a teenager, forming an interest in nature. Makes sculptures from natural materials. These often decay, so they are preserved only through photos and documents.

Francisco GOYA (1746-1828)
Spanish painter. Worked in Madrid, creating portraits of wealthy patrons in an elegant style inspired by **Velázquez**, **Gainsborough** and **Reynolds**. Also painted everyday scenes. Probably best-known for his shocking scenes of war and nightmares.

Juan GRIS (1887-1927)
Spanish painter and sculptor. Real name José Gonzalez. Became friends with **Picasso** in Paris and joined the avant-garde movement. Made slow progress until an art dealer gave him a contract. Then he could afford to focus more on his art and became a leading Cubist.

Walter GROPIUS (1883-1969)
German architect and teacher. Set up Bauhaus, an art school where all students studied arts, crafts and design.

George GROSZ (1893-1959)
German painter. Deeply marked by his experiences fighting in WWI. Fiercely critical of post-war Germany, he made satirical drawings attacking the German government. A founding member of the Berlin Dada group. When the Nazis rose to power, he emigrated to the U.S.

The GUERILLA GIRLS (founded 1985)
Anonymous group of women artists based in New York. Formed to campaign on issues such as sexism and racism in film, art and politics. Members use the names of dead women artists and wear gorilla masks to hide their identities.

Richard HAMILTON (born 1922)
British artist. His art studies were interrupted by WWII, when he worked as a draughtsman. After the war, became a leading Pop artist. Also an influential teacher and writer.

William Michael HARNETT (1848-92)
Irish-born U.S. painter. Trained as a silverware engraver before turning to painting. Specialized in detailed *trompe l'oeil* still lifes, painting objects so accurately they almost look real.

Mona HATOUM (born 1952)
Palestinian-born artist. Has lived in Britain since 1975. Became known in the 1980s for her performance work. Since then, has concentrated on video, installations and sculptures, focusing on themes such as violence and oppression.

John HEARTFIELD (1891-1968)
German artist. Born Helmut Herzfelde, but changed his name in 1916 to protest against German nationalism. Best known for his satirical photomontages.

Erich HECKEL (1883-1970)
German painter. Formed the German Expressionist group, *Die Brücke*, with **Kirchner, Schmidt-Rottluff** and **Bleyl**. During WWII the Nazis condemned his art as "degenerate" and much was destroyed.

Barbara HEPWORTH (1903-1975)
British sculptor. Created geometric and organic forms pierced with holes. Was friends with **Moore** and influenced his work.

Damien HIRST (born 1965)
British artist. Achieved recognition and notoriety through his provocative works using dead animals suspended in formaldehyde preservative. Has also made works inspired by pharmaceutical products. Once created an arrangement of rubbish for a London gallery, only to have a cleaner clear it away by mistake.

Meindert HOBBEMA (1638-1709)
Dutch painter. His natural-looking landscapes were popular after his death, but he was poorly paid in his lifetime and had to work as a customs officer.

David HOCKNEY (born 1937)
British artist. Born in the north of England, but moved to California in the 1960s. Associated with Pop art, though hates the label. Known for his portraits and pictures of swimming pools, painted in a clean, flat style. Also experimented with photos, faxes and photocopies, and designed stage sets for operas.

William HOGARTH (1697-1764)
British painter. Trained in print-making. Popular as a caricaturist as well as a painter. Celebrated for his depictions of contemporary English society and illustrations of moral tales.

Hans HOLBEIN the younger (about 1497/98-1543)
German artist. Designed woodcuts for books, and painted portraits and religious scenes. Met the English king, Henry VIII, then spent much of his time working for him, painting portraits and designing court costumes, silverware, jewelry and triumphal arches.

Pieter de HOOCH (1629-84)
Dutch painter. Started out as a footman for a rich merchant. Painted scenes of middle-class life, like his fellow Dutch artist and contemporary **Vermeer**. Later turned to painting upper-class life in Amsterdam, but with less success.

Edward HOPPER (1882-1967)
U.S. painter and commercial illustrator. Admired for his realistic, atmospheric landscapes. His use of moody lighting helped create a distinctive American style.

Gary HUME (born 1962)
British painter. Calls himself a "beauty terrorist." Known for his glossy images of everything from doors and flowers to Michael Jackson's face after plastic surgery.

Jean-Auguste-Dominique INGRES (1780-1867)
French painter. Made a living from portraits, including several for Napoleon. Painted in the Neoclassical style developed by David, though his choice of subjects was influenced by Romanticism. Leader of the Neoclassicists after **David**.

JEANNE-CLAUDE See **CHRISTO**

Donald JUDD (1928-1994)
U.S. artist. Known as a Minimalist sculptor though he disliked the label. Worked with industrial materials, such as sheet metal and plywood. His later works were built by professional metal workers.

Wilhelm KALF (1622-93)
Dutch painter. Worked mainly in Amsterdam creating still lifes.

Vassily KANDINSKY (1866-1944)
Russian painter. Studied law before turning to art. Worked in Germany, Russia and France. Founded the avant-garde group *Der Blaue Reiter* with **Marc**. One of the first abstract artists. Said he was inspired to create abstract art by seeing a painting which had fallen on its side. Taught at the German art school, the Bauhaus. Had many works confiscated by the Nazis. In 1933, moved to France, where he worked with **Miró**.

Anish KAPOOR (born 1954)
Indian-British sculptor. Grew up in Bombay, but came to London to study art. Creates abstract forms, sometimes covered with bright pigments imported from India. Says he wants his sculptures to look as if they have come "from another world."

Ernst Ludwig KIRCHNER (1880-1938)
German artist. Studied art and architecture. Helped found the avant-garde group *Die Brücke*. Discharged from the army during WWI because of a mental breakdown. Completed several frescoes while recovering. In 1937, the Nazis condemned his art as 'degenerate.' Committed suicide in 1938.

Yves KLEIN (1928-62)
French artist. Studied judo and languages before turning to art. Worked with natural substances such as pure pigment, gold leaf and real sponge. Loved intense colors and patented his own shade of blue. Also staged performances. In 1958, defied convention by exhibiting bare walls in a Paris gallery. Later experimented with fire and water.

Gustav KLIMT (1862-1918)
Austrian artist. Set up a firm in Vienna producing mosaics and murals, and had a great influence on decorative art. One of several Viennese artists who resigned from official posts in order to focus on modern art. His paintings of alluring women scandalized some people at the time. Perhaps best known for *The Kiss* (1908).

Jeff KOONS (born 1955)
U.S. artist. Creates sculptures out of inflatable toys and other kitsch objects. Also works with photography.

Joseph KOSUTH (born 1945)
U.S. artist. Trained in New York. Known for his Conceptual artworks using dictionary definitions of words.

Barbara KRUGER (born 1945)
U.S. artist. Started out designing magazines. Her art combines magazine-style photographs and slogan-like text. It is designed to challenge viewers to think about political issues such as feminism and consumer culture.

Nicholas LANCRET (1690-1743)
French painter. Studied with **Watteau** and imitated his work.

Michael LANDY (born 1963)
British artist. Creates installations and performances. Probably best-known for his work *Break Down*, where he catalogued and destroyed all his possessions.

Fernand LEGER (1881-1955)
French painter. Trained as an architect. His early Cubist paintings were nicknamed 'tubist' because of the tube-like shapes he created. Also designed film sets and costumes. Served in WWI and lived in the U.S. during WWII.

LEONARDO da Vinci (1452-1519)
Italian painter, sculptor, architect, inventor and engineer. Studied in Florence. Worked in Florence and Milan as an artist and military engineer. Moved to the French court in 1517 and remained in France till his death. Received many commissions, but left several unfinished. Perhaps best known for the *Mona Lisa* portrait (c.1505-14). His notebooks, in mirror writing, contain detailed studies of anatomy and perspective, as well as many inventions.

Percy Wyndham LEWIS (1882-1957)
British writer and painter. Influenced by the Futurists, he argued for the value of violence, energy and machines. Was an official War Artist in WWII. Stopped painting after he went blind in 1951, but continued writing.

Roy LICHTENSTEIN (1923-97)
American painter and sculptor. A university teacher and leading Pop artist. Began painting cartoons after one of his sons pointed to a comic book and challenged him to do better. Known for his striking comic-strip images, painted to mimic cheap printing processes.

The LIMBOURG brothers (worked in the early 1400s, all died by 1416)
Flemish artists. The three brothers – Paul, Jean and Herman – made illuminated manuscripts. *The Very Rich Hours*, created for the Duke of Berry, is a masterpiece of the International Gothic style.

El LISSITZKY (1890-1941)
Russian artist. Born Lazar Markovich Lisitskii. Studied architecture in Germany until WWI forced him to return to Russia. Taught architecture and graphics with **Malevich**. Also designed books. Made influential abstract paintings in the 1920s. Later concentrated on design.

Richard LONG (born 1945)
British artist. Known for making Land art based on long walks in remote areas, from the Arctic Circle to the Himalayas. Also uses natural materials such as mud and stones to create indoor works.

Sarah LUCAS (born 1962)
British artist. Associated with Britart. Uses everyday objects, often arranged in a humorous way, to create challenging works about subjects such as sex and death.

René MAGRITTE (1898-1967)
Belgian painter. Briefly earned a living designing wallpaper and drawing fashion advertisements. Knew the Surrealists, including **Dali** and **Miró**, and developed his own version of Surrealism. His paintings only received wide attention after WWII, and have since influenced posters and advertising.

Kasimir MALEVICH (1878-1935)
Russian painter. Experimented with various styles, and invented Suprematism, the abstract geometric style for which he is known. Designed opera costumes and scenery. Also an art teacher and theorist.

Edouard MANET (1832-83)
French painter. Greatly influenced by Spanish art. His work often provoked criticism at home, but was much admired by the Impressionists. *Olympia* (1865) was one of his most controversial paintings. It scandalized many people by breaking with convention and showing a female nude in modern surroundings, looking directly at the viewer. Although the writer Emile Zola defended him, he only found wide appreciation in his final years.

Franz MARC (1880-1916)
German painter. Son of a landscape painter. Founded the group *Der Blaue Reiter* with **Kandinsky**. Explored colors in a way partly inspired by **Delaunay**, and developed his own Expressionist style. He often painted animals, and gave lessons in animal anatomy. Killed in WWI.

F.T. MARINETTI (1876-1944)
Italian poet. Creator and leader of the Futurist movement. Author of the first Futurist Manifesto and the *Futurist Cookbook*.

MASACCIO (1401- about 1428)
Italian painter. Real name Tommaso di Giovanni. Worked in Florence. An inventive early Renaissance artist, he used his knowledge of perspective, anatomy and shading to paint religious scenes in a more realistic way. Influenced **Michelangelo**.

Henri MATISSE (1869-1954)
French painter and sculptor. Abandoned law studies to become an artist. Leader of the Fauve group and known for using bright, decorative colors. Mainly painted women, interiors and still lifes. Influenced the Expressionists but, unlike them, tried to represent happy emotions. With **Picasso**, one of the most influential artists of the 20th century. Admired **Cézanne** and bought his small painting *Bathers* in 1899, which he claimed sustained him spiritually through hard times. Claimed art should be comforting, "like a good armchair."

MICHELANGELO Buonarroti (1475-1564)
Italian sculptor, painter, architect and poet. Like **Leonardo**, one of the most important artists in Renaissance Italy. Nicknamed the 'divine Michelangelo,'

he worked for two popes, but found their demanding commissions frustrating. Created beautiful marble sculptures, including the famous statue of David in Florence. Probably best-known for his frescoes in the Sistine Chapel (1508-12). Also designed several important buildings, including St. Peter's in the Vatican.

John Everett MILLAIS (1829-96)
British painter. Studied art at the Royal Academy, London, from the age of 11. Founder member of the Pre-Raphaelite Brotherhood, along with **Rossetti**. Known for his detailed religious and historical paintings. Friend of influential art critic John Ruskin, until he married Ruskin's ex-wife. Later became Sir John and president of the Royal Academy.

Joan MIRO (1893-1983)
Spanish painter. Gave up work as a clerk after suffering a nervous breakdown. Exhibited with the Surrealists in Paris. Became known for his quirky, detailed paintings, though later simplified his style. Also did sculptures, etchings and murals.

Piet MONDRIAN (1872-1944)
Dutch painter. Began painting traditional landscapes, but soon made them brighter and more stylized. In 1909, he moved to Paris, where he was influenced by Cubism. His work became more linear and abstract, until it was a grid of black lines with blocks of primary colors. Leading member of Dutch art and design movement known as *De Stijl*.

Claude MONET (1840-1926)
French painter. Loved painting outside, directly from nature. His chief concern was the changing effect of natural light. Worked with **Renoir**, **Manet** and others to develop Impressionism – the name was taken from criticism leveled at his picture *Impression, Sunrise* (1872). Probably best-known for his water lily paintings, made in his own garden at Giverny in northern France.

Henry MOORE (1898-1986)
British sculptor. Influenced by ancient sculptures and by **Hepworth**, with whom he studied. Early in his career, he carved sculptures from wood and stone, often depicting figures or family groups. During WWII, a lack of available materials led him to turn to drawing. Famously sketched people sheltering from bombs in the London Underground. After the war, he turned mainly to large bronze castings, often of reclining women, or mothers and children.

Gustave MOREAU (1826-98)
French painter. Taught **Matisse**. Made detailed, mysterious paintings of religious and historical subjects. His style became known as Symbolism.

Berthe MORISOT (1841-95)
French painter. Studied in Paris and exhibited with the Impressionists. Encouraged **Manet**, her brother-in-law, to paint out of doors.

Ron MUECK (born 1948)
Australian-born artist. Started out making puppets and models for films. Creates extremely detailed figures using specialist techniques developed for films. Some of his sculptures are larger than life, and some smaller; none are actually life-size. Son-in-law of **Rego**.

Edvard MUNCH (1863-1944)
Norwegian painter. Influenced by **van Gogh**, he made intense, emotion-filled paintings and prints. His mother and sister died of TB during his childhood, and death is a recurring theme in his work. His best-known work, *The Scream* (1893), inspired the Expressionists.

Bartolomé Esteban MURILLO (1617-82)
Spanish painter. Contemporary of **Velázquez** and first president of the Seville Academy. His beautiful, sentimental images of the Virgin Mary were very popular in the 17th and 18th centuries.

Caspar NETSCHER
(about 1635/6-84)
Dutch painter. Settled in the Hague. Painted genre, religious and mythological scenes, then devoted himself to portraits.

Chris OFILI (born 1968)
British artist. His parents come from Nigeria and much of his work draws on his African roots, as well as cultural references and popular material ranging from contemporary black music to 1970s comics. Known for his use of elephant dung in his paintings.

Georgia O'KEEFFE (1887-1986)
U.S. painter. Early works included landscapes, townscapes and flowers. Married photographer and art dealer Alfred Stieglitz in 1924. Spent much of her later life in Mexico, painting buildings, landscapes and animal bones. Helped pioneer abstract art in America.

Giovanni Paolo PANINI (1691-1765)
Italian painter. Specialized in landscapes, picturesque ruins and architecture.

Cornelia PARKER (born 1956)
British artist. Best-known for large-scale installations involving violently destroyed objects, such as silver squashed by a steamroller and objects blown up, or burned by lightning or meteors.

Joachim PATINIR
(about 1485-1524)
Flemish painter. First known landscape specialist in European art.

James PEALE (1749-1831)
U.S. painter. Specialized in incredibly lifelike paintings of fruit and flowers and other still lifes. Also painted miniatures and landscapes.

Grayson PERRY (born 1960)
British ceramic artist. Makes pots decorated with challenging images addressing social and political issues. Enjoys attacking stereotypes, including gender, by dressing up as a female character named Claire. Critical of what he sees as the banality of society.

Pablo Ruiz PICASSO
(1881-1973)
Spanish painter and sculptor. A child prodigy, encouraged to paint by his father, an artist and art teacher. Visited Paris in the early 1900s, then settled there, meeting many writers and artists. Developed Cubism with **Braque**, inspired by African art and **Cézanne**. Continued to experiment all his life, creating many innovative works and becoming one of the most famous 20th-century artists. As well as paintings, made sculptures and ceramics, and designed stage sets. A very fast worker, he completed an average of 8.7 pictures each day of his adult life.

PIERO della Francesca (1415/20-92)
Italian painter and mathematician. Used geometry to work out perspective and create harmonious compositions. He was a central figure of the Renaissance and an inspiration to the Cubists. But his work was not very fashionable. In old age, devoted himself to studying math.

PISANELLO (about 1395-1455)
Italian painter and medal-maker. Real name Antonio Pisano. The last and most celebrated artist of the ornate International Gothic style. Known for his detailed, graceful paintings and frescoes. Also produced many portrait medallions.

Camille PISSARRO (1830-1903)
French painter. Knew **Manet** and **Monet**. Earned his living by teaching and painting decorative blinds and fans. A major Impressionist and a great influence on **Cézanne**.

Antonio POLLAIUOLO (about 1432-98)
Italian artist. Inspired by the classical past, he made a detailed study of anatomy. His brother Piero was also an artist, and often worked with him.

Jackson POLLOCK (1912-56)
American painter. Leading figure of Abstract Expressionism. His early work was influenced by ancient myths, and by the work of **Picasso** and the

Surrealists. In the late 1940s, he began his famous 'drip' paintings, splashing, dribbling and pouring paint onto canvases laid flat on the floor. Photographs of him at work looked so energetic, the technique was dubbed Action painting. He also experimented with using sand, glass, cigarette ends and other materials to create texture. He was killed in a road accident at the age of 44.

Lyubov POPOVA (1889-1924)
Russian painter and designer. Pioneered abstract painting with **Malevich**, but later joined the Constructivist movement and gave up painting to work on design projects. Died of scarlet fever.

Nicolas POUSSIN (1594-1665)
French painter. Moved to Rome, where he found inspiration in the hilly landscape and Roman ruins. In 1640, he was called back to France to run the prestigious Academy, but returned to Rome only two years later. He developed the genre of grand history paintings, much admired by the Academy.

Marc QUINN (born 1964)
British sculptor. Associated with Britart. Studied at Cambridge University. Many of his works use casts of his own body. Best known for *Self*, a model of his head made from his own blood. Has also worked with frozen flowers.

RAPHAEL (1483-1520)
Italian painter. Real name Raffaello Sanzio. A very successful Renaissance artist, along with **Michelangelo** and **Leonardo**. His big commissions included decorating the pope's rooms and designing tapestries for the Sistine Chapel in the Vatican. He also painted many fine portraits, pictures of the Virgin Mary and Classical scenes. His attention to gesture and expression inspired many later artists.

Robert RAUSCHENBERG (born 1925)
U.S. artist. Studied medicine, then drafted into the U.S. navy in WWII. Studied art after the war. Influenced by Dada and Surrealism, his work combines painting, collage and readymades. Also uses print and photographic processes, and has designed sets and costumes. In 1953, he erased a drawing donated by fellow artist Willem de Kooning to create a work called *Erased de Kooning*.

Odilon REDON (1840-1916)
French artist and writer. An important Symbolist. Fuelled by his imagination and love of literature, he created dramatic pastel drawings and prints, as well as richly colored paintings.

Paula REGO (born 1935)
Portuguese-born painter and illustrator, living in Britain since 1976. Says illustrated children's books were her greatest influence. Her work explores power, sexuality and social codes.

REMBRANDT Harmensz van Rijn (1606-69)
Dutch painter. Also worked as a teacher and art dealer. A prolific artist, painting everything from nudes to landscapes, biblical scenes and self portraits. He is known for his atmospheric use of light and shade. He made most of his money from portraits, but fell out with his patrons and went bankrupt.

Pierre-Auguste RENOIR (1841-1919)
French painter. Trained as a porcelain painter. Studied with **Monet** and was one of the most successful Impressionists. Painted outdoors, directly from the subject, using soft colors. In later life, he also made sculptures.

Joshua REYNOLDS (1723-92)
British painter and portrait artist. Worked for the British king, George III. Tried to develop a more formal kind of portrait, influenced by Classical sculpture. Founded the Royal Academy of Art in London, and was elected its first president. Later knighted, becoming Sir Joshua.

Alexander RODCHENKO (1891-1956)
Russian artist. Worked with the Constructivists. Also experimented with photography, created theater designs and made several film documentaries. Early in his career, he worked for **Tatlin**.

Dante Gabriel ROSSETTI (1828-82)
British painter and poet. Brother of the poet Christina Rossetti. Helped found the Pre-Raphaelite Brotherbood with **Millais**, but did not share the PRB's realistic approach to painting. Developed his own more Romantic style, making idealized paintings of beautiful women. He married the artist's model Elizabeth Siddal, who died tragically young. He threw a book of his poems into her grave, but dug them up later so he could publish them.

Mark ROTHKO (1903-70)
Russian-born U.S. painter. A leading Abstract Expressionist. Inspired first by **Miró** and the Surrealists, he later specialized in abstract images. Developed a style known as Color Field painting using huge, blurry blocks of color. In 1970, he committed suicide in his New York studio.

Henri ROUSSEAU (1844-1910).
French painter. Nicknamed *le douanier* (French for 'customs officer'). Worked for a lawyer and then the army, though he never saw action. Later

became a toll collector, painting in his spare time. Developed a deceptively child-like style. Began to paint full-time after he retired.

Peter Paul RUBENS (1577-1640)
Flemish painter. Traveled widely and spoke five languages. Worked as a diplomat for various European monarchs, as well as being a successful artist. Spent several years in Italy, where he was influenced by ancient Roman art and **Titian**. Also visited Spain, where he influenced **Velázquez**. Known for his grand mythological scenes and portraits. Knighted by Charles I.

Pieter SAENREDAM (1597-1665)
Dutch painter. Painstakingly recreated the perspectives of churches and town halls.

SASSOFERRATO (1605-85)
Italian painter. Real name Giovanni Battista Salvi. Influenced by **Raphael**, he made many paintings of the Virgin Mary in a style similar to his.

Egon SCHIELE (1890-1918)
German artist. Associated with Expressionism. His images of young women were considered so shocking, he was sent to prison in 1912 for obscenity.

Karl SCHMIDT-ROTTLUFF (1884-1976)
German artist. Added "Rottluff" to his name because it was where he was born. Helped found the group *Die Brücke*. Developed a harsh, angular style, influenced by African sculpture. During WWII, his work was confiscated by the Nazis. Afterwards, he became a professor in Berlin.

Kurt SCHWITTERS (1887-1948)
German artist. Associated with Dada. He developed a style known as 'Merz,' consisting of 2-D and 3-D collages made out of rubbish. Also wrote and performed nonsense poems.

Richard SERRA (born 1939)
U.S. sculptor. Worked in steel mills. Now makes huge abstract works using metal.

Paul SERUSIER (1863-1927)
French painter. Influenced by **Gauguin**. Founded the Nabis in 1889.

Georges SEURAT (1859-91)
French painter and theorist. His ideas on color led him to develop Pointillism, a technique using tiny dots of pure color.

Cindy SHERMAN (born 1954)
U.S. artist. Works with photography and film. Does series of pictures, often of herself as a variety of characters in different situations. More recently, she has represented herself in pictures that mimic famous old paintings.

Alfred SISLEY (1839/40-99)
Anglo-French painter. Born in Paris of British family, and worked mainly in France. A leading Impressionist.

Robert SMITHSON (1938-1973)
U.S. artist. Known for his Land art such as *Spiral Jetty*, a huge spiral of mud, rocks and salt crystals in the Great Salt Lake, Utah, U.S.A. Died in an aircrash near Amarillo while working on another piece, *Amarillo Ramp*.

Stanley SPENCER (1891-1959)
British painter. Known for his landscapes, portraits and Biblical scenes, painted with expressive and sometimes comic distortion. One critic described his work as "angels in jumpers." Served as a medic in WWI and as a war artist in WWII. Known for his scruffy appearance, he was once mistaken for a station porter.

Daniel SPOERRI (born 1930)
Romanian-born Swiss artist. Has worked as a poet and author, and in dance, mime and theater. Self-taught as an artist. Has done Kinetic sculptures and 'Happenings,' and collaborated with **Tinguely**.

Jan Havicksz STEEN (1625/6-79)
Dutch painter. Depicted everyday Dutch scenes and moral tales in a humorous, anecdotal manner.

Harmen STEENWYCK (1612-56)
Dutch painter. Specialized in still lifes, especially *vanitas* pictures designed to remind viewers of their own mortality.

Frank STELLA (born 1936)
U.S. artist. Studied at Princeton University. Associated with Minimalism. Creates paintings and prints using bands of color, sometimes in blacks and greys, sometimes in brighter shades.

Vladimir TATLIN (1885-1953)
Russian artist and architect. Often referred to as the "father of Constructivism." Worked as a painter and stage designer.

Sam TAYLOR-WOOD (born 1967)
British artist. Uses film, video and photography. Works with professional actors, dancers and celebrities, including pop star Kylie Minogue and footballer David Beckham.

Giovanni Battista TIEPOLO (1696-1770)
Italian painter. A brilliant Rococo artist, he worked all over Europe. Known for his frescoes and colorful decorative panels.

Jean TINGUELY (1925-1991)
Swiss sculptor. Best-known for his Kinetic sculptures – busy, electric machines that serve no function.

TITIAN (about 1487-1576)
Italian painter. Real name Tiziano Vecellio. Worked with **Giorgione**. Lived in Venice and rarely traveled, though his work (mainly in oils) became known across Europe and he made many paintings for European royalty. Admired for his range of subjects, brilliant colors and expressive style. Acknowledged as the greatest portrait painter of his time.

Joseph Mallord William TURNER (1775-1851)
British painter. The son of a barber, he began exhibiting pictures in his father's shop. Famous for painting seas, skies and weather. Even claimed to have tied himself to a ship's mast so he could sketch a storm. Developed a more modern style of landscape painting which had a great influence on the Impressionists. Shunned publicity and adopted the false name 'Admiral Booth.'

Paolo UCCELLO (about 1397-1475)
Italian painter. Worked in Florence and studied perspective. *Uccello* is Italian for 'bird,' and was probably a nickname – he was said to love animals.

Theo VAN DOESBURG (1883-1931)
Dutch artist. Founded *De Stijl* magazine and, with **Mondrian**, pioneered the style which became known by that name.

Anthony VAN DYCK (1599-1641)
Flemish painter. Later Sir Anthony. Was chief assistant to **Rubens** in Antwerp, then worked in Italy. In 1631, he became court painter to the English king, Charles I. His elegant, flattering portraits were hugely influential.

Jan VAN EYCK (about 1390-1441)
Netherlandish artist. Worked as a court painter and diplomat. Pioneered the use of oil paints. Created religious scenes and portraits. Much admired for his wonderfully detailed and lifelike style.

Vincent VAN GOGH (1853-90)
Dutch painter. An unsuccessful preacher, now one of the most famous artists in the world, though he sold only one painting during his lifetime. He began painting somber rural scenes. Then moved to Paris, met **Degas**, **Gauguin**, **Pissarro** and others, and started doing colorful pictures of flowers, people and local scenery. Later, moved south and tried to set up a studio with Gauguin, creating a now famous series of sunflower pictures for his friend. But after a violent argument with Gauguin, and suffering from mental illness, cut off part of his own ear. Shot himself two years later.

Jan VAN HUYSUM (1682-1749)
Dutch painter. Specialized in painting still lifes, creating detailed imaginary arrangements of flowers and fruit.

Jan VAN OS (1744-1808)
Dutch painter. Painted still lifes, imitating **van Huysum**. His son was also an artist.

Diego Rodriguez de Silva VELAZQUEZ (1599-1660)
Spanish painter. Worked for King Philip IV of Spain. Known for his history paintings and perceptive portraits of members of Philip's court. His work inspired many artists, including **Manet** and **Picasso**, who did a series of pictures based on *The Maids of Honour* (1656), often known by its Spanish title, *Las Meninas*.

Jan VERMEER (1632-75)
Dutch painter and art dealer. Did not seem to sell much of his own work – over half of it was found in his house and studio when he died. He was almost forgotten for years, but much admired when rediscovered. Famous for creating quiet, beautifully lit interior scenes.

VERONESE (about 1528-88)
Italian painter. Real name Paolo Caliari. Known as Veronese because he was born in Verona. Worked in Venice and became very successful, completing many large commissions in fresco and oils.

Elisabeth VIGEE-LEBRUN (1755-1842)
French painter. Studied art with her father. Her attractive, flattering portraits were popular with many patrons, among them Queen Marie-Antoinette of France.

Bill VIOLA (born 1951)
U.S. video and installation artist. Worked at a video studio in Italy and studied Buddhism in Japan, before returning to live in the U.S. Awarded many fellowships for his video work.

Maurice de VLAMINCK (1876-1958)
French artist. Started out as a mechanic with hopes of being a professional cyclist. Taught himself to paint. Shared a studio with **Derain** and became one of the Fauves.

Mark WALLINGER (born 1959)
British artist. Works include sculptures, photographs and video installations.

Andy WARHOL (1928-1987)
U.S. artist. Worked in advertising before getting involved with the U.S. Pop art movement. One of the most famous artistic personalities of modern times, known for his repeated prints of images taken from advertising and the media. Also made experimental films, including a six-hour film of a man sleeping, and an eight-hour film of the Empire State Building.

Jean-Antoine WATTEAU (1684-1721)
Flemish painter. Worked in Paris. Painted theater scenery, then worked with a court painter. Became a successful Rococo artist. Influenced by **Rubens**, he developed his own elegant, poetic style of dream-like landscapes, known as *fêtes galantes*.

James McNeill WHISTLER (1834-1903)
American painter. Studied art after failing to qualify for the army. He based many paintings on delicate arrangements of color. After the art critic John Ruskin attacked his painting *Nocturne in Black and Gold* (1875), he sued for libel. He won the case, but was ruined by the legal costs.

Rachel WHITEREAD (born 1963)
British sculptor. Known for making casts of objects ranging from a kitchen sink to a whole house.

Wolf WILLRICH (1867-1950)
German painter. Produced Nazi propaganda images and helped organize the 'Degenerate Art Exhibition' in 1937. Much of his work was destroyed during and after the war.

Richard WILSON (1713/14-82)
British painter. Born in Wales. Painted landscapes in England, Wales and Italy, where he was inspired by the scenery near Rome and by the works of **Poussin** and **Claude**. Sometimes called the "father of English landscape painting."

Johan ZOFFANY (about 1733-1810)
German painter. Studied in Rome, then moved to Britain. Mainly painted portraits, and theatrical and domestic scenes.

Glossary

There are lots of specialist words used in art. This glossary explains the names and terms used in this book, as well as some other common terms you may come across. Words in **bold** have their own entries.

👁 For a link to websites where you can look up lots more technical terms used in art, go to www.usborne-quicklinks.com

2-D – abbreviation of two-dimensional. Used to describe something which is (or seems to be) flat, such as a drawing of a square.

3-D – abbreviation of three-dimensional. Used to describe something which is (or seems to be) solid, such as a cube or a picture of a cube.

abstract art – art that has no recognizable subject matter, but is an arrangement of shapes and colors. Pioneered by Kandinsky.

Abstract Expressionism – an art **movement** which flourished in New York in the 1940s and 50s. It centred on dramatic abstract paintings. Rothko and Pollock were leading members. See also **Action Painting** and **Color Field Painting**.

acrylic paint – paint made from **pigment** and acrylic resin. Invented in the 1950s and now widely used.

Action Painting – a technique developed by Pollock, which involved dribbling and splashing paint onto a horizontal canvas to try to get an emphatic, expressive effect.

AD – used for dates, to indicate the years numbered forwards from the supposed year of Christ's birth, or 'year 1.' AD stands for *Anno Domini*, which is Latin for 'year of the Lord.' Some people prefer to express AD dates as CE, or 'Common Era.'

aerial perspective – an effect caused by distance which makes colors seem to fade and turn blue.

allegory – something which has a hidden symbolic meaning.

altarpiece – a large painting, often made up of many panels, made to stand behind an altar.

Analytical Cubism – an early form of **Cubism** developed by Picasso and

Braque in about 1907-12. It involved analysing real objects and breaking them down into separate elements.

ancient art – art from the ancient cultures of Egypt, Greece and Rome.

applied art – art which has a practical purpose, such as pottery.

art movement – a group of artists who work together and share ideas, and who often exhibit together too.

assemblage – **3-D collages**. Pioneered by Picasso and Braque, later taken up by Rauschenberg and others.

automatic drawing – a technique invented by the **Surrealists**. It involved trying to draw without thinking, as a way of trying to access their unconscious mind.

avant-garde – innovative, cutting-edge art. The term comes from the French name for the advance unit of an army.

Baroque – a dramatic, 17th-century style of art. Also used to describe the period when this style was popular. The term derives from the Portuguese word *barocco*, meaning 'misshapen pearl.'

Bauhaus, the – an influential German art school where all the students learned art, architecture and design, with the aim of creating a better environment for everyone. It opened in Weimar in 1919, then moved to Dessau and later Berlin. It was closed down by the Nazis in 1933.

BC – used for very early dates, to indicate the years numbered backwards from the supposed year of Christ's birth, or 'year 1.' BC stands for 'before Christ.' Some people prefer to express BC dates as BCE, or 'Before the Common Era.'

Blaue Reiter, Der – an **Expressionist** art **movement** founded in Germany, in 1911, by Vassily Kandinsky and Franz Marc. It broke up in 1914. They chose

the name, which means 'The Blue Rider' in German, because they liked blue and horses. They also published a periodical with the same title.

book of hours – an illustrated book containing prayers for different times of day, different days and different seasons. It was used at home rather than in church.

Britart – abbreviation of 'British art.' **Movement** which emerged in Britain in the 1990s. It centred on controversial works by young British artists or **YBAs**.

Brücke, Die – a German **Expressionist** art **movement** founded in 1905. Its members included Ernst Kirchner, Erich Heckel and Karl Schmidt-Rottluff. The name was meant to signify a bridge to the future, to a new kind of art. It broke up in 1913, with the approach of WWI.

burnishing – polishing something to make it shine.

Byzantine art – art from the Byzantine empire (the eastern part of the Roman empire), which lasted from the 4th to the 15th century.

camera obscura – a device designed to help artists make accurate, **2-D** sketches of **3-D** scenes. There were several versions of it, but all projected images of real-life scenes onto flat surfaces – a bit like a simple camera. The name means 'dark room' in Latin.

cartoon – a full-scale drawing on paper, which can be traced onto a wall, panel or canvas as a basis for a painting. Nowadays, also used to mean a caricature or funny picture.

chiaroscuro – this means 'light-dark' in Italian. In art, it is used to describe pictures where there is strong light coming from one side of the scene, so it casts strong shadows on the other side.

Classical art – ancient Greek and Roman art, especially Greek art from the 5th century BC.

Claude glass – a tinted mirror used by landscape artists. It simplified the colors of what it reflected in a way that was meant to resemble a painting by Claude.

Carolingian art – art from the time of the emperor Charlemagne (742-814).

collage – a technique where newspaper, wallpaper, fabric and other materials are glued onto the picture surface. Pioneered by Picasso and popular with **Pop** artists.

Color Field Painting – a style of abstract painting where pictures are made up from large blocks of color, designed to provoke a strong emotional or spiritual response. Pioneered by Rothko.

color wheel – an arrangement of the three **primary colors** (red, yellow and blue) and the **secondary colors** (orange, green and purple) you get by mixing them. It is shown on page 94.

commission – to pay an artist to produce a work of art to order. Also used to describe a work produced in this way.

complementary colors – colors which lie opposite each other on the **color wheel**. Seen side by side, they contrast very strongly and make each other look brighter.

Conceptual art – art which emphasizes the idea behind a work of art, rather than the work itself. As a **movement**, it flourished in the late 1960s-70s, for example in the work of Kosuth and Long.

Constructivism – an **abstract** art **movement** which grew out of the Russian Revolution of 1917. Its members included Rodchenko and Popova. They wanted to help build a new society by designing clothes, buildings, furniture, etc. using geometric principles. Suppressed by Stalin in the early 1920s.

contemporary art – art of the present day (which is not necessarily the same thing as **modern** art).

court painter – a painter employed by a ruler to work at his or her court.

Cubism – a style which draws attention to the contradictions involved in making a **2-D** image of a **3-D** scene. It was first developed in the early 20th century by Picasso and Braque. The name came from Braque's painting *Houses at L'Estaque* (1908), which a critic described as looking like 'a pile of little cubes.' The style is sometimes separated into two versions, **Analytical** and **Synthetic Cubism**.

Dada – an art **movement** formed during WWI. Its members created unconventional, often shocking, art to protest against the war and the state of society, often staging shows which were an early kind of **Performance art**. The name (a French word for 'hobby horse') was chosen at random from a dictionary.

death mask – a cast or model of someone's face made after he or she has died.

decorative art – art, such as embroidery or ornate silverwork, made to decorate other things.

'Degenerate' art – a term used by the Nazis to condemn radical modern art, which they feared was subversive. It included works by Kirchner, Grosz and Picasso. The Nazis held an exhibition in Munich in 1937 to mock 'degenerate' works of art; this later toured to other German cities. Afterwards, most of the art was sold abroad; the rest was burned in Berlin in 1939.

diptych – a picture made up of two hinged panels.

drip painting – a technique made famous by Jackson Pollock, where paint is dripped and splashed from a brush, stick or pot onto a canvas laid horizontally on the floor.

Earthworks – another name for **Land art**.

egg tempera – paint made using **pigment** and egg, used widely before the 15th century.

engraving – a kind of **print**. First, a picture is 'engraved' or cut onto a metal plate. The plate is brushed with ink, so ink fills the hollows. Then a sheet of damp paper is pressed over the plate to pick up the ink.

Environmental art – the name given by French artists Christo and Jeanne-Claude to their kind of outdoor art. They prefer this term to **Land art** because they work in a range of different environments.

etching – a kind of **print** made using a metal plate coated with a protective wax. A picture is 'etched' or scratched into the wax, revealing the metal beneath, and acid is used to burn the exposed metal. Then the plate is brushed with ink and printed in the same way as an **engraving**.

Expressionism – an early 20th-century development where artists use exaggerated shapes and colors to try to convey feelings and ideas, rather than showing how things really look. It was inspired by the work of Munch and van Gogh. There were two main groups, *Die Brücke* and *Der Blaue Reiter*. See also **Abstract Expressionism**.

Fauves – the name given to a group of young painters around 1905-10 who used vibrant, unnatural colors. Matisse and Derain were leading members. The name means 'wild beasts' in French.

feminism – a political movement which emerged in the 1960s-70s, concerned with ensuring women are valued equally to men.

feminist art – art which supports the ideas behind feminism, for example by using traditionally feminine **media** such as embroidery.

fête galante – a scene of courtly entertainment, such as dancing or music-making in an outdoor setting. A popular subject with Rococo artists, especially Watteau.

fine art – a collective term used to describe painting, sculpture, drawing, print-making and, sometimes, music and poetry. Unlike **applied art** or **decorative art**, fine art has no practical purpose.

Flemish – from, or in the style of things from, the region of Flanders, (now part of Belgium, France and the Netherlands).

Florentine – from, or in the style of things from, Florence, Italy.

Fluxus – a 1960s-70s art **movement** inspired by **Dada**. It focused on spontaneous, unexpected kinds of art, often in the form of **Happenings**. The name was meant to evoke a continuous process of change, or 'flux.' Beuys was a leading member.

found object – an object which an artist has not made, but has chosen to exhibit as a work of art. It can be a natural object, such as driftwood, or a man-made object, such as a bottle. See also **readymades**.

fresco – a wall painting made by applying colors to wet plaster.

Futurism – an art **movement** founded in Italy in 1909 by Marinetti. Its members celebrated the energy and speed of machines and city life, and even praised war, stating their aims in aggressive manifestoes. It broke up around the start of WWI.

genre – a particular kind of paintings, such as **portraits, landscapes, history paintings** and **still lifes**.

gesso – a thick, white paste used to prepare a surface for painting.

gild – to cover something, such as a frame, with a thin layer of gold.

gothic – a term used to describe the art and architecture of the Middle Ages. See also **International Gothic**.

gouache – thick, water-soluble paint.

Graffiti art – pictures scrawled on walls in public places, or paintings made in this style.

Happenings – unscripted, bizarre **performances**, such as Joseph Beuys' *How to explain paintings to a dead hare* (see page 146). Developed in the 1960s.

harmonizing colors – colors, such as red and orange, which come next to each other on the **color wheel**. Seen side by side, they seem to blend together.

high culture – traditional art forms, such as paintings, which tend to be expensive and available only to small numbers of people. Often contrasted with **pop culture**.

history painting – a painting that tells a story, whether real or made-up.

Most show scenes from Classical history and myths, or Bible stories. Originally described by Alberti and, in the 17th century, considered the highest form of painting. See also **genre**.

hyperrealism – also known as super realism. An extremely lifelike style of art, often based on photographs.

iconoclasts – in the past, people who wanted to destroy religious art because they believed it led to idol-worship. This happened in the 8th century in the Byzantine empire, and in the late 16th and 17th centuries in northern Europe. Now the word is used to describe anyone who attacks traditional beliefs and ideas.

icons – holy images of religious figures, usually of saints, or the Virgin Mary and Jesus.

illuminated manuscripts – books written and decorated by hand.

impasto – a very thick layer of paint. From the Italian word for 'paste.'

Impressionism – the first major **avant-garde** art **movement**, formed in France in the 1860s. Its members wanted to paint outdoors and study the changing effects of natural light. Their work has a sketchy, spontaneous style. Leading members included Monet, Renoir and Pissarro. The name came from a hostile review of Monet's painting *Impression, Sunrise* (1874). See also **plein air**.

installation – a work of art designed to be set up, or installed, in a particular location. Pioneered by **Dada** and **Surrealist** artists.

International Gothic – name given to the decorative, colorful style of painting developed in Europe in the 14th and 15th centuries.

Kinetic art – sculptures which move, such as those made by Tinguely.

kitsch – something considered trashy or in bad taste, but sometimes ironically celebrated for that.

Land art – also known as **Earthworks**. An art **movement** which began in the 1960s where artists work within the landscape, creating simple arrangements of natural materials.

Often these are made in remote places, and are temporary, so they survive only in photographs and documents. See also **Environmental Art**.

landscape format – a rectangle which is wider than it is tall.

landscapes – paintings where landscape or scenery is the main subject.

linear perspective – see **perspective**.

lithograph – a kind of **print** made by drawing onto a stone or metal tablet. The tablet is wetted, then coated with ink, which sticks to the lines of the drawing. A print is then taken by laying paper over it.

manuscripts – texts written by hand. See also **illuminated manuscripts**.

medieval art – art from the Middle Ages (about 1000-1400).

medium/media – the material used to make an artwork, such as **pastels, oil paints**, or **collage**. Originally, 'medium' meant the liquid, such as oil or acrylic resin, that is mixed with dry **pigment** to make paint. 'Media' is the plural of medium.

memento mori – an object such as a skull or a dying flame, used by artists to make you think about death.

Merz – a **collage** technique developed by Schwitters using scraps of everyday rubbish. He also made 3-D, room-sized collages known as Merzbau.

Minimalism – an art **movement** developed in the U.S. in the 1960s-70s where there is little obvious content, so viewers have to examine what is there very closely. Not a formal group, but artists associated with it include Andre and Judd.

Minoans – ancient Greek people who lived on the island of Crete.

mixed media – used to describe art made from more than one material or **medium**.

modern – originally 'modern' just meant 'of the present.' However in art, it can be used to mean a particular period from the mid-19th to early 20th century, when artists made a radical break with the past. More generally, it is used for all art dating from this period onwards. See also **postmodern**.

Modernism – a term used to describe the new artistic and cultural trends which arose during the mid-19th and early 20th century. These were largely about rejecting tradition and experimenting with radical techniques, in the hope of approaching universal truths. **Impressionism** is one early example; **Abstract Expressionism** is another. See also **Postmodernism**.

mosaics – pictures made of tiny pieces of colored glass or stone set in plaster or cement on a wall or other surface.

movements – groups of artists who shared ideas and practices, and often exhibited together, as began happening in the 19th century.

Myceneans – ancient Greek people and famed warriors.

mythological – relating to Classical myths.

Nabis, the – a group of artists who exhibited together at the end of the 19th century. They were inspired by Gauguin to focus on color. The name is Hebrew for 'prophets.'

naive art – a term used to describe work by untrained artists.

Neo – Latin for 'new.' It is sometimes added to the name of earlier art **movements** to describe a more recent revival of their ideas or techniques. For example, Neo-Expressionism was a revival of **Expressionism** in the late 1970s-80s.

Neoclassicism – a revival of **Classical** style and subjects in art during the late 18th and early 19th centuries. Associated with David and Ingres.

Netherlandish – from, or in the style of art from, Flanders and Holland (now the Netherlands, Belgium and France).

New Realism – an art **movement** in 1960s France which explored modern consumer culture, often through works made from discarded items. Sometimes known by its French name, *Nouveau Realisme*.

oil paints – paints made by mixing **pigment** and oil, used widely from the 15th century until the 20th century. Often shortened to 'oils.'

old master – one of the many celebrated European painters between about 1400 and 1800, or a painting by one of them.

Op art – short for 'Optical art.' An art **movement** in the 1950s-60s where artists used abstract, geometric shapes and patterns to create optical illusions and the impression of movement.

palette – a board on which an artist mixes his or her colors. Also used to mean the range of colors used by a particular artist.

pastels – soft, colored crayons.

patrons – people who pay artists to produce work for them.

Performance art – an art **movement** begun in the 1960s where artists stage live performances. Unlike theater shows, they do not usually follow a plot. The art exists only as long as the performance, but photographs and documents are sometimes kept. See also **Happenings**.

perspective – the rules used to create a sense of **3-D** space in a **2-D** drawing. One rule is that objects look smaller as they get further away. The most accurate system, worked out during the **Renaissance**, is known as unified or linear perspective, and uses **vanishing points**. See also **aerial perspective**.

photomontage – the technique of combining sections of different photographs to make a new picture.

photorealism – an incredibly detailed, almost photographic style, such as in paintings by Close.

pieta – Italian for 'pity.' In art, it usually means a painting or sculpture of the Virgin Mary holding her dead son, Jesus.

pigments – powdered substances used to create paint colors. In the past, they were made by grinding anything from earth to precious stones. In the 19th century, bright chemical pigments were introduced.

plein air – French for 'open air.' This term is sometimes used to mean the Impressionists' technique of painting outdoors. It is also used to describe the effect they were trying to create.

Pointillism – a technique where painters apply tiny dots of pure, unmixed colors instead of blending colors on a palette, to try and achieve a brighter, more vibrant effect. Seen from a distance, the dots seem to blend together. Pioneered by Seurat, who called it 'Divisionism.'

Pop art – an art **movement** developed in the late 1950s-60s which used images taken from **pop culture**. It celebrated and commented on the boom of pop culture and consumerism which followed the austerity of the war years. Pioneered in London by Hamilton and others; U.S. members included Lichtenstein and Warhol.

pop culture – short for 'popular culture.' It means television programs, films, magazines, advertising and other productions aimed at a mass audience. Often contrasted with **high culture**.

portrait format – a rectangle which is taller than it is wide.

portraits – pictures of real people which try to capture a true likeness.

Post Impressionism – a term used to describe the variety of styles which developed in the 1880s-90s following **Impressionism**. It includes the work of Cézanne, Gauguin and van Gogh.

Pre-Raphaelite Brotherhood – a group of young British painters who wanted to return to what they saw as the simpler, purer style of art before Raphael's time. Also known by its initials, PRB. Members included Rossetti and Millais.

primary colors – red, yellow and blue. All other colors can be made by mixing these colors together.

prime – to prepare a canvas for painting.

primitive art – art from early or non-industrialized societies.

primitivism – an artistic trend inspired by early history, non-Western cultures and children's art. Includes works of art by Gauguin and Kirchner.

print – any picture made by taking an impression from somthing else, such as a piece of carved wood or linoleum covered in ink. Often used to make many copies of a picture. **Etchings, lithographs** and **woodcuts** are all kinds of prints.

pronk **still life** – a still life painting designed to show off expensive luxury items. The term comes from the Dutch for 'show off': *pronk*.

readymades – a name given by the artist Marcel Duchamp to works consisting of ordinary, factory-made objects, which the artist has chosen to present as art.

Realism – often used just to mean 'lifelike.' More specifically, it is the name of a 19th-century **movement** in art and literature, which focused on ordinary, everyday life.

Renaissance, the – the cultural revolution of the 15th and 16th centuries, which saw a rebirth of interest in Classical ideas and many new scientific discoveries, such as **perspective**.

representational art – see **figurative art**.

Rococo – an ornate, 18th-century style of art. The term comes from the French *rocaille*, meaning 'shells.'

Romanesque – the name given to the style of art and architecture which developed in western Europe between the 10th and 12th centuries.

Romanticism – a literary and artistic **movement** which emphasized the importance of emotions (especially feeling for nature) and the imagination. It flourished from about 1790-1840. Leading painters included Friedrich and Delacroix.

Secession – the name adopted by groups of avant-garde artists in Austria and Germany who broke away or 'seceded' from traditional art academies.

secondary colors – orange, green and purple. These are the colors you get when you mix two **primary colors** together.

sfumato – Italian for 'smoky.' In painting, it means blurring the transitions between highlights and shadows to create a softly lit, mysterious effect, like that in Leonardo's *Mona Lisa*.

silkscreen print – a kind of **print** made using a silk panel to help distribute ink evenly through a stencil onto paper or fabric. A photographic process can be used to create the stencil. Often used by Warhol.

Soviet Socialist Realism – a realistic but melodramatic style of art, developed for propaganda by the Russian Communist party.

spalliera **panel** – a long painted panel made to decorate a chest or other piece of furniture. Often made for newly married couples in Renaissance Italy.

Stijl, De – Dutch for 'The Style.' An early 20th-century art **movement** aimed at promoting a colorful, **abstract** geometric style in art, architecture and design. Pioneered by van Doesburg and Mondrian.

still life – a painting mainly of objects that can't move, such as flowers, food and pots and pans. It can also refer to the actual arrangement of objects. The plural is always written 'still lifes' (not 'lives'). See also *pronk* **still life** and *vanitas*.

Suprematism – an early 20th-century style developed by Malevich, based on abstract geometric shapes. With Dynmaic Suprematism, he used more complex compositions to convey a sense of energy and movement.

Surrealism – an art **movement** which developed in Paris in the 1920s-40s, inspired by **Dada** and the writings of psychiatrist Sigmund Freud. The Surrealists, including Dalí and Miró, aimed to explore our unconscious minds, often using bizarre, dream-like imagery.

Symbolism – a 19th-century artistic and literary **movement** which rejected realism, emphasizing feelings and dreams instead. Leading artists included Moreau and Redon.

Synthetic Cubism – a kind of **Cubism** developed by Picasso and Braque between about 1912-14. It involved 'synthesizing' or building up images from abstract parts, using readymade materials such as newspaper.

tableau-piège – this means 'picture-trap.' Used to describe a group of objects 'trapped' and made into a **3-D** picture. Also a 'trap' for the viewer, because what looks like a picture is made up of real objects.

three-dimensional – see **3-D**.

triptych – a picture made up of three panels.

trompe l'oeil – a highly realistic painted device which tries to deceive viewers into thinking they are looking at a real object instead of a painted image. The name means 'tricking the eye' in French.

two-dimensional – see **2-D**.

underpainting – the first layer of colors applied to a painting.

unified perspective – see **perspective**.

vanishing point – a term used in **perspective** drawing to mean the point where parallel lines, such as train tracks, seem to come together in the distance.

vanitas – a **still life** which is meant to remind viewers of the futility of earthly achievements and encourage spiritual thoughts, by reminding them that success is only temporary and death comes to us all. The name is Latin for 'vanity' or 'futility.'

Venetian – from, or in the style of things from, Venice, Italy.

Vorticism – an **avant-garde** movement based in London. Inspired by **Cubism** and **Futurism**, it tried to promote violent change. It began around 1910, but did not survive the brutal reality of WWI.

woodcut – a kind of **print** made by cutting a picture into a wooden block, leaving raised lines which are coated with ink (unlike an **engraving**, where the ink fills the hollows). The block is then pressed onto paper to make a print.

YBAs – short for young British artists. Young artists associated with the recent **Britart** phenomenon. They include Hirst, Lucas and Emin.

Using the Internet

To visit the websites recommended in this book, go to the **Usborne Quicklinks Website** at **www.usborne-quicklinks.com** and type the keywords **book of art**. There you will find links to click on to take you to all the sites.

Here are some of the things you can do on the recommended sites:

- Explore virtual exhibitions of paintings and zoom in on the details of individual pictures.

- Experiment with an interactive artist's toolkit, and create your own works of art.

- Escape from inside a painting in an on-line art adventure.

- Go on an online 'art safari,' looking at a selection of modern art.

What you need

Most websites described in this book can be accessed using a standard home computer and a web browser (the software that lets you look at information from the Internet). Some sites need extra programs (plug-ins) to play sound or show videos or animations. You can download plug-ins for free from the Internet.

If you go to a site and do not have the necessary plug-in, a message will come up on the screen. There is usually a button on the site that you can click on to download the plug-in. Alternatively, go to Usborne Quicklinks and click on Net Help. There, you can find links to download plug-ins.

COMPUTER NOT ESSENTIAL

If you don't have access to the Internet, don't worry. This book is a complete, self-contained reference book on its own.

Site availability

The links in Usborne Quicklinks are regularly reviewed and updated, but occasionally you may get a message that a site is unavailable. This might be temporary, so try again later, or even the next day.

Websites do occasionally close down and when this happens, we will replace them with new links in Usborne Quicklinks. Sometimes we add extra links too, if we think they are useful. So when you visit Usborne Quicklinks, the links may be slightly different from those described in your book.

Internet safety

When using the Internet, please make sure you follow these guidelines:

- Children should ask their parent's or guardian's permission before connecting to the Internet.

- When you are on the Internet, never tell anyone your full name, address or telephone number. Children should ask an adult before giving their email address.

- If a website asks you to log in or register by typing your name or email address, children should ask an adult's permission first.

- If you do receive an email from someone you don't know, do not reply to the email.

Internet disclaimer

The websites described in this book are regularly reviewed and the links in Usborne Quicklinks are updated. However, the content of a website may change at any time and Usborne Publishing is not responsible for the content of any website other than its own. We recommend that children are supervised while on the Internet, that they do not use Internet chat rooms, and that parents and guardians use Internet filtering software to block unsuitable material. Please ensure that children read and follow the safety guidelines printed on the left.

For more information, see the Net Help area on the Usborne Quicklinks Website.

Index

Cartoons by Uwe Mayer
Picture research by Ruth King
Diagrams by Glen Bird; sample paintwork by Antonia Miller
Digital manipulation: Mike Olley and John Russell; additional design work by Louise Flutter
Thanks to Abigail Wheatley, Rachel Firth, Minna Lacey and Katie Daynes for additional research, Brian Roberts for additional art historical advice, and Rebecca Gilpin, Georgina Andrews, Fiona Patchett, Alice Pearcey and Alex Frith for editorial assistance.

First published in 2005 by Usborne Publishing Ltd, 83-85 Saffron Hill, London EC1N 8RT. www.usborne.com
Copyright © 2003, 2004, 2005 Usborne Publishing Ltd. AE. First published in America in 2006.
The name Usborne and the devices ♈ ♉ are Trade Marks of Usborne Publishing Ltd. All rights reserved.

Acknowledgements

Every effort has been made to trace the copyright holders of the material in this book. If any rights have been omitted, the publishers offer their sincere apologies and will rectify this in any subsequent editions following notification. The publishers are grateful to the following organizations and individuals for their contributions and permission to reproduce material:

All National Gallery (NG) images © The Trustees of The National Gallery, London

Cover details (left to right): *The Supper at Emmaus* see credit for pages 60-61, *Stables* see credit for pages 102-103, *Guitar on a Table* see credit for pages 18-19, *Self Portrait aged 63* see credit for pages 12-13, *Hunters in the Snow* see credit for pages 54-55, *Venus and Mars* see credit for pages 52-53. **Page 1** Detail from *The Beach at Trouville* see credit for page 93. **Pages 2-3** Detail from *Ophelia among the Flowers* see credit for page 87. **Pages 4-5** Detail from *Tiger in a Tropical Storm* see credit for page 95. **Pages 6-7** *Madame Moitessier* (1856) by Ingres, oil on canvas, 120 x 92cm (47 x 36in), NG; *Combing the Hair* (c.1896) by Degas, oil on canvas, 114 x 146cm (45 x 57in), NG; Detail from *A Sunday on La Grande Jatte* see credit for page 94; *Nocturne in Black and Gold* (1875) by Whistler, oil on wood, 60 x 47cm (24 x 18in), Detroit Institute of Art, Detroit/AKG-images/Erich Lessing. **Pages 8-9** *Vision of a Knight* (c.1504) by Raphael, egg tempera on poplar, 17 x 17cm (7 x 7in), NG; *At the Theatre* (1876-77) by Renoir, oil on canvas, 65 x 50cm (26 x 20in), NG. **Pages 10-11** *The Family of Darius before Alexander* (1565-70) by Veronese, oil on canvas, 236 x 475cm (93 x 187in), NG; *The Raft of the Medusa* (1818) by Géricault, oil on canvas, 490 x 720 cm (193 x 283in), The Art Archive/Musée du Louvre, Paris/Dagli Orti; *Liberty leading the People* (1831) by Delacroix, oil on canvas, 260 x 325cm (102 x 128in), The Art Archive/Musée du Louvre, Paris/Dagli Orti. **Pages 12-13** *Portrait of a Lady in Red* (c.1460-70) by an unknown artist, oil and egg tempera on wood, 42 x 29cm (17 x 11in), NG; *Self Portrait aged 63* (1669) by Rembrandt, oil on canvas, 86 x 71cm (34 x 28in), NG; *Self Portrait in a Straw Hat* (after 1782) by Vigée-Lebrun, oil on canvas, 98 x 71cm (39 x 28in), NG; *Portrait of Picasso* (1912) by Grís, oil on canvas, 74 x 93cm (29 x 37in) © Burstein Collection/CORBIS/ADAGP, Paris and DACS, London 2003. **Pages 14-15** *Saint John the Baptist retiring to the Desert* (1453) by Giovanni, egg tempera on poplar, 31 x 39cm (12 x 15in), NG; *An Autumn Landscape* (1636) by Rubens, oil on oak, 131 x 229cm (52 x 90in), NG; *The Water Lily Pond* (1899) by Monet, oil on canvas, 88 x 93cm (35 x 37in), NG; *Route 6, Eastham* (1941) by Hopper, oil on canvas, 71 x 97cm (28 x 38in) © Geoffrey Clements/CORBIS, by kind permission of Edward Hopper. **Pages 16-17** *Old Models* (1892) by Harnett, oil on canvas, 138 x 72cm (54 x 28in) © Burstein Collection/CORBIS; *Fruit, Flowers and a Fish* (1772) by van Os, oil on mahogany, 72 x 57cm (28 x 22in), NG; *The Attributes of the Arts* (1766) by Chardin, oil on canvas, 112 x 141cm (44 x 56in) © Archivo Iconografico, S.A./CORBIS; *Van Gogh's Chair* (1888) by van Gogh, oil on canvas, 92 x 73cm (36 x 29in), NG. **Pages 18-19** *Guitar on a Table* (1916) by Juan Gris © Christie's Images/CORBIS; *The Physical Impossibility of Death in the Mind of Someone Living* (1991) by Damien Hirst © Damien Hirst; *Vanitas* (1600s) by Unknown Artist, The Art Archive/Exhibition Asnieres/Seine 1991/Dagli Orti (A). **Pages 20-21** *The Snail* (1953) by Henri Matisse, The Art Archive/Tate Gallery London/Eileen Tweedy © Succession H. Matisse/DACS 2005; *Untitled* (1985) by Donald Judd, Stedelijk Museum Amsterdam, art © Judd Foundation, licensed by VAGA, New York/DACS, London 2005; *Girl with a Kitten* (1947) by Lucian Freud © Lucian Freud, British Council, London, U.K./Bridgeman Art Library; *Maman* (1999) by Louise Bourgeois © Louise Bourgeois/© FMGB Guggenheim Bilbao Museoa, 2005, photograph by Erika Barahona-Ede, all rights reserved, total or partial reproduction is prohibited. **Pages 22-23** Detail from *The Wilton Diptych* see credit for pages 32-33. **Pages 24-25** Egyptian tomb painting (c.1350BC) © Archivo Iconografico, S.A./CORBIS; scene from *The Book of the Dead*, British Museum/HIP; Minoan mural of bull jumping (c.1500BC) © Gustavo Tomsich/CORBIS; Mycenaean chariot krater (c.1400-1300BC), British Museum/HIP. **Pages 26-27** Greek cup with dancer (c.500-400BC), British Museum/HIP; discus thrower statue © Araldo de Luca/CORBIS; bust of Caesar (c.AD1-50) © Ruggero Vanni/CORBIS; mural from Pompeii © Mimmo Jodice/CORBIS. **Pages 28-29** *St. Matthew* from *The Book of Kells* (700s) © Bettmann/CORBIS; panel showing Miracle of Cana (800s), ivory, British Museum/HIP; Viking brooch (1000s), silver, British Museum/HIP; carved monster (c.1115-25), stone © Michael Busselle/CORBIS. **Pages 30-31** Photograph of church interior with mosaics (1100s) © Photo Scala, Florence/Palatine Chapel, Palermo 1990; mosaic panel of *The Multiplication of the Loaves and Fishes* (500s) © Photo Scala, Florence/Sant'Apollinare Nuovo, Ravenna 1990, courtesy of the Ministero Beni e Att. Culturali; Italian icon of Madonna and Child (900s) © Photo Scala, Florence/St. Mark's, Venice 1999; Russian icon of St. George (1400s), tempera on panel, Museum of the History of Religion, St. Petersburg, Russia/Bridgeman Art Library. **Pages 32-33** *The Wilton Diptych* (c.1395-99) by an unknown artist, egg tempera on oak, 57 x 29cm (22 x 11in), NG. **Pages 34-35** *The Coronation of the Virgin* (1370-71) by di Cione, egg tempera on poplar, 207 x 114cm (81 x 45), NG; *St. Michael and the Devil* (1468) by Bermejo, oil on wood, 179 x 82cm (70 x 32in), NG. **Pages 36-37** *May* from *The Very Rich Hours*, often known by its French title *Les très riches heures du Duc de Berry* (c.1416) by the Limbourg brothers, 14 x 16 cm (5.5 x 6in), Musée Condé, Chantilly/AKG-images; *To My One Desire* also known by its French title *A mon seul désir* (c.1410-20), tapestry, Musée de Cluny, Paris © Francis G. Mayer/CORBIS; *The Vision of St. Eustace* (c.1438-42) by Pisanello, egg tempera on wood, 55 x 66cm (22 x 26in), NG. **Pages 38-39** Detail from *Narcissus* see credit for page 50. **Pages 40-41** *St. Luke Painting the Virgin* (c.1530) by a follower of Quinten Massys, oil on oak, 114 x 35cm (45 x 14in), NG; *Man in a Turban* (1433) by van Eyck, oil on wood, 33 x 26cm (13 x 10in), NG; *The Virgin and Child before a Firescreen* (1500-25) by Campin, oil on oak, 63 x 49cm (25 x 19in), NG. **Pages 42-43** *The Virgin and Child* (1426) by Masaccio, egg tempera on poplar, 136 x 73cm (54 x 29in), NG; *The Annunciation* (1486) by Crivelli, egg tempera and oil on canvas, transferred from wood, 207 x 147cm (81 x 58in), NG; *The Battle of San Romano* (c.1450s) by Uccello, egg tempera on poplar, 182 x 320cm (72 x 126in), NG; photograph of Florence © Michael S. Lewis/CORBIS. **Pages 44-45** *Portrait of a Lady in Yellow* (1465) by Baldovinetti, egg tempera and oil on wood, 63 x 41cm (25 x 16in), NG; *Pope Julius II* (1522-12) by Raphael, oil on wood, 108 x 81cm (43 x 32in), NG; *Portrait of a Lady* (c.1511) by Titian, oil on canvas, 120 x 100cm (47 x 39in), NG; *The Ambassadors* (c.1533) by Holbein, oil on oak, 207 x 210cm (81 x 83in), NG. **Pages 46-47** *The Arnolfini Portrait* (1434) by van Eyck, oil on oak, 82 x 60cm (32 x 24in), NG. **Pages 48-49** *The Baptism of Christ* (1450s) by Piero, egg tempera on poplar, 167 x 116cm (66 x 46in), NG; *Creation of Adam* (1508-12) by Michelangelo, fresco, 280 x 570 cm (110 x 224in) © Bettmann/CORBIS; *The Virgin of the Rocks* (c.1508) by Leonardo, oil on wood, 190 x 120cm (75 x 47in), NG; *The Virgin and Child with St. Anne and St. John the Baptist* (c.1507-08) by Leonardo, charcoal, black and white chalk on tinted paper, 142 x 105cm (56 x 41in), NG. **Pages 50-51** *Cupid complaining to Venus* (1530s) by Cranach, oil on wood, 82 x 56cm (32 x 22in), NG; *Apollo and Daphne* (c.1470-80) by del Pollaiuolo, oil on wood, 30 x 20cm (12 x 8in), NG; *Narcissus* (c.1490-99) by a follower of Leonardo, oil on wood, 23 x 26cm (9 x 10in), NG; *Bacchus and Ariadne* (1521-23) by Titian, oil on canvas, 172 x 188cm (68 x 74in), NG. **Pages 52-53** *Venus and Mars* (c.1485) by Botticelli, egg tempera and oil on poplar, 69 x 173cm (27 x 68in), NG. **Pages 54-55** *The Agony in the Garden* (c.1465) by Bellini, egg tempera on wood, 81 x 127cm (32 x 50in), NG; *St. Jerome in a Rocky Landscape* (c.1515-24) by Patinir, oil on oak, 36 x 34cm (14 x 13in), NG; *Hunters in the Snow* (1565) by Bruegel, oil on panel, 117 x 162cm (46 x 64in), The Art Archive/Kunsthistorisches Museum, Vienna; *The Sunset* (1506-10) by Giorgione, oil on canvas, 73 x 92cm (29 x 36in), NG. **Pages 56-57** Detail from *The Vision of St. Joseph* see credit for pages 62-63. **Pages 58-59** *The Ecstasy of St. Theresa* (1647-52) by Bernini, marble, height approx. 350cm (138in), Santa Maria della Vittoria, Rome © Massimo Listri/CORBIS; *Perseus turning Phineas and his Followers into Stone* (c.1680) by Giordano, oil on canvas, 285 x 366cm (112 x 144in), NG; *Self Portrait* (1670-73) by Murillo, oil on canvas, 122 x 107cm (48 x 42in), NG; *Belshazzar's Feast* (c.1635) by Rembrandt, oil on canvas, 168 x 209cm (66 x 82in), NG. **Pages 60-61** *The Supper at Emmaus* (1601) by Caravaggio, oil and egg tempera on canvas, 141 x 196cm (56 x